Fundamentals of Export Management: Change and Continuity

Fundamentals of Export Management: Change and Continuity

By

Mitlesh Dhunna

2008

CYBER TECH PUBLICATIONS
4264/3, Ansari Road, Daryaganj, New Delhi-110002 (India)
Ph.: 011-23244078. Fax: 011-23280028
E-Mail: cybertechpublicationsdelhi@yahoo.com

FUNDAMENTALS OF EXPORT MANAGEMENT: CHANGE AND CONTINUITY

MITLESH DHUNNA

First Edition 2008

Published by :

G.S. Rawat for Cyber Tech Publications
4264/3, Ansari Road, Daryaganj, New Delhi-110002 (India)
Ph.: 011-23244078. Fax: 011-23280028
E-Mail: cybertechpublicationsdelhi@yahoo.com

Printed at : **Amit Enterprises**, Maujpur, Delhi, (9810878184)

PREFACE

When we switched over from barter trade to monetary trade our trading got increased manifold. Gradually we begin to produce more and more and started exporting them to foreign countries in exchange of foreign currency or goods of the same monetary value.

But when this trade developed need of management aroused to keep it functioning property in our interest and hence we brought to arena a management machinery— Export Management.

It has its own principles and guidelines. It has to abide with the laws of the countries concerned— importing and exporting. Today it is not so as it was at the time of inception, a lot of things are changed in its journey, but still it is continuing and developing further.

In this book I have tried to bring all those major changes and other broad features of the export management which are helpful.

I hope that this book will be of immense help of the readers.

However your valuable suggestions for the improvement of the book are always welcome.

—Author

Contents

1

Introduction to Export Management Systems

The Commerce Department's Bureau of Industry and Security (BIS), has responded to the changing world events by focusing much of its attention on items and services that could be used to develop or deliver weapons of mass destruction.

The terrorist attacks of September 11, 2001, emphasize the importance of controls on the export of dual-use items-controls that are maintained to combat terrorism, stem the proliferation of chemical, biological and nuclear weapons, and protect U.S. national security and foreign policy interests. Under the Export Administration Regulations (EAR), items that might not otherwise require a license based upon a review of the Commerce Control List (CCL) and country requirements, could require a license from BIS because of the nature of the end-use/user. The Enhanced Proliferation Control Initiative was issued in 1991 and placed greater emphasis on the end-use or end-user of exported items. As a result, exporters need to be more vigilant in screening their customers and export transactions.

In response to requests from the business community, BIS has published the EMS Guidelines (The Guidelines) to assist companies in establishing internal control procedures for vigilant screening of export/reexport transactions. The Guidelines provide ideas, examples of best practices and tools that have proven effective in U.S. businesses. This brochure provides a summary of the Guidelines, including an overview of administrative and screening elements that can help companies exporting under both license exceptions and licenses. Screening elements have been cross-referenced to the General Prohibitions identified in Part 736 of the EAR. The key is to tailor the best practices to your company's specific operations and activities.

MEANING AND DEFINITION

An Export Management System (EMS) is an optional program to assist exporters in complying with the Export Administration Regulations (EAR). A vital part of an EMS is the establishment of mechanisms within the company that provide checks and safeguards at key steps in the order processing system, helping to better manage the overall export process.

Such checks and safeguards help to ensure that the right questions are being asked to preclude exporters from making shipments that are contrary to U.S. export controls and, therefore, inconsistent with the exporter's best interests.

An EMS is a program that helps ensure that each export/reexport is treated consistently and in compliance with U.S. export laws and regulations. It is a map to consistent export compliance.

NEED AND SIGNIFICANCE

An EMS:

- reinforces senior management policy to comply with U.S. export laws and regulations.
- provides management structure and organization for the processing of export transactions.
- ensures accountability for export control tasks by identifying who is responsible for performing each part of the process and who is responsible for overall effectiveness of the system.
- provides a map of the order processing flow and export control safeguards to ensure consistent compliance with export decisions.
- provides written instructions for employees to "screen" export transactions against general prohibitions of exports, reexports and selected transfers to certain end-uses and end-users.

- provides personnel with tools to help ensure they are performing their export control functions accurately and consistently.
- identifies transactions that could normally be exported without a license, but because of the end-use or end-user, require a license.
- streamlines the process and reduces time spent on compliance activities because employees have written instructions, tools and ongoing training.
- provides training and awareness programs to help employees understand and comply with the EAR.
- protects a company, through implementing an ongoing compliance program, against violations of the EAR.

The establishment of an EMS soundly implemented, coupled with good judgment, can greatly reduce the risk of inadvertently exporting to an unauthorized party or for an unauthorized end-use. The establishment of an EMS, in and of itself, will not relieve an exporter of criminal and administrative liability under the law if a violation occurs. Companies and/or persons that act contrary to the EAR could lose their export privileges, be fined, or even be criminally prosecuted. An EMS is not a U.S. Government-mandated requirement. However, in a changing export control environment, it is a program that companies may consider establishing to ensure their actions are handled in a way that they comply with the EAR.

MAIN FACTORS

Understanding the EAR: If an individual or company exports, facilitates exports or engages in other controlled activities, a working knowledge of the EAR and its application is necessary. BIS suggests that company personnel responsible for export controls attend one of the many seminars offered by the Office of Exporter Services (OEXS). Identifying the factors that will form the foundation for the system: Some questions exporters may want to ask as you begin to develop an EMS are:

- In what type of international business activities is the company engaged?

- What resources are dedicated to effecting export transactions and what internal controls are in place, i.e., written procedures, oversight delegation of authority, etc.?
- What does the company export?
- Where are the company's customers located?
- What are the Export Control Classification Numbers for the products exported? Is a license required for export of the products to customers' destinations?
- Does my company hire foreign nationals or allow visits by foreign nationals where U.S. controlled technology may be released?
- Does the company perform contracts, services or employment that it knows or has reason to know will assist in the design, development, production, or use of missiles or chemical or biological weapons or nuclear-related activities?
- What is the business nature of your customers and what is the stated end-use for your products?

Know the Customer: A key objective of an effective EMS is to be able to detect and react to information that raises questions about the legitimacy of a customer or transaction. This guidance refers to the provisions in the regulations that prohibit the use of license exceptions when an exporter "knows that a proscribed end-use, end-user, destination, activity or other violation is involved." The EAR also prohibits specific activities with "knowledge" that a violation is about to occur. These duties require a certain standard of care.

STRUCTURE OF AN EMS

Certain principles have been developed to assist exporters with the establishment of an export management system. Without operational implementation and maintenance of principles, an EMS cannot remain useful and reliable. Each of these principles is considered a link in the chain. One weak link can create a vulnerability that could negatively impact the entire system. These principles are referred to as "Elements" in the Guidelines and include an Order Processing Element, Administrative Elements and Screening Elements:

Administrative Elements:	Screening Elements:
1. Management Commitment	1. Denied Persons & Other Lists
2. Responsible Officials	2. Product Classification/License Determination
3. Record Keeping	3. Diversion Risk
4. Training	4. Nuclear End-Uses/Users
5. Internal Reviews	5. Missile End-Uses/Users
6. Notification	6. Chemical & Biological Weapons End-Uses/Users
	7. Antiboycott Questions
	8. Informed By Letter/Entity List

The content of these elements can be incorporated into your company's existing office procedures. Such elements help establish that export control issues play an important role in a company's day-to-day operation.

Throughout each of the EMS elements, the importance of "documentation" is stressed. The purpose of "documentation" is to provide a method of assurance that the system and procedures are being maintained according to established company policy and consistent with the EAR. If your company is moving toward a paperless environment, "documentation" may need to evolve into other methods of assurance. In thinking about what those other methods might be, consider Part 762.5 of the EAR which may be found on the Government Printing Office Web site, and which describes acceptable records.

ADMINISTRATIVE ELEMENTS

Administrative elements of an Export Management System are designed to help establish the foundation upon which the system will be built.

Management Policy: When establishing an EMS, a company should formulate a clear and concise export control policy statement that outlines senior management's commitment to export compliance. This statement should be communicated to all levels of the company involved in export, reexport, traffic, and related activities; and should emphasize the importance of compliance with U.S. export regulations. The statement of policy should be supported by a sufficient allocation of resources [e.g., time, money, and personnel] in order to make the export compliance program effective.

Responsible Officials: The next step is to identify those positions within the company that are responsible for export control compliance. Personnel given export control functions should have authority commensurate with their responsibilities, including the authority to stop export transactions when export control questions arise.

Record Keeping (required by the EAR): The EAR requires that records of all export transactions be kept for a period of five years. This includes exports made under license exceptions. These records include commercial invoices, copies of Shipper's Export Declarations, and air waybills or bills of lading, etc. A program for maintaining records of export transactions in accordance with the EAR should be developed.

Training: The EAR is frequently amended to reflect changing U.S. national security and foreign policy concerns. Consequently, any EMS should include a program for keeping employees, with export control responsibilities, fully informed and up-to-date on how EAR changes affect their responsibilities.

Internal Review: A qualified person or team should conduct regular internal reviews to ensure that the company's EMS is operating effectively ensuring compliance with all the applicable export regulations. These reviews include verifying that appropriate screening procedures have been implemented and that records are being maintained, as required. The reviewer is a person who is not involved with sales or the day-to-day operation of export control functions, including the EMS, and can be a person who is not a regular employee of the company.

Notification: A system should be established for consulting with BIS when questions arise regarding the propriety of specific export transactions.

ORDER PROCESSING SYSTEM ELEMENT

This element consists of flow charting the entire order process from beginning to end, identifying the areas of highest export control risk, and implementing internal controls that eliminate those risks and ensure continuous compliance with the EAR. There are many different types of internal controls that can be used throughout the process that: require a series of questions be asked or steps be accomplished prior to further processing, deflect and hold the transaction for further review by a designated official, or create an immediate cancellation of the order. For example, at an early step in the process, evaluate whether your customer is a denied person, terrorist or other prohibited party. This action of comparing your customer against various U.S. Government lists is one type of export control screen. Other safeguards you may want to build into your Order Processing Element are described in the Screening Elements:

SCREENING ELEMENTS

These Screening Elements are designed to provide a mechanism to alert companies to red flags and to prevent them from entering into prohibited transactions based upon the end-uses and/or end-users. Although the following screens are presented as individual principles, they are frequently combined and developed into checklist and questionnaire-type tools.

Denied Persons Screen: Denied persons are those individuals and businesses, and any "related persons," that have been denied export privileges by the Commerce Department because they have, or are believed to have, violated the Export Administration Act, the EAR or other trade statutes. No denied persons can legally participate in any transaction that may involve the export of an item subject to the EAR unless authorization is specifically given by BIS. In addition, any person who deals with a denied person in an export-related transaction involving U.S.-origin goods or technical data is subject to administrative sanctions and/or criminal prosecution.

Denial orders are designed to prevent the access of denied persons from exporting or reexporting to denied persons overseas items subject to the EAR. If you export to a denied person, you have violated the EAR. General Prohibition Four, prohibits engaging in actions prohibited by a denial order.

Exporters should be aware that other U.S. Government Agencies publish notices in the Federal Register that may impact international transactions, (e.g., Department of Treasury, Office of Foreign Assets Control Terrorism List).

Product Classification/Licensing Determination Screen: General Prohibition One, prohibits the export/reexport of item(s) subject to the EAR without the proper authorization (license or license exception). There should be a procedure for the classification of each item your company wants to export. The classification of the item is the first step in deciding if a license is required and whether a license exception is available. Using this screen, exporters should be able to determine which authorization should be used for the export of an item to a destination. The most common tool used to perform this procedure is a Product/Country Matrix, supplemented by written narrative instructions that communicate conditions, specific parameters of license exceptions, and other transaction sensitivities.

Diversion Risk Screen: The Diversion Risk Screen is based upon the Know Your Customer Guidance and the Red Flag Indicators. The objective of creating this tool is to ensure that personnel are aware of red flags associated with your company products and know to question transactions that raise hints about the legitimacy of the end-use/end-user. This element may be used as a tool to prevent violations of General Prohibitions Six, Seven and Ten found in Part 736 of the EAR. General Prohibition Six prohibits the export or reexport of items to embargoed destinations [Part 746 of the EAR] without the proper license authorization (license or license exception). General Prohibition Seven prohibits Support of Proliferation Activities. General Prohibition Ten prohibits proceeding with transactions with knowledge that a violation has occurred or is about to occur. A person/company may not sell, transfer, export, reexport, finance, order, buy, remove, conceal, store, use, loan, dispose of, transport, forward, or otherwise service, any item subject to the EAR with knowledge that a violation of the EAR, the Export Administration Act, order, license, license exception, or other issued authorization has occurred, is about to occur in connection with the item.

Sensitive Nuclear End-Uses/End-Users Screen: Exporters can establish a system to ensure that transactions do not involve prohibited nuclear end-uses. A license is required to ship certain items identified on the CCL as controlled for nuclear non-proliferation reasons because of the nature of the product. This screen would also be used to determine whether items otherwise eligible for license exception require a license because of specific nuclear related end-uses. Some questions an exporter might ask are:

- Is a license required under the CCL?
- Some items are controlled to all destinations or some countries.
- Is the customer involved either directly or indirectly in any prohibited nuclear activities, whether or not the commodity is specifically designed or modified for such activities?
- Is the item going to be used in one of the activities described in Part 744.2?
- Has BIS "informed" you individually or publicly via a notice in the Federal Register that a license is required for export/reexport of specified items to specified end-users?

Missile End-Uses/End-Users Screen: Exporters can establish a system to ensure that transactions do not involve prohibited missile end-use or end-users. A license is required to ship certain items related to the design, development, production or use of missiles to all destinations. These items are identified in the CCL as controlled for missile technology reasons. In addition, sales of items that normally are eligible for license exceptions require a license to prohibited missile-related activities. Some questions exporters might ask include:

- Does the transaction involve an item on the CCL subject to missile technology controls?
- Is the export destined for activities involving the design, development, production or use of missiles?
- Is it being shipped to a country, region, or project specially designated in the EAR as a missile concern?
- Has BIS "informed" you individually or publicly via a notice in the Federal Register that a license is required for export/reexport of specified items to specified end-users?

Chemical/Biological Weapons End-Uses/End-Users Screen: Exporters can establish a system to ensure that transactions do not involve prohibited chemical or biological weapons end-uses or end-users. A license is required to all destinations except Australia Group members of chemical precursors and related technical data; for all destinations except Canada for biological agents and related technical data; and to listed items that are normally eligible for license exceptions require a license because of the end-use or end-user. Some questions exporters might ask include:

- Does the transaction involve an item on the CCL subject to control for chemical or biological weapons reasons?
- Is the item going to be used in one of the activities described in Part 744.4 of the EAR on the Government Printing Office Web site?
- Is the export destined for a country specially designated in the EAR?
- Has the customer made requests for safety/security devices/measures that would be excessive for the end-use, or is there a lack of familiarity with appropriate safety/security measures?
- Is the customer reluctant to provide information on the location of the plant or place where the materials or technical data are to be used or the equipment is to be installed?
- Has BIS "informed" you individually or publicly via a notice in the Federal Register that a license is required for export/reexport of specified items to specified end-users?

Antiboycott Compliance Screen: This is a tool that can be used to alert and remind personnel of restrictive trade practices or boycotts that the U.S. prohibits. The questions listed are a sample of what you can create for use in your company operations for assessing proposed transactions against conduct prohibited under the Export Administration Act:

- Is there a request to take any action which has the effect of supporting or furthering the Arab Boycott of Israel?

- Is there a request to agree to refuse or actual refusals to do business with Israel or with blacklisted companies?
- Is there a request to agree to discriminate or actual discrimination against other persons based on race, religion, sex, national origin, or nationality?
- Has a request been made to furnish information about business relationships with Israel or with blacklisted companies?
- Has a request been made to furnish information about the race, religion, sex, or national origin of another person?
- Does the letter of credit include requests to take boycott related actions prohibited by the antiboycott regulations?

Informed Letter/Entity List Screen: A screen can be established to ensure that transactions involving items subject to the EAR do not involve parties who are on the Entity List without proper review and documentation. The Department of Commerce maintains export controls to prevent the proliferation of chemical or biological weapons, nuclear weapons or explosive devices, and missile systems. General Prohibition Five (Part 736.2(b)(5) of the EAR) prohibits exports and reexports to certain end-users or end-uses without a license. In the form of Supplement No. 4 to Part 744, BIS maintains an Entity List to provide notice informing the public of certain entities subject to such licensing requirements.

Part 744.1 provides that a license is required for exports and reexports to parties on the Entity List for specified items. For example, if the specified items are "all items subject to the EAR," then a license is required for all exports and reexports to the named party. However, if the Entity List specifies a narrower product category such as computers, then each export or reexport of a computer to that party requires a license. The license requirement for specified items exists regardless of the actual end-use.

2

Trade

Trade is the voluntary exchange of goods, services, or both. Trade is also called commerce. A mechanism that allows trade is called a market. The original form of trade was barter, the direct exchange of goods and services. Modern traders instead generally negotiate through a medium of exchange, such as money. As a result, buying can be separated from selling, or earning. The invention of money (and later credit, paper money and non-physical money) greatly simplified and promoted trade. Trade between two traders is called bilateral trade, while trade between more than two traders is called multilateral trade.

Trade exists for many reasons. Due to specialisation and division of labor, most people concentrate on a small aspect of production, trading for other products. Trade exists between regions because different regions have a comparative advantage in the production of some tradable commodity, or because different regions' size allows for the benefits of mass production. As such, trade at market prices between locations benefits both locations.

Trading can also refer to the action performed by traders and other market agents in the financial markets.

HISTORICAL BACKGROUND

Trade originated with the start of communication in prehistoric times. Trading was the main facility of prehistoric people, who bartered goods and services from each other when there was no such thing as the modern day currency. Peter Watson dates the history of long-distance commerce from circa 150,000 years ago.

Trade is believed to have taken place throughout much of recorded human history. There is evidence of the exchange of obsidian and flint during the stone age. Materials used for creating jewelry were traded with Egypt since 3000 BC. Long-range trade routes first appeared in the 3rd millennium BC, when Sumerians in Mesopotamia traded with the Harappan civilization of the Indus Valley. The Phoenicians were noted sea traders, travelling across the Mediterranean Sea, and as far north as Britain for sources of tin to manufacture bronze. For this purpose they established trade colonies the Greeks called emporia.

From the beginning of Greek civilization until the fall of the Roman empire in the 5th century, a financially lucrative trade brought valuable spice to Europe from the far east, including China. Roman commerce allowed their empire to flourish and endure. Their widespread empire produced a stable and secure transportation network that enabled the shipment of trade goods without fear of significant piracy.

The fall of the Roman empire, and the succeeding Dark Ages brought instability to Western Europe and a near collapse of the trade network. Nevertheless some trade did occur. For instance, Radhanites were a medieval guild or group (the precise meaning of the word is lost to history) of Jewish merchants who traded between the Christians in Europe and the Muslims of the Near East.

From the 8th to the 11th century, the Vikings and Varangians traded as they sailed from and to Scandinavia. Vikings sailed to Western Europe, while Varangians to Russia. The Hanseatic League was an alliance of trading cities that maintained a trade monopoly over most of Northern Europe and the Baltic, between the 13th and 17th centuries.

Vasco da Gama restarted the European Spice trade in 1498. Prior to his sailing around Africa, the flow of spice into Europe was controlled by Islamic powers, especially Egypt. The spice trade was of major economic importance and helped spur the Age of Exploration. Spices brought to Europe from distant lands were some of the most valuable commodities for their weight, sometimes rivaling gold.

In the 16th century, Holland was the centre of free trade, imposing no exchange controls, and advocating the free movement of goods.

Trade in the East Indies was dominated by Portugal in the 16th century, the Netherlands in the 17th century, and the British in the 18th century.

In 1776, Adam Smith published the paper An Inquiry into the Nature and Causes of the Wealth of Nations. It criticised Mercantilism, and argued that economic specialisation could benefit nations just as much as firms. Since the division of labour was restricted by the size of the market, he said that countries having access to larger markets would be able to divide labour more efficiently and thereby become more productive.

Smith said that he considered all rationalisations of import and export controls "dupery", which hurt the trading nation at the expense of specific industries.

In 1799, the Dutch East India Company, formerly the world's largest company, became bankrupt, partly due to the rise of competitive free trade.

In 1817, David Ricardo, James Mill and Robert Torrens showed that free trade might benefit the industrially weak as well as the strong, in the famous theory of comparative advantage. In Principles of Political Economy and Taxation Ricardo advanced the doctrine still considered the most counterintuitive in economics:

When an inefficient producer sends the merchandise it produces best to a country able to produce it more efficiently, both countries benefit.

The ascendancy of free trade was primarily based on national advantage in the mid 19th century. That is, the calculation made was whether it was in any particular country's self-interest to open its borders to imports.

John Stuart Mill proved that a country with monopoly pricing power on the international market could manipulate the terms of trade through maintaining tariffs, and that the response to this might be reciprocity in trade policy. Ricardo and others had suggested this earlier. This was taken as evidence against the universal doctrine of free trade, as it was believed that more of the economic surplus of trade would accrue to a country following reciprocal, rather than completely free, trade policies.

This was followed within a few years by the infant industry scenario developed by Mill anticipated New Trade Theory by promoting the theory that government had the "duty" to protect young industrics, although only for a time necessary for them to develop full capacity. This became the policy in many countries attempting to industrialise and out-compete English exporters.

The Great Depression was a major economic recession that ran from 1929 to the late 1930s. During this period, there was a great drop in trade and other economic indicators.

The lack of free trade was considered by many as a principal cause of the depression. Only during the World War II the recession ended in United States. Also during the war, in 1944, 44 countries signed the Bretton Woods Agreement, intended to prevent national trade barriers, to avoid depressions.

It set up rules and institutions to regulate the international political economy: the International Monetary Fund and the International Bank for Reconstruction and Development (later divided into the World Bank and Bank for International Settlements).

These organisations became operational in 1946 after enough countries ratified the agreement. In 1947, 23 countries agreed to the General Agreement on Tariffs and Trade to promote free trade.

Free trade advanced further in the late 20th century and early 2000s:

- 1992 European Union lifted barriers to internal trade in goods and labour.
- January 1, 1994 NAFTA took effect
- 1994 The GATT Marrakech Agreement specified formation of the WTO.

- January 1, 1995 World Trade Organization was created to facilitate free trade, by mandating mutual most favoured nation trading status between all signatories.
- 2005, the Central American Free Trade Agreement was signed; It includes the United States and the Dominican Republic.

Development of Money

The first instances of money were objects with intrinsic value. This is called commodity money and includes any commonly-available commodity that has intrinsic value; historical examples include pigs, rare seashells, whale's teeth, and (often) cattle. In medieval Iraq, bread was used as an early form of money. In Mexico under Montezuma cocoa beans were money.

Currency was introduced as a standardised money to facilitate a wider exchange of goods and services. This first stage of currency, where metals were used to represent stored value, and symbols to represent commodities, formed the basis of trade in the Fertile Crescent for over 1500 years.

Numismatists have examples of coins from the earliest large-scale societies, although these were initially unmarked lumps of precious metal.

Ancient Sparta minted coins from iron to discourage its citizens from engaging in foreign trade.

The system of commodity money in many instances evolved into a system of representative money. In this system, the material that constitutes the money itself had very little intrinsic value, but none the less such money achieves significant market value through scarcity or controlled supply.

SILENT TRADE

Silent trade, also called dumb barter, or depot trade, is a method by which people with no common language could barter goods. Group A would leave trade goods in a prominent position and signal, by gong, fire, or drum for example, that they had done so. Group B would then arrive at the spot, examine the goods and deposit their trade goods that they wanted to exchange and withdraw. Group A would then return and either accept the trade by taking the goods from Group B or withdraw again leaving Group B to add to or change out items to create an equal valuc. The trade ends when Group A accepts Group B's offer and removes the offered goods leaving Group B to remove the original goods.

The practice was certainly well established between tribes in Africa in their trade with India. Cosmas Indicopleustes describes this practiced in Azania, where officials from Axum bartered for gold with beef 1. Prince Henry the Navigator of Portugal recorded this practice when he occupied Ceuta in 1415.

3

Effective Export Control System

Effective export controls must be a combined effort between governments and companies. This section will discuss three distinct aspects of a good export control system, as well as offer some possible solutions to challenges that may arise. It will discuss:

- The government's role in developing policies to better regulate export controls and create an environment supportive of nonproliferation efforts;
- Industry's role in developing internal compliance systems to ensure strict adherence to governments' policy;
- The need for companies and governments to work together to enforce those policies; and
- Specific challenges and possible solutions to problems in implementing export controls.

INTRODUCTION

The purpose of nuclear export controls is not to deny the export of every nuclear weapon-related commodity, but to create obstacles and bottlenecks in secret nuclear programs by recognizing key items and blocking their transfer.

The German Peace Research Institute has identified several functions of export controls: Delaying and Increasing costs. Export controls can delay the acquisition of nuclear weapons and increase the costs of success.

Deterrence: The threat to punish violations of foreign trade restrictions is a deterrent against those who would illegally export and import items. Two conditions, however, must be met. First, a significant probability of detection must exist. Second, the severity of the punishment must outweigh the potential benefits.

Detecting and Preventing Proliferation: Export controls increase the probability that illicit procurement is uncovered and the sinister intentions of would-be proliferants discovered. If a country is detected trying to import items illicitly, an effective export control system can increase scrutiny of that country and improve the chance of preventing future illicit efforts.

Intelligence Gathering: The process of operating an effective export control system provides governments with opportunities to identify and analyze clandestine nuclear programs.

Confidence-building: An effective export control system, particularly in conjunction with international safeguards and national intelligence activities, can create confidence within the international community that a state is abiding by its international obligations. If no violations of export control regulations are registered, states can more credibly believe that these countries are not engaged in clandestine nuclear activities.

Triggering Safeguards or Broadened Declarations: Export controls provide the mechanism to define items subject to international safeguards. Internationally agreed lists of controlled items serve to define what a state must declare or report to the International Atomic Energy Agency (IAEA) under advanced safeguards agreements.

Supplier's Treaty Compliance: By controlling the foreign trade activities of their citizens and of firms under their jurisdiction, states fulfill their obligations under Article III of the Nuclear Non-Proliferation Treaty (NPT) and the Nuclear Suppliers Group.

For export controls to be effective, governments and companies need to work together. In the United States, the Department of Energy has initiated the International Nuclear Export Control Program (INECP) that aims to strengthen international export control practices. Although written mainly from the perspective of the government, the INECP has summarized the roles of companies and governments regarding effective export control:

- Export controls rest on an interlocking set of national and international laws, regulations, and agreements. These laws require a transparent and standardized national licensing system and competent technical review of proposed transfers of nuclear-related materials, equipment, and technologies. These reviews must take into account national laws, international obligations, and proliferation risks associated with a particular item or technology, as well as the reliability of the end-user and intermediate consignees.
- Industry awareness and compliance are the prerequisites for the success of any nation's system of nuclear export controls. Key goals are promoting communication between government and industry and establishing procedures for industry to regulate the export of controlled commodities. The government should promote industry use of internal compliance programs and other tools-of-the-trade to reinforce export control 'best practices' at facilities that produce nuclear related commodities.
- The last line of defense in export controls is a government's ability to prevent illicit shipments while facilitating legitimate commerce. Weaknesses in this area are a leading proliferation risk today. This risk is particularly acute for states engaging in significant transshipment trade. In collaboration with other agencies, the governments should provide tools that enable customs personnel, border guards, and other officials in partnering countries to enforce their national nuclear export control requirements.

POLICIES AND PROCEDURES BY GOVERNMENTS

Governments need to develop a sustainable infrastructure designed to control sensitive exports without unduly limiting trade. Moreover, governments need to establish and reinforce an export control "culture" that emphasizes nonproliferation security over specific sales and company contracts. Guarding against illicit exports of advanced technology or other dual-use items should be an ongoing effort, not just a passing concern with each scare over Iraq, Iran, or another country. Responsible export attitudes must be cultivated and encouraged. Without the government's support and positive reinforcement, individual companies might not take the initiative to proactively limit sensitive trade on their own.

On the most basic level, governments need to draft export laws and adopt a standard set of export control procedures. These policies are the foundation upon which everything else is built. These regulations should be in depth and comprehensive. The Lawyer's Alliance for World Security (LAWS) developed a compilation of 14 generic concepts that export laws should incorporate, which should serve as a basis for export control regulations. Although this compilation does not represent the exact language for adoption, governments have used this as working model on which to fashion their export control policy.

The 14 areas covered include:

- Policy-states the government's position on export controls and how it will proceed to accomplish the goals;
- Right to Export-states that one has the inherent right to export unless the item or country to which you are exporting are pursuant to government regulations;
- Authority-identifies the person or agency ultimately responsible for enacting the policies;
- Control List-lists specific states and items that are subject to licensing requirements;
- Controlled Countries-lists countries to which exports are limited or prohibited;
- Licensing-explains the various types of licenses and what is required for what export;
- Special Licensing Authority-provides guidelines for a special license for specifically named "dual-use" exports;
- Notification of the Public-accounts for the government's responsibility to keep the public informed on all the export control policies;

- Advisory Committees-establishes a committee of experts to assist and advise on matters relating to export control policy and procedures;
- Negotiations with Other Countries-verifies that authority heads and officials, in consultation with the various heads of other appropriate agencies dealing with export controls, negotiate and cooperate with other nations when establishing and enforcing export control policies;
- Record Keeping-mandates that all records of licenses and transactions be properly maintained and made available to other agencies if requested;
- Confidentiality-states that all information submitted by an exporter is not to be made public without the consent of the applicant or as authorized by law;
- Penalties-states that there should be an agency established to review suspect exports and enforce penalties as designated by officials and experts; and
- Transshipments-states that items in transit through the country are subject to control laws and regulations.

In order to cultivate a culture sensitive to the need for export controls, however, merely having strongly worded policy is not enough. The ultimate goal is for companies to do more than just obey the letter of the law.

Governments should make a concerted effort to engage companies and government enterprises. Governments should do this by acting as a liaison to the companies to facilitate a better understanding of the laws. The government should establish programs geared towards training companies and company representatives through workshops and seminars. The government also needs to provide assistance by disseminating information and be better prepared to respond to inquires or problems in a timely and efficient manner. The government needs to construct user-friendly aides and resources to assist the companies with adhering to the regulations. These resources need to be provided in a variety of forums, through personal contacts with representatives, seminars and workshops, hardcopy print, and electronic resources.

Each government needs to collaborate with experts in the nonproliferation, commerce, and border control fields to develop appropriate export control licensing policies. It then needs to train government and industry officials regarding those policies to make sure these policies are properly executed.

For example, the government needs to work hand-in hand with the customs and border control guards to ensure that the items listed on the export declaration are identical to the actual items being shipped. This ensures that undeclared or illegal exports are not permitted to leave the country under false pretenses.

The government should also take into consideration international export controls as well. It should look at the Zangger Committee Trigger List, which implements supplier commitments in the Nonproliferation Treaty, and the Nuclear Supplier's Group, which places additional controls on the transfer of nuclear commodities.

Governments have met for over two decades to work out satisfactory arrangements for exporting dual-use items. The results of such meetings can be seen in agreements such as the Wassenaar Arrangement on Export Controls for Conventional Arms and Dual-Use Goods and Technologies (WA) was established to promote transparency and greater responsibility in transfers of conventional arms and dual-use goods and technologies. Participating states seek, through their respective national policies, to ensure that transfers of these items do not contribute to the development or enhancement of military capabilities, which undermine nonproliferation goals.

Towards this aim, WA obtained from its member states a collection of the "best practices" for effective export control policies, including:

- Consultations occur among relevant government agencies within the exporting country with respect to license applications to export very sensitive list (VSL) items. During these consultations, the appropriateness of the quantity and technological level of the item to the stated end-use, and bona fides of the end-user are among the criteria considered;

- In order to determine, inter alia, the risk of diversion or unauthorized use, additional information on end-users may be gathered, as necessary, using appropriate means ranging from documentation to visitation (with consent of the visiting country) prior to the licensing decision;
- As necessary, post-shipment verification may be carried out through appropriate means by the exporter, supplier or officials of the exporting country.

While these examples are specifically for items considered most sensitive, the same careful procedures would be required for other, less sensitive items, as well. For more detailed examples of WA's best practices, click here.

The United States has a good web site, the Export Administration Regulation Database, which contains more helpful practices and additional information on the U.S. export control system. Other countries in the NSG also maintain informative web sites in different languages.

THE GERMAN EXAMPLE

Germany is a useful model of a specific country that drastically improved its national export control laws in a relatively short period of time. In the late 1980s and early 1990s, several German companies were found to have exported numerous sensitive items that had greatly assisted Iraq's clandestine weapons of mass destruction (WMD) programs, particularly its nuclear weapons program. Blame for these exports fell not only on the companies and individuals, but also on the German government.

When it was discovered that German companies had been providing vital assistance to Iraq's weapons program, that knowledge prompted dramatic reform of Germany's export control system. Prior to the Gulf War, the German government did not have strict export control laws, and the laws that it did have were poorly enforced. Therefore, in order to regain the confidence of the international community, Germany severely tightened its export control policies and enforcement procedures. Formerly a weak system overrun with loopholes was transformed, within the course of a few years, into one of the world's strongest systems.

In the late 1980s, the German government was becoming increasingly aware that something was wrong with its export control system. As early as 1988, the government conducted a parliamentary inquiry into doubtful nuclear trade. Based on its findings, the government tightened the interagency process for licensing to give Germany's Foreign Office a stronger role in trade with sensitive countries. In 1989, Germany sought to strengthen export control legislation. These efforts, however, were inadequate and significant illicit exports continued to occur. After the Gulf War, the UN-mandated inspection process revealed how German companies easily manipulated Germany's weak and over-burdened export control system with false and misleading end-user information. Other governments condemned Germany's illicit exports to Iraq and elsewhere, and Germany was accosted as a "black sheep" of export controls.

The German media played an extremely important role in creating a strong political constituency demanding fundamental change. Extensive publicity about these illicit or questionable exports damaged the reputations of many German companies. They not only suffered legal consequences, but also were condemned publicly as amoral.

In order to regain its image and international respect, the German government radically tightened its export control system twice-once in 1990, and again in 1992. The penalties for foreign trade violations were drastically increased and the range of mechanisms for effective export control was expanded.

In Germany, exports are not prohibited, per se. Rather, exports are subject to an extensive authorization process. This approval process became more extensive in the post Gulf War years. The government also provided the export classification system with the general "catch-all clause," which says that all products are subjected to approval requirements to the extent that the exporter has knowledge of an actual or intended use for weapons production.

Under the new laws, German companies are required to create stringent internal compliance systems and senior officials are now legally responsible for the actions of their employees. The law permits the prosecution of senior company officials for the illegal exports of lower level employees, creating a powerful incentive for companies to create stringent internal controls.

Despite the tightening of German governmental standards, a major burden still resides on the companies to act with honesty and moral integrity. The companies are recognized as playing a major role in achieving nonproliferation goals. In several cases, their internal compliance systems have become models for both other companies and governments. For a more in-depth discussion of German export control laws and practices, please click here.

MODELS OF INTERNAL COMPLIANCE SYSTEMS

Corporations and government-owned entities must share in the responsibility to halt the proliferation of sensitive nuclear or nuclear-related technology. Officials, management, and employees of companies must make a firm commitment to proactively address nonproliferation through strict export control regulations and implementation. The most common method for a company to accomplish this goal is the creation of an internal compliance system.

An internal compliance system is an arrangement in which a company ensures that it is completing legal transactions, obeying the regulations enacted by the government, and fulfilling company export policies. Internal compliance systems typically include a set of procedures that company officials must satisfy before an item leaves the company. Such procedures include a thorough investigation of the buyer and end-user prior to the shipment of a purchased item off-site.

However, many companies lack procedures or resources to establish effective internal compliance systems. In some cases, the internal compliance systems that are established do not have the resources that they require to function effectively. In other cases, company officials lack even rudimentary knowledge of their government's export laws and regulations, let alone the expertise to create an internal compliance system. Many models of internal compliance systems exist. One particularly effective system was created by the German company Leybold in the early 1990s. It provides an excellent example of how a company confronted the challenge of internally strengthening export controls. In the early 1990s Leybold developed an internal compliance system that not just met the requirements for Germany's strengthened export laws but exceeded them. Click here for an in-depth discussion of this development. Since the early 1990s, Leybold has changed owners and split into many smaller companies, but the different entities have tried to maintain the internal compliance system.

KEY QUESTIONS AND RED FLAGS

There are several steps a company can take to ensure its transactions are viable and legal. Most important, a company must develop a set of procedures specifically intended to guard against sales of sensitive or dual-use technology to unauthorized parties. The procedures must be applied throughout the entire framework of the company, including any separate divisions and subsidiaries.

Internal compliance systems should address several specific goals:

- To develop contacts and good-standing relationships between the company and export agencies;
- To remain informed of updates to the government's export control laws and regulations;
- To centralize export-related questions and issues;
- To standardize procedures;
- To provide early warning and screening of all inquires and orders;
- To generate coherent and complete documentation of all sensitive export transactions; and
- To train all employees engaged, either directly or indirectly, with exports.

The most important aim of an internal compliance system is to prevent doing business with unauthorized parties. There are several measures that can be taken to ensure that company officials are not dealing with unauthorized parties. First and foremost, one must know the customer. A thorough background check of any customer requesting sensitive items should be performed. Many supplier countries publish databases containing lists of names of individuals and companies who are known to be associated with illicit procurement efforts.

The U.S. Bureau of Industry and Security, for example, has developed a comprehensive "Denied Persons List" as a reference tool to help companies recognize potential violators of export laws and other parties who are known to have previously engaged in illicit procurement behavior. To view this list, click here. Checking national lists should be done routinely. Such checks should include any freight forwarding companies, as well as intermediate consignees and the ultimate consignee.

Companies should develop and apply routinely a specific set of questions to examine each potential sale prior to completing the transaction. Questions should include:

- Careful screening of the customer
    - o Is the identity of the customer or end-user requesting the item transparent?
    - o Is there any intermediary agent involved?
    - o Is the customer or its address similar or the same to that found on the governmental denied persons list or on a governmental or company database of known front companies?
    - o Is the customer or purchasing agent hesitant to provide information regarding the end-use of the item in question, or the future research and development or the industrial production of the item in question?
    - o Does the product's capabilities coincide with the buyer's line of business?
    - o Is the item in question incompatible with the technical level of the country?
    - o Is the customer willing to pay in cash for an expensive item that normally requires financing? Or are there unusual favorable payment terms, prices or other conditions offered or accepted by the customer?

   - o Does the customer have little or no business background?
   - o Is the customer unfamiliar with the item and its capabilities but still wishes to purchase it?
   - o Is the customer related to military business or under the control of the defense ministry or armed forces?

- Careful screening of end-use or end-user
   - o Is the buyer evasive and unclear about whether the product is intended for domestic use, for export or for reexport when questioned?
   - o Have the nonproliferation credentials of the recipient country been thoroughly screened?
   - o Has particular attention been paid to whether or not the product or service is intended for military use or subject to licensing?
   - o Careful screening of final destination
      - * Is the requested order suitable to improve existing equipment or plants for military use?
      - * Are there excessive safety or security measures in light of the nature of the equipment?
      - * Is equipment to be installed in an area under strict security control or adjacent to military-related facilities?
   - o Careful screening of shipping procedures
      - * Are delivery dates vague or are deliveries planned for out of the way destinations or is a freight-forwarding firm listed as the product's final destination?
      - * Is the shipping route abnormal for the product and destination?
      - * Is the packaging inconsistent with the shipping mode or destination?
      - * Are there unusual requests concerning labeling or shipment of goods?

- o Careful screening of terms of sale
    - * Are there any requests for normally unnecessary devices or no request for usually necessary devices and lack of a convincing explanation for the request or non-request?
    - * Was there no request for performance guarantee, warranty or normal service?
    - * Are routine installation, training or maintenance services declined by the customer?
    - * Does the customer request completion of a partly finished product?

The company should also evaluate whether the recipient country is a member of an international nonproliferation agreement or regime. In addition, it should determine the degree to which the importing government cooperates with nonproliferation policies, and whether or not the buyer or end-user has been previously denied by another supplier for an item they are requesting.

In carrying out the normal procedures of evaluating purchases, authorities also recommend that officials do not "self-blind" themselves, meaning that they do not cut off or ignore the flow of information that is received in the normal course of business. For company officials, the best advice is: Ask questions and be alert!

The United States has developed a set of indicators, or "red flags," that can indicate that the customer is attempting to engage in illegal or potentially illegal transactions. These indicators are similar to some of the above questions, but are designed to alert company officials to the need for increased suspicions and scrutiny. The following is a list of examples of red flags published by the U.S. Bureau of Industry and Security Export Enforcement web site:

- o If the customer or purchasing agent is reluctant to offer information about the end-use of the item.
- o If the product's capabilities do not correspond with the buyer's stated line of business, such as an order for sophisticated computers from a small restaurant.

- o If the item ordered is incompatible with the technical level of the country to which it is being shipped, such as semiconductor manufacturing equipment bring shipped to a country that has no electronics industry.
- o If the customer is willing to pay cash for an expensive item that ordinarily requires financing.
- o If the customer has little or no business background or if the customer is unfamiliar with the product but still wants to purchase the item.
- o If routine installation, training or maintenance services are declined by the customer.
- o If delivery dates are vague, or deliveries are planned for out of the way destinations.
- o If a freight forwarding firm is listed as the product's final destination.
- o If the shipping route is abnormal for the product destination.
- o If the packaging is inconsistent with the stated method of shipment or destination.
- o If when questioned, the buyer is evasive and remains especially unclear about whether the purchased item is for domestic use, export, or re-export.
- o If the customer or its address is similar to one of the parties found on the Denied Persons List.

Should a company official be asked to participate in a transaction that is suspicious or illegal, authorities recommend refraining from the transaction, disclosing the information to the government's established export control agency, and waiting for the agency's response. Any information that a company gathers could be useful to prosecuting the suspicious customer or building a dossier on the individual or company in question.

Other useful lists of questions or procedures exist. The Wassenaar Arrangement established a list of end-use assurances that helps provide a checklist for both governments and companies of what information needs to be obtained for a particular transaction. Items on this list include:

- o Making sure to provide a detailed description of goods, which discloses their true identity;
- o Describe the specific end-use of the goods;
- o Provide assurances that the goods will not be used other than for the stated purposes and/or provide an undertaking that the goods will be used for civil end-uses;
- o Provide certification that the goods will be installed at the premises of the end-user or will only be used by the end-user;
- o The final consignee/end-user's undertaking not to transship or re-export the goods covered by the End-use Certificate/Statement;
- o The final consignee/end-user's undertaking not to divert the goods covered by the End-use Certificate/Statement to another destination or location in the importing country;
- o Provide a commitment by the final consignee to provide the exporter or the exporting government with proof of importation, upon request (e.g., provide a Delivery Verification Certificate); and
- o Obtaining signature and end-use certification by the final consignee's/end-user's government or other authority as to the authenticity of the primary details provided in the document.

Internal Export Control Hierarchy

An export control hierarchy creates at a company or government-owned entity a system of checks and balances within separate divisions and ensures that these different divisions work together to examine the sale of products, services, or technology. The company should also establish a senior group to oversee and take responsibility for the internal compliance system's integrity, effectiveness, and compliance.

The U.S. Lawrence Livermore National Laboratory (LLNL) developed a unique and thorough way to implement U.S. export control laws and regulations that uses a hierarchical system.

It developed a panel whose members consist of various managers of its export control programs and its chair is the Export Control Officer. These members include:

- o Commodity Export Manager-who is responsible for assessing and ensuring that all LLNL commodity exports are in full compliance with U.S. export control laws and regulations. This manager also serves as LLNL's policy and licensing liaison with the federal government's export control community on commodity export matters.
- o Technology Export Manager-who is responsible for assessing whether or not a proposed technology (or software) export requires a license, and also serves as LLNL's policy and licensing liaison with the federal government on technology export matters.
- o Sensitive Countries Information Logging System Manager-who is responsible for overseeing the Sensitive Countries Information Logging system, a Department of Energy (DOE) system to track requests for and transmittal of technical information (including software) to countries on the DOE Sensitive Countries List.
- o Foreign Visit/Assignment/Travel Coordinator-who is responsible for coordinating approvals for foreign visits and assignments to the Laboratory and foreign travel by the LLNL personnel.
- o Export Counsel-who is responsible for providing legal guidance to the Laboratory's Export Control Office and Panel.
- o Topical/Functional Experts-Individuals from throughout the Laboratory may be called upon to provide technical expertise to the Export Control Office or Panel on an as-needed basis.

Fewer people are used at Argonne National Laboratory (ANL) to control its exports and ensure that ANL adheres to U.S. export laws. ANL assigned certain individuals specific topical areas and developed an internal contact list so that anyone who has questions regarding a specific area can contact the right person. The contact list contains the current name, telephone extension, and organizational affiliation of the technical and administrative personnel responsible for different aspects of ANL's export control processes. Moreover, it also developed the position of Export Control Manager to assist employees in different sections of the laboratory with any general matters related to export control and export control determinations. To look at the list in depth, please click here.

While few companies have the resources or expertise of ANL or LLNL, they serve as models that show the functions a company must perform and the types of responsibilities that must be assigned to officials, which in most companies will involve a smaller group of people.

ADDITIONAL RESPONSIBILITIES FOR AN EFFECTIVE INTERNAL COMPLIANCE SYSTEM

Authority Approval A top company official, such as a chief executive officer (CEO) or the president, needs to act as an export officer and be ultimately responsible for the final approval of all export transactions. This official must have confidence that strong oversight is maintained over all the departments involved in exporting an item.

No product should be allowed to leave the company unless all internal compliance procedures have been met, the proper signatures have been obtained, and the transaction is officially approved by the highest authority. It is imperative that the sales decision be the responsibility of a senior official of the enterprise. A mid-level manager often is most concerned with meeting a sales quota and may have different objectives than that of a top official, who bears the responsibility of ensuring the future of the company.

Training All employees must be informed of their duty to adhere to the established export policies. Their attention to detail and their accurate examinations of export transactions are paramount in the decision making process of whether to proceed with a transaction. Extensive training, therefore, should be mandatory. Export control systems are continually evolving and must continually be monitored and updated. There needs to be a department or official whose purpose is to remain current on export policies on the corporate, national, and international levels, and to disseminate this information in a comprehensible and accessible manner to other employees. Ambiguities can lead to confusion and could contribute to unsatisfactory practices or performances. The better a complex law or policy is understood, the more likely it will be applied correctly in practice.

To do this, the department needs to develop a good-standing liaison with government export officials and maintain contacts with international export control groups so that they remain abreast of any changes. Moreover, the department needs to share its resources and export information with other companies, both domestically and internationally, to promote a community of free exchange and export control assistance.

Employees should be required to complete training courses to learn about not only specific export regulations, but also about the particular products the company exports, ways in which such products can be misused, how to identify illegalities, and how to detect suspicious and inconsistent behavior. Resource materials need to be made available to them, and frequent workshops and seminars dedicated to updating their knowledge base needs to occur on a regular basis. Important updates can also be made on an "as needed" basis through personal contacts and company memorandums.

Reviewing the System Internal compliance systems should be reviewed to ensure that policy procedures are enforced and that high standards are maintained. Two separate reviews should be conducted. One review evaluates policies to ensure that they meet legal, regulatory, and company requirements and expectations. The other review assesses the implementation of the system. Reviews can be done internally or by a third party.

Special attention should be paid to making sure that all the company export policies are being fully implemented by the employees, and that employees are not taking short-cuts that could undermine the effectiveness of the process. The findings of any review should be widely available internally and senior management should be promptly briefed on the results of the review. Following the review, any changes to policy or procedures should be implemented as quickly as possible. Taking Advantage of Available Resources Sometimes companies will encounter difficulties when implementing export control policies. If a company needs further assistance or technical advice, it should seek the expertise of other export control experts, such as representatives from government agencies, other groups specifically designed to monitor and develop export controls, or even other companies.

A company should consult available resources to familiarize itself with the export control system. These resources would assist in creating a step-by-step procedure on how to verify end-users, as well as work to ensure that the company remains up-to-date on export control laws and regulations. These resources should help to curb any potential problems that the company may face.

To ensure that an end-user is legitimate, the company can use a variety of resources. The internet provides a wide range of domestic and international databases and directories that list both private and public companies. These directories provide users with such company vitals as a listing of the board of directors, number of employees, products produced or services rendered, and some even delve into stock and financial information as well. Click here for links to additional export control resources.

Creation of Internal Resources & Databases Companies need to establish their own internal databases of denied persons, companies, and countries of concern. These databases should include any government lists and international lists. Moreover, the company needs to make sure that it is not in violation of any multilateral regime requirements. Therefore, it needs to establish dossiers on individual countries' laws and regulations as well as any trade organizations or other trade governing entities.

In order to establish these various lists and dossiers, the company should consult the proper government authorities and agencies both domestically and internationally, as well any domestic or international trade organizations, and nonproliferation organizations and experts. A variety of different resources are available.

Companies should develop a basic understanding of the process of proliferation and methods to stop it. Although expertise in nuclear weapon design and production is not necessary, company export control officials should be familiar with several known types of nuclear weapons, and with the processes to make the materials that go into them.

Senior company officials should be aware of the methods proliferant countries use to disguise their procurement networks. Dual-use items are hidden by using civilian-use cover stories and by routing the technology through countries that are not suspected of wanting nuclear weapons, but that are less careful about export controls. An awareness of these tactics is as important as knowing which countries are likely final destinations.

THE QUESTION OF APPROVAL

The company should use its discretion when rendering an export approval. The interests of a company may be best served by approving exports on a case-by-case basis. Items should be segregated into various lists depending on their sensitivity. The higher the sensitivity of the item, the stricter the background check and documentation evaluation. If a company has any doubt regarding the end-use of the product, it should take the responsibility upon itself not to proceed with the transaction, even if the company anticipates receiving an approval from the government's exporting agency. Some exports will inevitably require further research. A company must establish a policy and develop procedures to deal with these suspect exports. For example, once an export has been classified as "suspect," does the company stop the transaction until further research has been completed, and wait until the transaction has been researched and authorized to complete the export, or rather not proceed with the export at all?

Each internal compliance system must develop procedures to augment and improve itself. The system must be able to grow and adapt as company personnel changes, government laws change, or company policy changes. Preventing a system from becoming rigid or obsolete requires sustained commitment by senior management.

ENFORCEMENT

Governments must strictly prosecute export violations. Experience has shown that export control laws are not taken seriously without effective enforcement. In addition, governments must establish strict fines, significant prison sentences, and other penalties severe enough to deter violations of export regulations. Although states are responsible for creating and enforcing laws, companies should also maintain effective procedures to hold their employees responsible for their actions. The Wassenaar Arrangement assembled a collection of practices that illustrate an effective governmental enforcement program. Some of the recommendations include:

- Using threat assessment techniques and procedures for evaluating parties involved in a proposed export transaction, paying particular attention to those considered to be suspicious, unreliable, or presenting a high risk of diversion;
- Maintaining a list of problem end-users to identify license applications deserving closer inspection;
- Obtaining assurances regarding end-use and non re-export of licensed items, as appropriate;
- As necessary, confirming that exported goods have reached their intended destinations using appropriate means, ranging from documentation to on-site verification;
- Seeking voluntary compliance by industry. As appropriate, encourage development by industry of internal compliance programs;
- Providing adequate resources and training for enforcement officers;
- Ensuring that national laws and regulations have statutes of limitations sufficiently long to permit the detection and prosecution of export control violators; and
- Establishing effective penalties (including, as appropriate, criminal sanctions, civil fines, publicity and restriction or denial of export privileges) sufficient to punish and deter violations of export controls.

If a government denies a license to a company, the company should be required to conduct an audit to review its internal compliance measures to understand why it approved the export in the first place. The government should work with the company to rectify any problems that are identified.

On the corporate level, failures or individual acts of indiscretion or poor judgment require punishment and immediate rectification. Employees must know that if they are negligent or violate export control policies, they must bear the consequences of those failures. Punishments should vary, but include employment termination.

FACING OF CHALLENGES

Once a company has established an internal compliance system, it will face many challenges whose solution has proven difficult. Two recurring ones are keeping employees from being lured into illegal sales and obtaining reliable information about end users.

The Psychology of Illegal Exports

Despite the best internal controls, a company official may decide to violate export control laws. Understanding the psychology of those who would violate export control laws may prove useful in preventing a colleague from going too far to make a sale.

A lingering question in examining case studies of illicit exports is why highly skilled and educated technicians would choose to sell dangerous technology to a foreign government illegally. Simple explanations for these illegal activities include excessive greed and a basic moral depravity that permits someone to understand the real damage they may be doing without caring about the consequences. Some people have acted under these impulses, but in the majority of export control violations, these explanations do not hold up well.

Based on interviews conducted by ISIS staff, one particular trait of many businessmen or experts involved in illegal sales was their ability to rationalize their actions, and in some cases, block out the circumstances that would call into question the morality or legality of their actions. They appear to have created stories to justify their actions and repeated them to themselves long enough that they eventually believed their own lies.

They have argued that they had no way of knowing what their export was used for, or that the export was meant for an exclusively civil purpose. They also justified questionable activities by giving themselves a "higher purpose" of saving their companies or employees during times of economic uncertainty. In addition, they convinced themselves that someone would carry out the sales, so it would not prevent anything by refusing the business themselves.

This ability to rationalize and justify their actions appears to be recognized and exploited by proliferant states. These states created stories that would not hold up under intense investigation or scrutiny, but give enough cover to company officials or experts that they could consent to the cooperation. The stories often provide enough explanation for the item to allow the businessmen to avoid asking the questions for which the answers might cause legal or moral conflict.

One example of this type of justification is the repeated assertion by some German businessmen that their work for Iraq in the 1980s was, in fact, for academic research at a university in Baghdad. This rationalization required the Germans to ignore the fact that they had met with military officials during visits to Iraq, and that, in a dictatorship like that of Saddam Hussein's, there is no real independent academic community. In addition, the explanation provided enough of an excuse for the Germans to be able to cooperate without asking further questions which might have resulted in unpleasant answers.

Ensuring End-User Verification

If corporations are to play a major role in thwarting would-be proliferators, they require reliable, current information about the end-users of sensitive items. This type of information is vital in deciding whether to refuse sales or reject contractual commitments, especially in cases where the export is in fact legal, but the end-use of the export remains in question.

Companies often depend on governments for this kind of information. Unfortunately, despite the existence of many databases, key information about certain companies is unavailable or kept secret by governments.

In addition, many companies and governments do not have the resources or expertise to create a system to thoroughly examine end-users. One Russian export control expert, for example, said that more than 90 percent of all Russian enterprises do not have books or other resources with which to research the companies buying their items. Thus, a seller in Russia has a difficult time verifying whether the information the customer provides is reliable and accurate. There is no international centralized database of known front companies or otherwise denied persons. Many countries possess such lists, but often times access to the lists from outside organizations proves difficult. In some cases, the language barrier cannot be overcome, foreign companies are denied access to other country's established lists, or lists are classified and restricted to cleared national officials only.

There remains a need for an open international database on end-users that can be accessed by all companies. To create this database, countries must be more willing to share information on end users. A group of nations, such as the NSG, will need to provide the resources to create and maintain the site. Such a database cannot completely stop front companies from going undetected, but it would make it significantly more difficult for them to illicitly procure items for long.

The United States, Japan and the European Union need to provide additional resources to Russia and other countries that are struggling to implement effective export control systems both on the national and corporate level. A relatively small amount of funds and other resources can significantly increase the security of all.

4

Export Finance

Trade Finance is a specific topic within the financial services industry. It's much different, for example, than commercial lending, mortgage lending or insurance. A product is sold and shipped overseas, therefore, it takes longer to get paid. Extra time and energy is required to make sure that buyers are reliable and creditworthy. In addition, foreign buyers-just like domestic buyers-prefer to delay payment until they receive and resell the goods. Due diligence and careful financial management can mean the difference between profit and loss on each transaction.

This tutorial is intended as an introduction to the different types of trade finance and the different funding sources available. Understanding these alternatives will help borrowers avoid common mistakes like securing the wrong type of financing, miscalculating the amount required or underestimating the cost of borrowing the money.

INTRODUCTION

All sellers want to get paid as quickly as possible, while buyers usually prefer to delay payment, at least until they have received and resold the goods. This is true in domestic as well as international markets.

Increasing globalization has created intense competition for export markets. Importers and exporters are looking for any competitive advantage that would help them to increase their sales. Flexible payment terms has become a fundamental part of any sales package.

Selling on open account, which may be best from a marketing and sales standpoint, places all of the risk with the seller. In essence, the seller ships and turns over title of the product on a promise to pay from the buyer.

Cash-in-advance terms place all of the risk with the buyer as they send payment on a promise that the product will be shipped on time and it will work as advertised. Cash-in-advance often places the seller at a competitive disadvantage. Today, open account terms with extended dating are becoming more common despite the dangers.

Trade finance provides alternative solutions that balance risk and payment. In this overview, we'll outline the two broad categories of trade finance:

- Pre-shipment financing to produce or purchase the material and labor necessary to fulfill the sales order; or
- Post-shipment financing in order to generate immediate cash while offering payment terms to buyers.

GENERAL CONSIDERATIONS

The following factors and considerations apply to financing in general.

In some cases, favorable payment terms make a product more competitive. If the competition offers better terms and has a similar product, a sale can be lost.

In other cases, the exporter may need financing to produce the goods or to finance other aspects of a sale, such as promotion and selling costs, engineering modifications, and shipping costs. Various financing sources are available to exporters, depending on the specifics of the transaction and the exporter's overall financing needs.

Financing Costs

The costs of borrowing, including interest rates, insurance and fees will vary. The total cost and its effect on the price of the product and profit from the transaction should be well understood before a pro forma invoice is submitted to the buyer.

Financing Terms

Costs increase with the length of terms. Different methods of financing are available for short, medium, and long terms. Exporters need to be fully aware of financing limitations so that they secure the right solution with the most favorable terms for seller and buyer.

RISK MANAGEMENT

The greater the risks associated with the transaction, the greater the cost. The creditworthiness of the buyer directly affects the probability of payment to an exporter, but it is not the only factor of concern to a potential lender. The political and economic stability of the buyer's country are taken into consideration.

Lenders are generally concerned with two questions:

- Can the exporter perform? They want to know that the exporter can produce and ship the product on time, and that the product will be accepted by the buyer.
- Can the buyer pay? They want to know that the buyer is reliable with a good credit history. They will evaluate any commercial or political risk.

If a lender is uncertain about the exporter's ability to perform, or if additional credit capacity is needed, government guarantee programs are available that may enable the lender to provide additional financing.

EXPORT INTERMEDIARIES

Many times, small business owners may not have the time or resources to pursue international sales. If there is a demand for the company's product, use of export intermediaries may prove beneficial.

Export Trading Companies (ETCs) and Export Management Companies (EMCs) can help with international sales and marketing efforts. IN some instances, EMCs can help finance export sales. Some of these companies may provide short-term financing or may simply purchase the goods to be exported directly from the manufacturer. This eliminates any risks associated with the export transaction as well as the need for financing.

TYPES OF TRADE FINANCE

Trade Finance

Trade finance generally refers to the financing of individual transactions or a series of revolving transactions. In addition, trade finance loans are often self-liquidating-that is, the lending bank stipulates that all sales proceeds are to be collected, and then applied to payoff the loan. The remainder is credited to the exporter's account.

The self-liquidating feature of trade finance is critical to many small, undercapitalized businesses. Lenders who may otherwise have reached their lending limits for such businesses may nevertheless finance individual export sales, if the lenders are assured that the loan proceeds will be used solely for pre-export production; and any export sale proceeds will first be collected by them before the balance is passed on to the exporter.

Given the extent of control lenders can exercise over such transactions and the existence of guaranteed payment mechanisms unique to or established for international trade, trade finance can be less risky for lenders than general working capital loans.

Working Capital Loans

For exporters, working capital loan programs are normally associated with pre-shipment financing. Many small businesses need pre-export financing to cover the operating costs related to a sales order or contract. Loan proceeds are commonly used to finance three different areas:

- *Labor:* The people needed to build or buy the export product.
- *Materials:* The raw materials needed to produce the export product.
- *Inventory:* The costs associated with buying the export product.

Term Financing for Foreign Buyers

Frequently, foreign buyers don't have the cash on hand to pay for major purchases. So the buyers ask for extended credit terms and/or financing. Few exporters can manage the cash flow dilemma or commercial and political risks caused by these long-term contracts.

Buyer Credit Programs are often an effective solution that benefits the exporter, their buyer and commercial lenders providing the loans. Programs typically provide loan guarantees to commercial lenders. These kind of programs benefit all the parties involved.

The exporter benefits because they're paid cash on delivery and acceptance of the product or service. The foreign buyer benefits because they get extended credit terms at markets rates or better. And the lender benefits because guarantees, many backed by the U.S. Government, mean full repayment of the loan and a reasonable return on funds loaned.

Trade Port Export Finance Online (TEFO) provides Term Financing for foreign buyers. Detailed information is here.

TRADE FINANCE PRODUCTS

Factoring

Once a product has been shipped, that inventory is converted to an Account Receivable (A/R). A list of all Accounts Receivable are maintained on an aging report while the exporter waits for final payment. If there is a need for immediate cash, it's possible to sell the A/R at a discount. This solution is called Factoring.

Factoring is the discounting of foreign accounts receivable that do not involve drafts as the method of payment. A Factor (an organization that specializes in the financing of accounts receivable) takes title for immediate cash at a discount from the face value. Although factoring is often done without recourse to the exporter, verify these specific arrangements.

Factors typically provide 70% of the face value with 3-5 working days, and assume responsibility for collection from the buyer. After final payment, the Factor will pay the remaining 30%-less a service fee of 4%-5%.

FORFAITING

Forfaiting is the selling, at a discount, of longer term accounts receivable or promissory notes of the foreign buyer. These instruments may also carry the guarantee of the foreign government. Both U.S. and European forfaiting houses, which purchase the instruments at a discount are active in the U.S. market. Because forfaiting may be done either with or without recourse, verify all of the specific the specific arrangements.

PURCHASE ORDER FINANCING

A Purchase Order (P.O.) is a legal agreement signed by a buyer requesting a seller to provide goods or services. Purchase Orders normally list the amount of goods or services required and the terms and conditions of delivery and payment.

Major domestic buyers will normally issue a P.O. with Net 30 to 60 day terms. Overseas suppliers will usually ask for OD or sight draft Letter of Credit terms. For an importer, this difference in terms of sale means that there won't be any cash coming in during the manufacturing process or the transit period. Unless a bank or factor will finance the A/R period, the importer is out of cash until the invoices are finally paid off.

Purchase Order Financing can be an alternative solution to this cash flow dilemma. P.O. Financing is a short-term funding technique used to finance the purchase or manufacture of goods that have been presold to a creditworthy customer. Lenders that offer this specialized form of financing will assist in the purchase of product inventory by using the inventory and confirmed purchase orders as collateral.

Importers, Exporters, Distributors or Manufacturers can use Purchase Order Financing. Funds are used for issuing Letters of Credit, payment to suppliers for finished goods, raw materials or direct labor. Purchase Order Funding is a risky form of financing and therefore costs more than traditional financing. It requires extensive due diligence, and lenders are highly selective. If you can meet the prerequisites there are some excellent P.O. lenders available to offer you a financial solution

SOURCES OF EXPORT FINANCING

The Trade Port Export Finance Online (TEFO) Program is a managed financial network of banks, lenders and brokers focused on the small business market. The TEFO/Trade Port partnership brings together the international trade strengths of Trade Port, the Caltrade Coalition, California's trade promotion community, private sector banks and lenders, the U.S. Commercial Service, the U.S. Export-Import (EXIM) Bank and the Small Business Administration (SBA) for the benefit of small business trade development.

Commercial Banks

Large multinational banks are generally thought to be the most experienced in trade finance. Frequently these services are reserved for their major clients and maintain transaction minimums of $1M or more. These banks are less interested in working with small businesses because of smaller deal size and volumes accompanied by greater risk. In fact, small importers and exporters often present a business profile that creates obstacles to financing. Even SMEs with large trade deals are not attractive to larger banks due to risk and credit issues such as loan concentration, debt-earnings ratio restrictions or insufficient collateral.

It is important to select a lender that is sincerely interested in serving businesses of similar type or size. If your bank lacks an international department, it may refer you to a correspondent or partner bank. There are non-banks lenders and service providers that specialize in trade finance.

Due Diligence

As part of your due diligence when selecting a bank and a financial solution, ask the following questions:

- What are the charges for confirming a letter of credit, processing drafts, and collecting payments?
- Does the bank have foreign branches or correspondent banks? Where are they located?
- Can the bank provide buyer credit reports? At what cost?

- Does the bank have experience with U.S. and state government financing programs that support small business export transactions? If not, is it willing to consider participating in these programs?
- What other services, such as trade leads, can the bank provide?

APPLICATION INFORMATION

Banks and non-bank lenders will require business information as part of their due diligence. This information is packaged with a loan application and submitted to the lender. The typical information required may include some or all of the following:

- Year end financial statements for the last three years on the business and signed tax returns.
- Current interim financials, normally not older than 90 days.
- Current A/R and A/P agings and inventory details
- Personal Financial Statements on all owners of 20% or more and each of their last three years tax returns (signed).
- Product literature/Business Plan or narrative on how business is operated, number of products produced and sold (proof of ability to perform).
- Resumes on key management.
- Financial projections (P&L) and Cash Flow statement
- Proof of 50% US Content in product exported.
- Purchase Order copies from exporter from foreign buyers (basis for loan/line advances).
- Information on Foreign Buyers (ability to pay)

Assistance from the Federal Government

Several federal and local government agencies offer programs to assist exporters with their financing needs. Some are guarantee programs that require the participation of an approved lender, while others provide loans or grants to the exporter or a foreign government. Government programs generally are aimed at improving an exporter's access to credit. They are not intended to subsidize the cost of credit at below-market levels. With few exceptions, banks are allowed to charge market interest rates and fees; a portion of those fees are paid to the government agency to cover the agencies' administrative costs and default risks. Government guarantee and insurance programs are used by commercial banks to reduce the risk associated with loans to exporters. Lenders who are concerned with an exporter's ability to perform under the terms of sale, and with an exporter's ability to be paid, often use government programs to reduce the risks that would otherwise prevent them from providing financing.

Export Import Bank of the United States (EXIM Bank): EXIM Bank is an independent federal government agency responsible for assisting export financing of U.S. goods and services. It offers a variety of information services, insurance, loan, and guarantee programs.

Ex-Im Bank operates an export financing hotline that provides information on the availability and use of export credit insurance, guarantees, direct and intermediary loans extended to finance the sale of U.S. goods and service abroad.

Briefing programs are offered by Ex-Im Bank to the small business community. These programs includes regular seminars, group briefings, and individual discussions held both within the Bank and around the country.

U.S. Department of Agriculture (USDA): The Foreign Agricultural Service (FAS) of USDA administers several programs to help make U.S. agricultural exporters competitive in international markets and make U.S. products affordable to countries that have greater need than they have ability to pay.

These programs are designed to make it easier for commodity exporters to obtain bank financing by providing repayment guarantees to the lenders.

The USDA's Commodity Credit Corporation (CCC) operates Export Credit Guarantee Programs to provide United States agricultural exporters or financial institutions a guarantee that they will be repaid for short-and intermediate-term commercial export financing to foreign buyers. These programs protect against commercial or noncommercial risk if the importer's bank fails to make payment. Under one program, the CCC will guarantee credit terms of up to 3 years and under another, credit terms from 3 to 10 years are guaranteed.

Small Business Administration (SBA): The SBA has some services specifically designed to help the small business get started in exporting. The SBA provides financial assistance programs for U.S. exporters. Applicants must qualify as small businesses under the SBA's size standards and meet other eligibility criteria. The SBA has two main programs to assist U.S. exporters-the Export Working Capital Program and the International Trade Loan (ITL) program.

The SBA programs provide the small business owner with financing aids that will enable the business to obtain the capital needed to get into exporting.

This program is designed to help small business exporters obtain financing by reducing risks to lenders. The SBA will guarantee up to 90% of a loan from a private bank. The proceeds from the loan can be used for pre-shipment working capital, post-shipment exposure coverage, or a combination of both.

FINANCING EXPORT SALES

Few would disagree that small businesses must look overseas for profit opportunities in the 1990s. However, to compete successfully, small firms must offer financing arrangements that are competitive with exporters of other nations. This chapter will discuss three major influences on an exporter's ability to arrange competitive financing:

- today's banking environment
- how to approach a lender
- methods of payment

UNDERSTANDING THE BANKING ENVIRONMENT

In the United States, most small firms turn first to their local banks for export finance assistance. However, during the past decade many banks have decided not to focus on export financing. The banks' reasons for doing so have varied--many cut their international operations due to the huge losses they incurred on overseas debt; others may have chosen to concentrate on more lucrative lines of business, such as home equity loans or mergers and acquisitions.

Consequently, during the 1980s export finance expertise in many U.S. banks deteriorated. Even today, most smaller banks do not retain any staff with expertise in international trade. This is not to say, however, that such help is unavailable--only that small businesses must be persistent and tenacious in their efforts to find it. For example, if a small business loan officer is unwilling to work with his or her bank's international staff (or the bank is unwilling to work with a correspondent), exporters should consider establishing a second banking relationship or, if necessary, moving all their accounts to a more aggressive lender. Don't be afraid to shop.

Given the difficulty most small business exporters face when seeking financing, it is imperative that financial arrangements be made in advance.

Finding a lender willing to consider such a request requires that the borrower ensure that the purpose of the loan makes sense for the business, and that the request is a reasonable amount. Prospective borrowers also should understand some key distinctions before beginning discussions with a lender.

APPROACHING LENDER FOR EXPORT FINANCING

Venture Capitalists and Lenders

Before approaching a bank for financial assistance, small exporters should understand the distinction between venture capitalists and lenders. Venture capitalists invest in a business with the expectation that as the business grows, their equity in the business will grow exponentially. On the other hand, lenders are not in the venture capital business--they make their money on the difference between the rate at which they borrow money and the rate at which they lend to their customers.

International Trade Services and Export Lending: Small exporters should also understand the distinction between international trade services and international trade lending.

Although many banks offer international trade services, such as advising and negotiating letters of credit, the banks' international divisions are not authorized to lend money. International lenders, on the other hand, have the authority to make loans, as well as provide related services. Exporters should verify that the bank officer with whom they are dealing has the authority to lend for an export transaction.

WORKING CAPITAL FINANCING AND TRADE FINANCING

It is also important to note the difference between general working capital financing and trade financing. A small firm's ability to qualify for general working capital financing depends on, among other things, the strength of its balance sheet and its prospects for generating sufficient earnings over the life of a loan to repay it. Trade finance, on the other hand, generally refers to financing individual transactions (or a series of like transactions). In addition, trade finance loans are often self-liquidating--that is, the lending bank stipulates that all sales proceeds are to be collected by it, and then applies the proceeds to pay down the loan. The remainder is credited to the account of the borrower.

The self-liquidating feature of trade finance is critical to many small, undercapitalized businesses. Lenders who may otherwise have reached their lending limits for such businesses may nevertheless finance individual export sales, if the lenders are assured that the loan proceeds will be used solely for pre-export production; and any export sale proceeds will first be collected by them before the balance is passed on to the exporter. Given the extent of control lenders can exercise over such transactions and the existence of guaranteed payment mechanisms unique to--or established for--international trade, trade finance can be less risky for lenders than general working capital loans.

Pre-export, Accounts Receivable and Market Development Financing

Exporters should understand the distinctions between the various types of trade finance. Most small businesses need pre-export financing to help with the expense of gearing up for a particular export sale. Loan proceeds are commonly used to pay for labor and materials or to acquire inventory for export sales. Others may be interested in foreign accounts receivable financing.

In that case, exporters can borrow from their banks an amount based on the volume and quality of such accounts receivable. Although banks rarely lend 100 percent of the value of the accounts receivable, many will advance up to 80 percent of the value of qualified accounts. Foreign credit insurance (such as Exim bank's Export Credit Insurance Program) is often used to enhance the quality of such accounts.

Financing for foreign market development activities, such as participation in overseas trade missions or trade shows, is often difficult for small businesses to arrange. Most banks are reluctant to finance such activities because, for many small firms, their ability to repay such loans depends on their success in consummating sales while on a mission--prospects that in many cases are speculative. Although difficult for many small firms to do, the recommended source for financing such activities is through the working capital of the firm or, in certain cases, through the use of personal credit cards.

Finally, take time to make sure your banker understands your business and products. Have a detailed export plan ready and, most important, be able to clearly show how and when a loan will be repaid.

METHODS USED TO FINANCE EXPORTS

A small business exporter's principal concern should be to ensure that he or she will be paid in full and on time. Foreign buyers may have concerns as well, including uncertainty that the goods ordered will meet the necessary specifications and arrive in a timely manner. As a result, it is imperative that the terms of payment be agreed upon in advance and in a manner satisfactory to both parties.

The payment method exporters use can significantly affect the financial risk of a particular export sale. In general, the more generous the sales terms are to a foreign buyer, the greater the risk to the exporter. The primary methods of payment for international transactions, ranked in order of most secure to the exporter to least secure, include:

- payment in advance
- letters of credit
- documentary collections (drafts)
- consignment
- open account

Advance Payment

Paying in advance is often too expensive and risky for foreign buyers. Yet, this method of payment is not uncommon. Requiring full payment in advance may cause lost sales to a foreign (or even another domestic) competitor who is able to offer more attractive payment terms. In some cases, however, where the manufacturing process is specialized, lengthy or capital-intensive, it may be reasonable to insist upon partial payment in advance, or on progress payments.

Letters of Credit (LC)

A letter of credit is an internationally recognized instrument issued by a bank on behalf of its client, the purchaser. The LC actually represents the bank's guarantee to pay the seller, provided the conditions specified on it are fulfilled. Of course, the purchaser pays its bank a fee to render this service.

The rationale behind the use of an LC is reliance by the seller on the credit worthiness of the bank, which is normally more reliable than that of the purchaser. It is also easier to verify by the seller's bank. Moreover, this vehicle can be structured to protect the purchaser because no payment obligation arises until the goods have been satisfactorily delivered as promised.

The conditions of the LC are spelled out on the LC itself. When the conditions of delivery have been satisfied (usually by the documented, satisfactory and timely delivery of the goods), the purchaser's bank makes the required payment directly to the seller's bank in accordance with the terms of payment (in 15, 30, 60 or 90 days, whichever is specified).

The greatest degree of protection is afforded to the seller when the LC has been issued by the buyer's bank and confirmed by the seller's bank.

LCs may be utilized for one-time transactions, or they can cover multi-shipments, depending upon what is agreed between the parties. Also, make sure you can deliver within the terms of the LC. It is suggested that you review the details of such documentation with a bank that has LC experience.

Letter of Credit

Buyer	Seller
. Agrees to buy product	. Agrees to ship goods if LC is opened
. Requests bank to issue LC	. LC assures payment if proper documents are presented
	. Ships goods and submits shipping documents to bank for payment
. Verifies documents for compliance	
. Payment is made when documents received or accepted	. Payment received immediately or upon maturity of accepted draft

Documentary Collection (Drafts)

Documentary collections involve the use of a draft, drawn by the seller on the buyer, requiring the buyer to pay the face amount either on sight (sight draft) or on a specified date in the future (time draft). The draft is an unconditional order to make such payment in accordance with its terms, which specify the documents needed before title to the goods will be passed.

Because title to the goods does not pass until the draft is paid or accepted, both the buyer and seller are protected. However, if the buyer defaults on payment of the draft, the seller may have to pursue collection through the courts (or possibly, by arbitration, if such had been agreed upon between the parties). The use of drafts involves a certain level of risk; but they are less expensive for the purchaser than letters of credit.

Documentary Collections

Buyer	Seller
. Agrees to buy products	. Agrees to be paid via documentary collection . Ships goods and submits shipping documents to bank for collection or acceptance
. Documents released to buyer against payment or acceptance	. Seller receives payment at sight or upon acceptance

Consignment

When goods are sold subject to consignment, no money is received by the exporter until after the goods have been sold by the purchaser. Title to the goods remains with the exporter until such time as all the purchase conditions are satisfied. As a practical matter, consignment is very risky. There is generally no way to predict how long it might take to sell the goods; moreover, if they are never sold, the exporter would have to pay the costs of recovering them from the foreign consignee.

Open Account

An open account transaction means that the goods are manufactured and delivered before payment is required (for example, payment could be due 14, 30, or 60 days following shipment or delivery). In the United States, sales are likely to be made on an open-account basis if the manufacturer has been dealing with the buyer over a long period of time and has established a secure working relationship.

In international business transactions, this method of payment cannot be used safely unless the buyer is credit worthy and the country of destination is politically and economically stable. However, in certain instances it might be possible to discount open accounts receivable with a factoring company or other financial institution, referred to above.

The following diagram assesses the relative strengths and weaknesses of each method of payment:

Method	Usual Time	Goods Available of Payment	Risk To To Buyer	Risk To Exporter Importer
Cash in Advance	Before shipment	After payment	None	Dependent upon exporter shipping goods
Letter of Credit	After shipment, when documents complying with LC are presented	After payment	Very little or none depending on LC terms	Relies on exporter to ship goods
Documentary Collection Sight Draft	On presentation of draft to buyer	After payment	If draft unpaid, must dispose of goods	Relies on exporter to ship goods
Documentary Collection Time Draft	On maturity of draft	Before payment	Relies on buyer to pay draft; no control of goods	Almost none
Consignment	After sale	Before payment	High	Low
Open Account	After shipment, as agreed	Before payment	Relies on buyer to pay his account	None

Private Sector Export Financing Resources

Commercial Banks

International trade transactions traditionally have been financed by commercial banks. Commercial banks can make loans for pre-export activities. They can also help process letters of credit, drafts and other methods of payment discussed in this chapter. Banks have also become increasingly involved in making export loans backed by United States government export loan guarantees.

Many larger banks have international departments which can help with your company's particular export finance needs. If your bank does not have an international department, it probably has a correspondent relationship with a larger bank that can assist you.

Private Trade Finance Companies

Private trade finance companies are becoming increasingly more commonplace. They utilize a variety of financing techniques in return for fees, commissions, participation in the transactions or combinations thereof. International trade associations, such as a District Export Council, can assist you in locating a private trade finance company in your area.

Export Trading and Management Companies

Both EMCs and ETCs provide varying ranges of export services, including international market research and overseas marketing, insurance, legal assistance, product design, transportation, foreign order processing, warehousing, overseas distribution, foreign exchange and even taking title to a supplier's goods. All of these services can leverage the limited resources of small businesses.

Factoring Houses

Factoring houses, also called factors, purchase export receivables on a discounted basis. Using factors can enable the exporter to receive immediate payment for goods while at the same time alleviating the hassles associated with overseas collections.

Factors purchase export receivables for a percentage fee at 2-7 percent below invoice value, depending on the market and type of buyer. The percentage rate will depend on whether the factor purchases the receivables on a recourse or non-recourse basis. In the case of a non-recourse purchase, the exporter is not bound to repay the factoring house if the foreign buyer defaults or other collection problems arise. Therefore, the percentage charge will be greater with non-recourse purchases.

Forfaiting Houses

Similar to factoring, exporters relinquish their rights to future payment in return for immediate cash. Where a debt obligation exists between the parties, it is sold to a third party on a non-recourse basis, but is guaranteed by an intermediary bank. One U.S. exporter which used forfaiting found the benefits substantial:

Government Export Financing Resources

Because private sector financing providers will only assume limited risk regarding foreign transactions, the U.S. government has become increasingly involved in providing export financing assistance.

U.S. government export financing assistance comes in the form of guarantees made to U.S. commercial banks which in turn make the loans to exporters. Federal agencies, as well as certain state governments, have their own particular programs as noted below:

U.S. Small Business Administration (SBA)

SBA provides financial and business development assistance to help small businesses develop export markets. The SBA assists businesses in obtaining the capital needed to explore, establish or expand international markets. SBA's export loans are available under SBA's guarantee program. As a prospective applicant, you should request that your lender seek SBA participation, if the lender is unable or unwilling to make a direct loan. The financing staff of each SBA district and branch office administers the financial assistance programs. You can contact the finance division of your nearest SBA office for a list of participating lenders. The business development staff of each SBA district and branch office can provide counseling on how to request export financial assistance from a lender.

Borrowers can use different SBA loan programs and types of loan guarantees simultaneously, as long as the total SBA-guaranteed portion does not exceed the agency's $750,000 statutory loan guarantee limit to any one borrower. The lender may charge a maximum interest rate of 2.75 percentage points above the New York prime interest rate, or 2.25 percentage points above New York prime if the maturity is less than seven years.

Regular Business Loan Program

The SBA can guarantee up to 90 percent of a bank loan up to $155,000. For larger loans, the maximum guaranty is 85 percent up to $750,000. Small businesses that need money for fixed assets and for working capital may be eligible for the SBA's regular 7(a) business loan guarantee program. Loan guarantees for fixed-asset acquisition have a maximum maturity of 25 years. Guarantees for general purpose working capital loans have a maximum maturity of seven years. Export trading companies (ETCs) and export management companies (EMCs) also may qualify for the SBA's business loan guarantee program.

To be eligible, the applicant's business generally must be operated for profit and fall within size standards set by SBA. Loans cannot be made to businesses involved in creation or distribution of ideas or opinions, such as newspapers, magazines and academic schools. Other types of ineligible borrowers include businesses engaged in speculation or investment in rental real estate.

Export Revolving Line of Credit Program

The Export Revolving Line of Credit (ERLC) Program offers a credit line up to 36 months. Any number of withdrawals and repayments can be made as long as they do not exceed the dollar limit of the credit line, and the disbursements are made within the stated maturity period. Loan maturities are generally for 12 months, with options to renew. Loans can be used to finance labor and materials for manufacturing or wholesaling for export, to develop foreign markets or to finance foreign accounts receivable. Foreign business travel and participation in trade shows are also among the eligible uses, but a regular 7(a) business loan may be more appropriate for these purposes.

Applicants must satisfy eligibility criteria established for all SBA loans. Also, the applicant must have been in business--not necessarily exporting--for at least 12 months' continuous operation before filing an application. The 12-month requirement may be waived by the SBA regional office, if the firm's management has sufficient export experience or enough management ability to warrant an exception.

The International Trade Loan Program

The International Trade Loan Program provides long-term financing to help small businesses compete more effectively and to expand or develop export markets.

Loan maturities cannot exceed 25 years, excluding the working capital portion of the financing. The SBA's guarantee cannot exceed 85 percent of the loan amount. The agency's maximum share for facilities or equipment loans is $1 million, plus $250,000 for working capital.

Proceeds may be used to purchase or upgrade facilities or equipment, and to make other improvements that will be used within the U.S. to produce goods or services.

No debt payment is allowed. Proceeds can be used to buy land and buildings; build new facilities; renovate, improve or expand existing facilities; and purchase or recondition machinery, equipment and fixtures. The working capital portion of the borrowing could be in the form of either an ERLC or a portion of the term loan.

Applicants must establish either of the following to meet eligibility requirements:

- Loan proceeds will significantly expand existing export markets or develop new ones.
- The applicant's business is adversely affected by import competition.

Small Business Investment Company (SBIC) Financing

A Small Business Investment Company (SBIC), approved and licensed by the SBA, may also provide equity or working capital exceeding the agency's $750,000 statutory maximum. SBICs can invest in export trading companies in which banks have equity participation as long as other SBIC requirements are met.

Export-Import Bank of the United States (Exim Bank)

Exim bank is an independent federal government agency responsible for assisting the export financing of U.S. goods and services through a variety of information service and insurance, loan and guarantee programs. Exim bank has undertaken a major effort to reach more small business exporters with better financing facilities and services, to increase the value of these facilities and services to the exporting community, and to increase the dollar amount of Exim bank's authorizations supporting small business exports. Exim bank's export financing hotline provides information on the availability and use of export credit insurance, guarantees, direct and intermediary loans extended to finance the sale of U.S. goods and service abroad. Briefing programs are offered by Exim bank to the small business community. The program includes regular seminars, group briefings and individual discussions held both within the Bank and around the country.

Export credit insurance programs reduce an exporter's risk and can be obtained through an insurance broker or from Exim bank's Insurance Division.

A wide range of policies is available to accommodate many different export credit insurance needs. Insurance coverage:

- protects the exporter against the failure of foreign buyers to pay their credit obligations for commercial or political reasons;
- encourages exporters to offer foreign buyers competitive terms of payment;
- supports an exporter's prudent penetration of higher risk foreign markets; and
- gives exporters and their banks greater financial flexibility in handling overseas accounts receivable.

During the first two years, the new-to-export insurance policy offers a short-term (up to 180 days) insurance policy geared to meet the particular credit requirements of smaller, less experienced exporters. Under the policy, Exim bank assumes 95 percent of the commercial and 100 percent of the political risk involved in extending credit to the exporter's overseas customers. This policy frees the smaller exporter from "first loss" commercial risk deductible provisions that are usually found in regular insurance policies. The special coverage is available to companies which are just beginning to export, or have an average annual export credit sales volume of less than $2,000,000 for the past two years, and meet the SBA definitions of small business.

The umbrella policy also covers short-term receivables of companies with only limited experience in export trade. These policies are available to commercial lenders, state agencies, finance companies, export trading and management companies, insurance brokers and similar agencies to insure their clients' receivables. Exporters are eligible if they have average annual export credit sales of less than $2,000,000 for the past two years and meet the SBA definitions of small business.

LOAN PROGRAMS

The Working Capital Loan Guarantee Program assists small businesses in obtaining crucial working capital to fund their export activities. The program guarantees 100 percent of the principal and interest on working capital loans extended by commercial lenders to eligible U.S. exporters.

The loan may be used for pre-export activities such as the purchase of inventory, raw materials, the manufacture of a product or for marketing. Exim bank requires the working capital loan to be secured with inventory of exportable goods, accounts receivable or by other appropriate collateral.

Direct and Intermediary Loans

Exim bank provide two types of loans, direct loans to foreign buyers of U.S. exports and intermediary loans to fund responsible parties that extend loans to foreign buyers of U.S. capital and quasi-capital goods and related services. Both the loan and guarantee programs cover up to 85 percent of the U.S. export value, with repayment terms of one year or more.

Direct loans of any size and long-term loans to intermediaries are offered at the lowest interest rate permitted under the Organization for Economic Cooperation and Development (OECD) arrangement for the market and term.

Medium-term intermediary loans are structured as "standby" loan commitments.

Under this arrangement, the intermediary may borrow against the remaining undisbursed loan at any time during the term of the underlying debt obligation. There is a prepayment fee if it is triggered by prepayment of the foreign borrower.

GUARANTEE PROGRAMS

Guarantees of the Exim bank provide repayment protection for private sector loans to credit worthy buyers of U.S. capital equipment and related services. The guarantee is available alone or may be combined with an intermediary loan.

Most guarantees provide comprehensive coverage of both political and commercial risks but political risks only coverage is also available. The guarantee covers 100 percent of principal and interest. In the event of a default, the guaranteed lender must file a claim no less than 30 and no more than 150 days after the default. The claim will be paid within five business days after receipt.

Customary repayment terms for capital goods in international trade are:

Contract Value	Maximum Term
Less than $75,000	2 years
$75,000-$150,000	3 years
$150,000-$300,000	4 years
$300,000 or more	5-10 years

depending on the nature of the sale and the OECD classification of the buyers' country.

Loans for projects and large product acquisitions, such as aircraft and capital-intensive machinery, are eligible for longer terms while lower unit value items such as automobiles and appliances receive shorter terms.

Commodity Credit Corporation (CCC)

The United States Department of Agriculture's Commodity Credit Corporation (CCC) operates Export Credit Guarantee Programs to provide United States agricultural exporters or financial institutions a guarantee that they will be repaid for short-and intermediate-term commercial export financing to foreign buyers. These programs protect against commercial or noncommercial risk if the importer's bank fails to make payment. Under one program, the CCC will guarantee credit terms of up to 3 years and under another, credit terms from 3 to 10 years are guaranteed.

STATE EXPORT FINANCING PROGRAMS

A number of state-sponsored export financing and loan guarantee programs are available. Many cities and states have established cooperative programs with the Exim bank and can provide specialized export finance counseling.

Arkansas, California, Delaware, Georgia, Indiana, Louisiana, Maine, Maryland, Massachusetts, Michigan, Minnesota, New Jersey, New York, Nevada, North Carolina, Oklahoma, Pennsylvania, South Carolina, Texas, Utah, Virginia, Washington, and Wisconsin all provide direct or indirect export financing assistance.

Once an exporter determines the kind of export financing assistance to be used and which payment method, the next step is to arrange for delivery of the goods to the buyer's destination. It is important to assess the various transportation options available, the subject of Chapter 6, "Transporting Goods Internationally."

5

Foreign Relations of India

The Republic of India, the second most populous country and one of the fastest growing economies in the world, is considered as a major power and a potential superpower. It is India's growing international influence that gives it a prominent voice in global affairs.

India has a long history of collaboration with several countries and is considered as a leader of the developing world. India was one of the founding members of the United Nations and the Non-Aligned Movement and is an active member of several international organizations, most notably the WTO, ADB, SAARC and G20.

During the Cold War, India adopted a foreign policy of not aligning itself with any major power bloc. However, India developed close ties with the Soviet Union and received extensive military support from the U.S.S.R.. The end of the Cold War significantly affected Indian foreign policy, as it did for much of the world. The country now seeks to strengthen its diplomatic and economic ties with the United States, the People's Republic of China, European Union, Japan, Israel, Latin America, and the Association of Southeast Asian Nations. India also has close ties with the African Union, the Commonwealth states and the Arab World. India continues to have strong a military relationship with Russia.

India has actively participated in several UN peacekeeping missions. India is currently the largest troop contributor to the UN and currently seeking a permanent seat in the UN Security Council.

BRIEF HISTORY

After India gained independence from the United Kingdom, New Delhi tried to establish friendly diplomatic relationship with several countries. The communal riots following the Partition of India and dispute over Junagadh and Kashmir created tense relations between newly-born India and Islamic Republic of Pakistan. Within a year after attaining independence, Pakistan attacked Kashmir, which subsequently acceded to India resulting in the full-scale war. The region continues to be a bone of contention between the neighbours.

In the 1950s, India showed keen interest in establishing close relationship with the People's Republic of China. The Panchsheel was seen as a landmark agreement between the two. However, several border disputes and the Chinese invasion of Tibet continued to plague Sino-Indian relations. Pakistan gave a part of Kashmir to China.

India played a key role in establishing the Non-Aligned Movement in 1961. Though India pursued close relations with both US and USSR, it decided not to join any major power bloc and refrained from joining military alliances. India, however began establishing close military relationship with the Soviet Union.

In 1962, India detected Chinese infiltration into Indian territory, which resulted in a brief war between the two. India has remained suspicious towards China since then. China also became a close ally of Pakistan, India's neighbor, adding to the rift between the two. Even though, there has been a significant improvement in trade and diplomatic relations, India remains wary of China.

After the Sino-Indian War and the Indo-Pakistani War of 1965, India made considerable changes to its foreign policy. It developed a close relationship with the Soviet Union and started receiving massive military equipment and financial assistance from the USSR. This had an adverse effect on the Indo-US relationship. USA saw Pakistan as a counter-weight to pro-Soviet India and started giving the former military assistance. This created an atmosphere of suspicion between India and US. The US-India relationship suffered a considerable setback during the Soviet invasion of Afghanistan when India openly supported the Soviet invasion.

ALLIES

India has friendly relations with several countries in the developing world. Though India is not a part of any major military alliance, it has close strategic and military relationship with most of the major powers. India's large growing economy, strategic location and friendly foreign policy has won it more allies than enemies.

Countries considered India's closest allies include Russia, Israel and South Africa. India has a key strategic alliance with several other countries including the United States, United Kingdom, France, Germany, Japan, Australia, Mexico, Brazil, Nepal, Bhutan, Persian Gulf countries, African Union and South East Asian countries. After economic liberalization in 1992, India has forged its relationship with other developing countries especially South Africa, Brazil, Mexico, and People's Republic of China. India's decade old "Look East" policy has helped it develop greater economic and strategic partnership with ASEAN, South Korea and Taiwan.

BILATERAL AND REGIONAL RELATIONS

African Union

India has had historically good relationships with most sub-Saharan African nations for most of its history. In the Prime Minister's visit to Mauritius in 1997, the two countries secured a deal to a new Credit Agreement of 10.50 crore INR (3 million USD) to finance import by Mauritius of capital goods, consultancy services and consumer durable from India. The government of India secured a rice and medicine agreement with the people of Seychelles. India continued to build upon its historically close relations with Ethiopia, Kenya, Uganda and Tanzania. Visits from political ministers from Ethiopia provided opportunities for strengthening bilateral cooperation between the two countries in the fields of education and technical training, water resources management and development of small industries. This has allowed India to gain benefits from nations that are generally forgotten by other Western Nations. The

South African Thabo Mbeki has called for a strategic relationship between India and South Africa to avoid imposition by Western Nations. India continued to build upon its close and friendly relations with Angola, Botswana, Lesotho, Malawi, Mozambique, Namibia, Swaziland, Zambia and Zimbabwe. The Minister of Foreign Affairs arranged for the sending of Special Envoys to each of these countries during 1996-97 as a reaffirmation of India's assurance to strengthening cooperation with these countries in a spirit of South-South partnership. These relations have created a position of strength with African nations that other nations may not possess.

United Kingdom & Commonwealth nations

Since 1947, India's relations with the United Kingdom have been through bilateral, as well as through the Commonwealth of Nations framework. Although the Sterling Area no longer exists and the Commonwealth is much more an informal forum, India and the UK still have many enduring links. This is in part due to the significant number of people of Indian origin living in the UK. The large South Asian population in the UK results in steady travel and communication between the two countries. The British Raj allowed for both cultures to imbibe tremendously from the other. The English language and cricket are perhaps the two most evident British exports, whilst in the UK Indian music and food are fixtures in daily life. It's also notable that there are many words of Indian origin now common to the language.

Economically the relationship between Britain and India is also strong. Britain is one of the largest investors in India. The millions of pounds invested annually sustain a wide range of industries, including the controversial "call centres". Money flowing back to India from Indian expatriates in Britain is also quite substantial. These expatriates also tend to invest in real estate in India. The Indian diaspora in UK is one of the most influential minority ethnic groups in Europe.

In the late 1980s, Britain agreed on selling SEPECAT Jaguar to India further enhancing the military cooperation between the two. In the sphere of politics relations are mostly through multilateral channels, namely the Commonwealth,

WTO and ADB. India has remained staunchly sovereign and has rejected any type of British intervention in regional affairs. Despite the occasional spats, such as the 1997 row when the Foreign Secretary Robin Cook offered to mediate a dispute over Kashmir, relations between London and New Delhi are warm. The Queen's visits to India have been enormously successful along with those by other members of the Royal Family. Britain has also supported India's rise to prominence on the international stage, including advocating a permanent seat on the Security Council.

France

France and India established diplomatic relationships soon after India achieved independence in 1947. India's strong diplomatic ties with France resulted in the peaceful cession of Pondicherry to India in 1964 without any military opposition from France.

France was the only country that did not condemn India's decision to go nuclear in 1998. In 2003, France became the largest supplier of nuclear fuel and technology to India and remains a large military and economic trade partner. India's permanent member aspirations in the UN Security Council have found very strong support from French President Chirac. The Indian Ministry of Defence is currently in talks with the French government regarding the possible purchase of more than 200 Dassault Rafale aircraft for the Indian Air Force. The recent decision by the Indian government to purchase French Scorpene class submarines worth 3 billion USD and 43 Airbus aircraft for Indian Airlines worth 2.5 billion USD has further cemented the strategic, military and economic cooperation between India and France.

South Asia

Certain aspects of India's relations within the subcontinent are conducted through the South Asia Association for Regional Cooperation (SAARC). Its members are Afghanistan, Bangladesh, Bhutan, India, Maldives, Nepal, Pakistan, and Sri Lanka. Established in 1985, SAARC encourages cooperation in agriculture, rural development, science and technology, culture, health, population control, narcotics control and anti-terrorism.

SAARC has intentionally stressed these "core issues" and avoided more divisive political issues, although political dialogue is often conducted on the margins of SAARC meetings. In 1993, India and its SAARC partners signed an agreement gradually to lower tariffs within the region. Forward movement in SAARC has come to a standstill because of the tension between India and Pakistan, and the SAARC Summit originally scheduled for, but not held in, November 1999 has not been rescheduled.

In November 1988, at the behest of the Maldivian government, Indian paratroopers and naval forces crushed a coup attempt by mercenaries. India's action, viewed by some critics as an indication of Indian ambitions to be a regional hegemon, were regarded by the United States, the Soviet Union, Britain, Nepal, and Bangladesh as legitimate assistance to a friendly government, and to be fully in keeping with India's strategic role in South Asia.

Pakistan

The principal source of contention between India and its western neighbour has been Kashmir, the Hindu Maharaja of which, Hari Singh of Dogra, and its Muslim Prime Minister, Sheikh Abdullah, chose in 1947 to join India conditionally and provisionally. A Standstill Agreement with Pakistan was in place, so the matter is still much disputed, since the decision was hastened by the loss of territory to invading irregulars from Pakistan, backed by the Pakistan Army. India maintains that this decision was the norm for every other princely state at Independence and that subsequent elections in Kashmir for over 40 years have made it an integral part of India. Pakistan asserts the Kashmiris' rights to self-determination through a plebiscite in accordance with an earlier Indian statement and a UN resolution. This dispute triggered wars between the two countries in 1947 and 1965 and a limited conflict in 1999. The state remains divided between the two countries by the Line of Control (LoC), which demarcates the cease-fire line agreed upon in the 1947 conflict. Pakistan refers to its part of the state as Azad Kashmir with external affairs limited to Pakistan and Indian Occupied Kashmir (IOK) (Kashmir in general)--what India refers to Jammu and Kashmir. India terms it Pakistan Occupied Kashmir (PoK).

In December 1971, following a political crisis in what was then East Pakistan and a subsequent genocide of Bengalis by the Pakistani army, millions of Bengali refugees fled to India. The situation soon spiralled out of control in East Pakistan and India was forced to intervene. Pakistan has always claimed that the armed insurrection in the troubled state was abetted by India. The brief conflict left the situation largely unchanged in the west, where the two armies reached an impasse (although India is regarded to have held the upper hand), but a decisive Indian victory in the east resulted in the creation of Bangladesh and over 90,000 Pakistani POWs.

Since the 1971 war, Pakistan and India have made only slow progress towards the normalization of relations. In July 1972, Indian Prime Minister Indira Gandhi and Pakistani President Zulfikar Ali Bhutto met in the Indian hill station of Shimla. They signed an agreement by which India would return ıll personnel (over 90,000) and captured territory in the west ınd the two countries would "settle their differences by peaceful neans through bilateral negotiations." Diplomatic and trade elations were re-established in 1976.

After the 1979 Soviet invasion of Afghanistan, new strains ppeared in Indo-Pak relations. Pakistan actively supported he Afghan resistance, while India was a friend of the USSR. n the following eight years, India voiced increasing concern ver Pakistani arms purchases, U.S. military aid to Pakistan, nd Pakistan's nuclear weapons program. In an effort to curtail ensions, the two countries formed a joint commission to examine isputes. In December 1988, Prime Ministers Rajiv Gandhi and Benazir Bhutto concluded a pact not to attack each other's uclear facilities. Agreements on cultural exchanges and civil viation were also initiated.

In 1997, high-level Indo-Pakistan talks resumed after a 3-ear pause. The Prime Ministers of India and Pakistan met vice and the foreign secretaries conducted three rounds of lks. In June 1997, the foreign secretaries identified eight utstanding issues" around which continuing talks would be cused. The dispute over the status of Kashmir, (referred by dia as Jammu and Kashmir), an issue since partition, remains e major stumbling block in their dialogue. India maintains that the entire former princely state is an integral part of the Indian union, while Pakistan insists that UN resolutions calling for self-determination of the people of the state must be taken into account. It however refuses to abide by the previous part of the resolution, which calls for it to vacate all territories occupied.

In September 1997, the talks broke down over the structure of how to deal with the issues of Kashmir, and peace and security. Pakistan advocated that the issues be treated by separate working groups. India responded that the two issues be taken up along with six others on a simultaneous basis. In May 1998 India, and then Pakistan, conducted nuclear tests. Attempts to restart dialogue between the two nations were given a major boost by the February 1999 meeting of both Prime Ministers in Lahore and their signing of three agreements. These efforts turned out to be a trick, as three months later the Northern Light Infantry of the Pakistani Army, along with full artillery support infiltrated Indian territory in the Kargil sector, which launched the Kargil War. This stab in the back severely hurt the bilateral relations between both countries, as did a subsequent military coup in Pakistan that overturned the democratically elected Nawaz Sharif government in October of the same year also proved a setback to relations.

In 2001, a summit was called in Agra, India and Pakistan's military president, Pervez Musharraf turned up to meet Indian Prime Minister Atal Behari Vajpayee. The talks broke down when the Pakistani dictator repeatedly dubbed terrorists in Kashmir 'freedom fighters' at a press conference. The Indians appeared miffed and the talks fell through.

On June 20, 2004, with a new government in place in India, both countries agreed to extend a nuclear testing ban and to set up a hotline between their foreign secretaries aimed at preventing misunderstandings that might lead to a nuclear war.

India has granted Pakistan unilateral "most favoured nation" trade status under WTO guidelines, but Pakistan is yet to reciprocate. As of early 2005, both countries are committed to a process of dialogue to solve all outstanding issues.

South America

The Government has also strengthened relations with Latin America and the Caribbean both at the mutual and bilateral stances and with the regional groups. Visits on the behalf of the Foreign Ministers of Mexico, Venezuela, Suriname and the visit of Shri Rao Inderjit Singh, Minister of State, to Panama, Colombia, Dominican Republic and El-Salvador has maintained high-level interaction with the countries of the region. India's commonalities with Brazil have continued to grow as both works together on Security Council reform and the WTO. The process of finalizing Preferential Trade Agreement (PTA) with MERCOSUR (Brazil, Argentina, Uruguay, and Paraguay) is on the itinerary and negotiations are being held with Chile.

Soviet Union Bloc

The collapse of the Soviet Union and the emergence of the Commonwealth of Independent States (CIS) had major repercussions for Indian foreign policy. Substantial trade with the former Soviet Union plummeted after the Soviet collapse and has yet to recover. Longstanding military supply relationships were similarly disrupted due to questions over financing, although Russia continues to be India's largest supplier of military systems and spare parts.

Russian Federation

Russia and India have decided not to renew the 1971 Indo-Soviet Peace and Friendship Treaty and have sought to follow what both describe as a more pragmatic, less ideological relationship. Russian President Yeltsin's visit to India in January 1993 helped cement this new relationship. Ties have grown stronger with President Vladimir Putin's 2004 visit. The pace of high-level visits has since increased, as has discussion of major defence purchases.

Tajikistan

India's intention to station defense forces personnel on foreign soil was first reported in 2002. At that time, some reports claimed that the Farkhor/Ayni facility in Tajikistan was already operational. The origins of this base lie in Pakistan's closure of its air space to Indian commercial aircraft during the crisis following the December 13, 2001 attack on the Indian Parliament by Pakistan-based terrorist suicide bombers. This led to India's resolve to find ways and means to neutralise this restriction for both its commercial and military aircraft, while at the same time gaining an ability to strike Pakistan from its rear.

The potential implications of this base go far beyond the Indo-Pakistani rivalry on the subcontinent. The Ayni base is a tangible manifestation of India's move to project its power in Central Asia, a policy goal formally enunciated in 2003-2004. It not only signifies India's determination to play a role in Central Asian security, but its genuine ability to do so.

The Ayni base represents a major element in India's efforts to promote stability in Afghanistan, and to enhance New Delhi's ability to contain Islamic terrorism both in South Asia and Central Asia. India obviously will not accept being confined to an exclusively South Asian geo-strategic role any longer.

India's determination to project power throughout Central Asia is not just for military purposes. Access to Central Asian energy is vitally important for India. New Delhi seeks access to Kazakh oil and gas and involvement in "mega-projects," such as an Iran-Afghanistan-Pakistan-India pipeline and another linking Turkmenistan, Afghanistan, Pakistan, and India. Either or both of these pipelines would substantially improve India's reliable access to energy supplies, while encouraging better Indo-Pakistani relations.

India wants to develop a new power grid that integrates Central Asian states with those of the subcontinent, an idea that has received strong backing from the United States of late. While India would use a new grid to enhance its overall economic profile in Central Asia, Washington sees the project as a way to counter the growing economic and political influence of Russia and China in Central Asia.

The importance of India's Ayni base does not end here. Its appearance suggests that India's long-standing strategic ties with Russia remain on a sound footing. In the strategic sphere, India and Russia share a common enemy in Islamic terrorism, and India needs Russian energy as much as Russia needs Indian diplomatic support and arms deals.

Although both India and Pakistan are observers in the Shanghai Cooperation Organization, China is undoubtedly wary of the Indian presence at Ayni. Moreover, Indian policy intellectuals continue to view China as a strategic rival in Central Asia, as well as closer to home. Thus, India's power-projection ambitions are in a certain sense directed toward China. India's Ayni base helps illustrate one of the ways in which the regional security agenda is being militarized. The proliferation of foreign bases in Central Asia, it ought to be stressed, predates 9/11 and the U.S. strategic move into the region. The presence of so many bases is prompting a far-ranging re-evaluation of the region's geo-strategic importance.

Middle East

The government has been clear cut about not sending troops to Iraq, a move that has increased its relations with the Middle East, while it hasn't proliferated weapons, allowing it to maintain relations with the west. India has the world's second largest Muslim population, and has vowed to increase its amount of Haj pilgrims. This has led to a connection between the Muslim world and the Indian democracy. India's long standing friendship with the Palestinian people and its support for their cause was reaffirmed when Shri K. Natwar Singh, Minister for External Affairs, led a multi-party delegation to Cairo to pay homage to the memory of Yasser Arafat, the much revered leader of the Palestinian people. In September, Minister of State for External Affairs, Shri E. Ahamed, had visited Ramala with a goodwill message from Prime Minister Dr. Manmohan Singh reiterating India's unwavering support to Palestine, which was greatly appreciated by the late President Arafat. Despite these actions, India has not lost good relations with Israel and the United States. A considerable feat considering the state of the modern world.

Israel

India and Israel were on opposite sides during the Cold War, with Israel siding with the NATO countries and India leaning in the direction of the Soviet Union. The creation of Israel supported by India's first prime minister Jawaharlal Nehru and openly supported by Hindu revivalists such as Vinayak Damodar Savarkar.

However, Israel and India shared a clandestine relationship that involved cooperation between their respective intelligence agencies and the purchase of military hardware by India from Israel. Israel shared India's concerns about the growing danger posed by Pakistan, a nation hostile to India and one that supplied weapons and training to the Arabs against Israel. After the end of the Cold War, formal relations with Israel started improving significantly.

Since the establishment of full diplomatic relations with Israel in 1992, India has had a highly productive relation with the Jewish State. India is regarded as Israel's strongest ally in Asia, and Israel is India's second largest arms supplier. Both countries perceive a common problem with Islamic Terrorism and Islamic Fundamentalism, and have engaged in joint military ventures in an effort to combat this problem.

India has entertained Israeli Prime Minister Ariel Sharon in a visit in 2003, and Israel has entertained Indian dignitaries such as Finance Minister Jaswant Singh in diplomatic visits. India and Israel collaborate extensively in scientific and technological endeavours. Israel's Minister for Science and Technology has expressed interest in collaborating with the Indian Space Research Organization (ISRO) towards utilizing satellites for better management of land and other resources. Israel has also expressed interest in participating in ISRO's Chandrayaan Mission involving an unmanned mission to the moon.

People's Republic of China

Despite lingering suspicions remaining from the 1962 Sino-Indian War and continuing territorial/boundary disputes in Kashmir and Arunachal Pradesh, Sino-Indian relations have improved gradually since 1988. Both countries have sought to reduce tensions along the frontier, expand trade and cultural ties, and normalize relations.

A series of high-level visits between the two nations have helped improve relations. In December 1996, PRC President Jiang Zemin visited India on a tour of South Asia. While in New Delhi, he signed, with the Indian Prime Minister, a series of confidence-building measures for the disputed borders. This included troop reductions and weapons limitations, which appear to have taken place.

Sino-Indian relations received a setback in May 1998 when the Indian Defencc ministcr justified the country's nuclear tests by citing potential threats from the PRC. However, in June 1999, during the Kargil crisis, External Affairs Minister Jaswant Singh visited Beijing and stated that India did not consider China a threat. Relations between India and the PRC are on the mend, and the two sides handled the move from Tibet to India of the 17th Karmapa in January 2000 with delicacy and tact. In 2003, India formally recognized Tibet as a part of China, and China recognized Sikkim as a formal part of India in 2004. Both India and China are members of the East Asia Summit.

United States

Historically, relations between India and the United States were somewhat cool following Indian independence, as India took a leading position in the Non-Aligned Movement, and attempted to pursue even-handed economic and military relations with the Soviet Union. For most of the Cold War, the US tended to have warmer relations with Pakistan, primarily as a way to contain Soviet-friendly India and to use Pakistan to back the Afghan Mujahideen against the Soviet occupation of Afghanistan. An Indo-Soviet twenty year friendship treaty, signed in 1971, also positioned India against the US.

India played a key role in establishing the Non-Aligned Movement in 1961. Though India pursued close relations with both US and USSR, it decided not to join any major power bloc and refrained from joining military alliances. India, however began establishing close military relationship with the Soviet Union.

After the Sino-Indian War and the Indo-Pakistani War of 1965, India made considerable changes to its foreign policy. It developed a close relationship with the Soviet Union and started receiving massive military equipment and financial assistance from the USSR. This had an adverse effect on the Indo-US relationship. USA saw Pakistan as a counter-weight to pro-Soviet India and started giving the former military assistance. This created an atmosphere of suspicion between India and US. The US-India relationship suffered a considerable setback during the Soviet invasion of Afghanistan when India openly supported the Soviet invasion.

Relations between India and the United States came to an all-time low during the early 1970s. Despite reports of atrocities in East Pakistan, and despite being told-most notably in the Blood telegram-of 'genocidal' activities being perpetrated by Pakistani forces, U.S. Secretary of State Henry Kissinger and U.S. President Richard Nixon did nothing to discourage then Pakistani President Yahya Khan and the Pakistan Army. Kissinger was particularly concerned about Soviet expansion into South Asia as a result of a treaty of friendship that had recently been signed between India and the Soviet Union, and sought to demonstrate to the People's Republic of China the value of a tacit alliance with the United States.

In recent years, Kissinger came under fire for comments made during the Indo-Pakistan War in which he described Indians as "bastards." Kissinger has since expressed his regret over the comments.

However, since the end of the Cold War era, India-US relations have improved dramatically. This has largely been fostered by the fact that the US and India are both democracies and have a large and growing trade relationship.

During the Gulf War, the economy of India went through an extremely difficult phase. The Government of India liberalized the Indian economy. After the break up of the Soviet Union, India started looking for new allies and tried improving diplomatic relations with the members of the NATO particularly the United States, Canada, France and Germany. In 1992, India established formal diplomatic relations with Israel.

In the mid-1990s, India tried to attract world attention towards the Pakistan backed terrorism in Kashmir. The Kargil

War resulted in a major diplomatic victory for India. The United States and European Union recognized the fact that Pakistani military had illegally infiltrated into Indian territory and pressurized Pakistan to withdraw from Kargil. Several anti-India terrorist groups based in Pakistan were labelled as terrorist groups by the United States and European Union.

In 1998, India tested nuclear weapons which resulted in several U.S., Japanese and European sanctions on India.

India's then defence minister, George Fernandes, said that India's nuclear program was necessary as it provided a deterrence to potential Chinese nuclear threat. Most of the sanctions imposed on India were removed by 2001. India has categorically stated that it will never use weapons first but will defend if attacked. In fact Pakistan is the first country that India informs if any nuclear tests are on the agenda.

The economic sanctions imposed by the United States in response to India's nuclear tests in May 1998 appeared, at least initially, to seriously damage Indo-American relations. President Bill Clinton imposed wide-ranging sanctions pursuant to the 1994 Nuclear Proliferation Prevention Act. U.S. sanctions on Indian entities involved in the nuclear industry and opposition to international financial institution loans for non-humanitarian assistance projects in India. The United States encouraged India to sign the Comprehensive Test Ban Treaty (CTBT) immediately and without condition. The U.S. also called for restraint in missile and nuclear testing and deployment by both India and Pakistan. The non-proliferation dialogue initiated after the 1998 nuclear tests has bridged many of the gaps in understanding between the countries.

After the September 11 attacks, Indian intelligence agencies provided the U.S. with significant information on Al-Qaeda and related groups' activities in Pakistan and Afghanistan. India's extensive contribution to the War on Terrorism has helped India's diplomatic relations with several countries. Over the past three years, India has held numerous joint military exercises with U.S and European nations that have resulted in a strengthened U.S.-India and E.U.-India bilateral relationship. India's bilateral trade with Europe and U.S. has more than doubled in the last five years.

However, India has yet to sign the CTBT, or the NPT, claiming the discriminatory nature of the treaty that allows the 5 declared nuclear countries of the world to keep their nuclear arsenal and develop it using computer simulation testing. Prior to its nuclear testing, India had pressed for a comprehensive destruction of nuclear weapons by all countries of the world in a time-bound frame. This was not acceptable to the US and other countries. Presently, India has declared its policy of "no-first use of nuclear weapons" and the maintenance of a "credible nuclear deterrence". The US, under President George W. Bush has also lifted most of its sanctions on India and has resumed military cooperation. Relations with US have considerably improved in the recent years, with the two countries taking part in joint naval exercises off the coast of India and joint air exercises both in India as well as in the United States.

India has been pushing for reforms in the UN and WTO with mixed results. India's candidature for a permanent seat at the UN Security Council is currently backed by several countries including United Kingdom, France, Germany, Japan, Brazil and African Union nations. In 2005, the United States signed a nuclear cooperation agreement with India even though the latter is not a part of the NPT. The US argued that India's strong nuclear non-proliferation record made it an exception and persuaded other NSG members to sign similar deals with India.

On 2 March 2006 India and US has signed a pact on cooperation in civilian nuclear field. This was signed during the four days state visit of US president George Bush in India. On its part, India would separate its civilian and military nuclear programs, and the civilian programs would be brought under the safeguards of IAEA. The United States would sell India the reactor technologies and the nuclear fuel for setting up and upgrading its civilian nuclear program. The US Congress needs to ratify this pact since US laws prohibits the trading of nuclear technologies and materials outside the framework of the Nuclear Suppliers Group (NSG).

United States Congress, hitherto a staunch defender of the Nuclear Non-Proliferation Treaty and all it stands for, is poised to allow America's laws to be amended to accommodate civilian nuclear trade with India, despite that country's bomb-building. There will then be pressure on the Nuclear Suppliers Group to carve an India-shaped hole in its global nuclear export restrictions and on the board of the International Atomic Energy Agency (IAEA) to agree to "India-specific" safeguards on any nuclear materials or technology sold. The Bush administration defends its India deal as good for combating Global warming, good for friendship with the world's biggest democracy and good for jobs in America. By lifting restrictions on India's ability to buy nuclear technology and fuel from abroad, America will be helping it out of a uranium squeeze: its usable stocks of the enriched stuff (lower enriched for power generation, higher for weapons) have been dwindling fast. If the NSG goes along, and makes an exception to its rule that nuclear exports can go only to countries with all their nuclear facilities under safeguards, India will no longer have to eke out its nuclear materials. It will be able to use foreign uranium for power generation.

India's ties with the US have grown stronger since the 9/11 attacks on the US. Two million diaspora of Indians in the United States is a factor in this relationship. Levels of cooperation between the Armed Forces of both countries have increased in recent years, and have been taking part in various joint drills. Indian and U.S. Military leaders have also met to consider ways for the two countries to further expand their military partnership. Also India is the world's largest arms importer and the United States is one of the key exporters.

AIR INDIA

Air India is the largest international airline in India and the national flag carrier of India with a worldwide network of passenger and cargo services. It is one of the two state-owned airlines in the country, the other being Indian Airlines. Its main bases are Chhatrapati Shivaji International Airport, Mumbai and Indira Gandhi International Airport, New Delhi with hubs at Chennai International Airport. The airline connects 95 destinations around the world, including 12 gateways in India with Air India Express, which is a fully-owned subsidiary of Air India.

Brief History

Air India was founded as Tata Airlines in 1932, a division of Tata Sons Ltd. (now Tata Group) by J. R. D. Tata.

On October 15, 1932 the founder, J. R. D. Tata flew a single engined De Havilland Puss Moth registered VT-and carrying air mail (postal mail of Imperial Airways) from Karachi's Drigh Road Aerodrome to Bombay's Juhu Airstrip via Ahmedabad. The aircraft continued to Madras via Bellary piloted by Royal Air Force pilot Neville Vincent.

Following the end of World War II, regular commercial service was restored in India and Tata Airlines became a public limited company on 29 July 1946 under the name Air India.

In 1948 49% of the airline was acquired by the Government of India, with an option to purchase an additional 2%. In return, the airline was granted status to operate international services from India as the designated flag carrier under the name Air India International. On June 8, 1948 a Lockheed Constellation L-749A named Malabar Princess and registered VT-CQP took off from Bombay bound for London via Cairo and Geneva. This marked the airline's first long haul international flight, soon followed by service in 1950 to Nairobi via Aden.

On 1 August 1953, the Government of India exercised its option to purchase a majority stake in the carrier and Air India International Limited was born as one of the fruits of the Air Corporations Act that nationalised the air transportation industry. At the same time all domestic services were transferred to Indian Airlines. In 1954, the airline took delivery of its first L-1049 Super Constellations and inaugurated services to Singapore, Bangkok, Hong Kong and Tokyo.

Air India International entered the jet age in 1960 when its first Boeing 707, named Nandadevi and registered VT-DJJ, was delivered. Jet services to New York via London were inaugurated that same year in May 1960. On June 8, 1962 the airline's name was officially truncated to Air India. On June 11, 1962 Air India became the world's first all-jet airline.

In 1970, Air India moved its offices to down town Bombay. The next year, the airline took delivery of its first

Boeing 747-200 named Emperor Ashoka and registered VT-EBD. This coincided with the introduction of the 'Palace In The Sky' livery and branding. A distinctive feature of this livery is the paintwork around each aircraft window, in the cusped arch style of windows in Indian palaces.

In 1986 Air India took delivery of the Airbus A310. The airline is the largest operator of this type in passenger service. In 1988, Air India also took delivery of two Boeing 747-300s in mixed passenger-cargo configuration.

In 1989, to supplant its "Flying Palace" livery, Air India introduced a new livery that was mostly white but had a golden sun on a red tail. Only applied to around a half of Air India's fleet, the new livery did not succeed, as the Indian flying public complained about the phasing out of the classic colours. The new livery was dropped after two years and the old scheme was returned. Since then, Air India has been hesitant to radically change the paint scheme, instead opting for minor updates and face lifts.

In 1993, Air India took delivery of the flagship of its fleet when the first Boeing 747-400 named Konark and registered VT-ESM made history by operating the first non-stop flight between New York and Delhi.

In 1994 the airline was registered as Air India Ltd. In 1996, the airline inaugurated service to its second US gateway at Chicago's O'Hare International Airport. In 1999, the airline opened its dedicated Terminal 2-C at the newly renamed Chatrapati Shivaji International Airport in Mumbai.

The 21st century has seen Air India introduce new services to Shanghai in China, as well as two new US gateways at Newark Liberty International Airport (EWR) and Los Angeles (LAX).

Air-India has registered a profit of Rs 133.85 crores (approx USD 30 million) in the financial year ending March 31, 2003, after taking into account the deferred tax benefit. In the year 2002, it recorded a net profit of Rs 15.44 crores. Air-India earned a total revenue of Rs 5658 crores (approx USD 1.26 billion) in 2002-03 as against Rs 5017 crores (approx USD 1.1 billion) in the previous year. The newly elected Government of

India has appointed Mr.Praful Patel as the Minister for Civil Aviation. In March 2004, Air India started non-stop flights from Ahmedabad's Sardar Vallabhbhai Patel International Airport to London, Heathrow, making it the third station from India (after Mumbai and Delhi). In December 2004, Air India leased three Boeing 777-222ER aircraft from United Airlines. With these three new B777s, Air India was able to introduce three new routes: Delhi-Frankfurt-Los Angeles, Delhi-Amritsar-Birmingham-Toronto, and Delhi-Dhaka-Kolkata-London.

In early 2006, it was announced that Air India and the other state-run carrier, Indian Airlines may merge.

The International Federation of Air Line Pilots' Associations has imposed a recruitment ban for pilots thus hindering the ability of the airline to recruit qualified pilots.

Incidents and Accidents since 1970

- Air India Flight 855 Ashoka crashed into the Arabian Sea after take-off from Sahar International Airport (now Chatrapati Shivaji International Airport) in Bombay (now Mumbai) on 1 January 1978, killing all on board (213 persons-190 passengers, 23 crew).
- On 21 June 1982 a Boeing 707 crashed at Bombay airport while trying to land in a heavy rainstorm. 2 crew and 15 passengers were killed.
- At 07:13 on Sunday June 23, 1985 an explosion in the New Tokyo International Airport (now Narita International Airport) baggage terminal killed two baggage handlers, and injured four. The bomb in that bag was intended for Air India Flight 301 with 177 passengers and crew on board, bound for Bangkok.
- Air India Flight 182-Kanishka was blown up mid-flight on 23 June 1985 by a bomb. The flight was on the first leg on its Montreal-London-Delhi-Bombay (Mumbai) flight when it exploded off the coast of Ireland. The plane crashed into the Atlantic Ocean. All 307 passengers and 22 crew on board died. After this incident Air-India suspended all services to Canada, which resumed after 20 years in 2005.

Destinations

Passenger Operations

Air India has 50 (two of them only covered by Air India Express) worldwide destinations.

It also has code-sharing agreements with international airlines to expand coverage. The airline carried 3.39 million passengers during the financial year ending March 2003 and achieved a load factor of 71.6 per cent, substantially higher than the 66 per cent load factor recorded in the preceding year.

The airline has received a 4 star rating for cabin safety procedures from skytrax airline quality review. Three classes of seats are offered-First class, Executive class and Economy class. Flat bed seats are offered for first class passengers. The airline also offers a frequent flyer programme alone and in collaboration with many of its alliances.

The airline also offers luxury lounges in its ground terminals for its First and Executive class travellers in select destinations within India. Air-India has duty free sale on board its flights, named 'Sky Bazaar'.

Fleet

Air India and its low-cost subsidiary Air India Express operate a fleet consisting of the following 45 aircraft:

- 19 Airbus A310
- 11 Boeing 747
    - o 2 Boeing 747-300M Combi
    - o 8 Boeing 747-400
    - o 1 Boeing 747-400M Combi
- 4 Boeing 777
    - o 3 Boeing 777-200ER
    - o 1 Boeing 777-200A
- 10 Boeing 737-800
- 1 Boeing 767-300ER

Ordered Fleet

Air India placed an order for the following 68 aircraft from Boeing:

- 8 Boeing 777-200LR "Worldliners"
- 15 Boeing 777-300ER
- 27 Boeing 787-8 "Dreamliners"
- 18 Boeing 737-800 (for its fully-owned subsidiary Air-India Express)

Air India plans to use the Boeing 777-300ER aircraft to replace their Boeing 747-300 aircraft and Boeing 747-400 leased aircraft. They will operate on routes to Europe and the U.S. They plan to use their Boeing 787-8 aircraft to replace their ageing A310-300 aircraft on routes to the Middle East and Southeast and East Asia. The Boeing 777-200LR will operate on non-stop routes to North America. These new aircraft will also allow Air India to open up new routes to Australia, Canada, Europe, East Asia, and the U.S.

Air India plans to refurbish the interiors of its 6 owned Boeing 747-400s. This refurbishment will include PTVs in all classes. Air India is set to merge with Indian Airlines to create a mega airline consisting of 130 to 140 aircraft. This will occur in the 2006 fiscal year. The combined entity is leaning toward joining Star Alliance to expand coverage and to be one of the biggest South Asian airlines. Air India will replace the remainder of its Boeing 747-400 by 2011 and is evaluating the Boeing 747-8 and the Airbus A380.

Cargo Operations

In 1954, Air-India started its freighter operations with a Douglas DC-3 Dakota aircraft, giving Air India the distinction of being the first Asian airline to operate freighters. The airline operates cargo flights to many destinations. The airline also has ground truck-transportation arrangements on select destinations.

A member of IATA, Air-India carries all types of cargo including dangerous goods (hazardous materials) and live animals, provided such shipments are tendered according to

IATA Dangerous Goods Regulations and IATA Live Animals Regulations. At the warehouse in Mumbai, Air India has developed a system of inventory management for cargo handling of import/export functions. This takes care of the entire management of cargo, supports Electronic Data Interface (EDI) messages with Indian Customs and replaces to a great extent existing paper correspondence between Customs, Airlines, and the custodians. This also replaces manual handling and binning of cargo at the warehouse in Mumbai by Air India.

Livery

Air India's livery is mostly painted in red and white colours. The bottoms of the aircraft remain metal and unpainted but the upper portion is given a white background along with the airline's name written in red. The name is in Hindi on one side and in English on the other. The painted on red palace style carvings on the outside of the windows refer to their slogan "your palace in the sky" which is written on the back of the aircraft. Near the noses of Air India aircraft, the air plane is given a name. Most planes are named after powerful Indian kings or landmarks. Finally, the tail is mostly red with again, the carrier's name written in Hindi on one side and English on the other. The airline once proposed a new livery with a golden sun on the tail, however passengers missed the old traditional livery and found the new one less authentic and Indian. Eventually, the airline returned to its regular livery, pleasing customers.

As of January 2007, Air India has given its livery a refresh, making the Rajasthani Arches along the windows slightly smaller, extending a stylized cheatline from the vertical tail of the aircraft to the nose, and painting a small portion of the underbelly red. Additionally, engine nacelles are now deep red, and a gold-colored version of the airline's stylized centaur trademark now adorns both the vertical tail and engine nacelles. This livery can be seen on Air India's first 777-237/LR aircraft, registered VT-ALA.

SPECIAL ECONOMIC ZONE

A Special Economic Zone (SEZ) is a geographical region that has economic laws that are more liberal than a country's typical economic laws. Usually the goal is an increase in foreign investment. One of the earliest and the most famous Special Economic Zones were founded by the government of the People's Republic of China under Deng Xiaoping in the early 1980s. The most successful Special Economic Zone in China, Shenzhen, has developed from a small village into a city with a population over 10 million within 20 years.

The article Special Economic Zone of the People's Republic of China provides more information about the Special Economic Zones in China. Following the Chinese examples, Special Economic Zones have been established in several countries, including India, Iran, Jordan, Poland, Kazakhstan, the Philippines and Russia. North Korea has also attempted this to a degree, but failed. Currently, Puno, Peru has been slated to become a "Zona Ecomomica" by its president Alan Garcia. In the United States, SEZ are referred to as "Urban Enterprise Zones".

According to World Bank estimates, as of 2007 there are more than 3,000 projects taking place in SEZs in 120 countries worldwide.

In India

Considering the need to enhance foreign investment and promote exports from the country and realising the need that a level playing field must be made available to the domestic enterprises and manufacturers to be competitive globally, The Government of India had in April 2000 announced the introduction of Special Economic Zones policy in the country, deemed to be foreign territory for the purposes of trade operations, duties and tariffs. As of 2007, more than 500 SEZs have been proposed, 220 of which have been created. This has raised the concern of the World Bank, which questions the sustainability of such a large number of SEZs. The Special Economic Zones in India closely follow the PRC model.

List of SEZs in India

The policy provides for setting up of SEZ's in the public, private, joint sector or by State Governments. It was also envisaged that some of the existing Export Processing Zones would be converted into Special Economic Zones. Accordingly, the Government has converted Export Processing zones located at:

- Kandla and Surat (Gujarat)
- Cochin (Kerala)
- Santa Cruz (Mumbai-Maharashtra)
- Falta (West Bengal)
- Chennai (Tamil Nadu)
- Vishakhapatnam (Andhra Pradesh)
- NOIDA (Uttar Pradesh)
- Nanguneri, Tirunelveli (Tamil Nadu)

Currently, India has 15 SEZs, each an average size of 200 acres. The government has approved 285 sez's more. 8 Export Processing Zones (EPZs) have been converted into SEZs. These are fully functional. All these SEZs are in various parts of the country in the private/joint sectors or by the State Government.

But this process of planning and development is under question, as the states in which the SEZs have been approved are facing intense protests, from the farming community, accusing the government of forcibly snatching fertile land from them, at heavyily discounted prices as against the prevailing prices in the commercial real estate industry.

Also some reputed companies like Bajaj and others have commented against this policy and have suggested using barren and wasteland for setting up of SEZs. Also the suggested cost of setting up SEZs is under speculation.

In the People's Republic of China

The word "special" mainly means special economic systems and policies. In the People's Republic of China, the central government gives SEZs special policies and flexible measures, allowing SEZs to utilize a special economic management system.

1. Special tax incentives
2. Greater independence on international trade activities.

3. Economic characteristics are represented as "4 principles":
   - Construction primarily relies on attracting and utilising foreign capital
   - Primary economic forms are sino-foreign joint ventures and partnerships as well as wholly foreign-owned enterprises
   - Products are primarily export-oriented
   - Economic activities are primarily driven by market

SEZ are listed separately in the national planning (including financial planning) and have province-level authority on economic administration. SEZs local congress and government have legislation authority.

6

Foreign Trade of the Soviet Union

Soviet foreign trade played only a minor role in the Soviet economy. In 1985, for example, exports and imports each accounted for only 4 percent of the Soviet gross national product. The Soviet Union maintained this low level because it could draw upon a large energy and raw material base and because it historically had pursued a policy of self-sufficiency. Other foreign economic activity included economic aid programs, which primarily benefited the less developed Council for Mutual Economic Assistance (Comecon) countries of Cuba, Mongolia, and Vietnam, and substantial borrowing from the West to supplement hard-currency export earnings.

The Soviet Union conducted the bulk of its foreign economic activities with communist countries, particularly those of Eastern Europe. In 1988 Soviet trade with socialist countries amounted to 62 percent of total Soviet foreign trade. Between 1965 and 1988, trade with the Third World made up a steady 10 to 15 percent of the Soviet Union's foreign trade. Trade with the industrialized West, especially the United States, fluctuated, influenced by political relations between East and West, as well as by the Soviet Union's short-term needs. In the 1970s, during the period of detente, trade with the West gained in importance at the expense of trade with socialist countries. In the early and mid-1980s, when relations between the superpowers were poor, however, Soviet trade with the West decreased in favor of increased integration with Eastern Europe.

The manner in which the Soviet Union transacted trade varied from one trade partner to another. Soviet trade with the Western industrialized countries, except Finland, and most

Third World countries was conducted with hard currency, that is, currency that was freely convertible. Because the ruble was not freely convertible, the Soviet Union could only acquire hard currency by selling Soviet goods or gold on the world market for hard currency. Therefore, the volume of imports from countries using convertible currency depended on the amount of goods the Soviet Union exported for hard currency. Alternative methods of cooperation, such as barter, counter trade, industrial cooperation, or bilateral clearing agreements were much preferred. These methods were used in transactions with Finland, members of Comecon, China, Yugoslavia, and a number of Third World countries.

Commodity composition of Soviet trade differed by region. The Soviet Union imported manufactured, agricultural, and consumer goods from socialist countries in exchange for energy and manufactured goods. The Soviet Union earned hard currency by exporting fuels and other primary products to the industrialized West and then used this currency to buy sophisticated manufactures and agricultural products, primarily grain. Trade with the Third World usually involved exchanging machinery and armaments for tropical foodstuffs and raw materials.

Soviet aid programs expanded steadily from 1965 to 1985. In 1985 the Soviet Union provided an estimated US$6.9 billion to the Third World in the form of direct cash, credit disbursements, or trade subsidies. The communist Third World, primarily Cuba, Mongolia, and Vietnam, received 85 percent of these funds. In the late 1980s, the Soviet Union reassessed its aid programs. In light of reduced political returns and domestic economic problems, the Soviet Union could ill afford ineffective disbursements of its limited resources. Moreover, dissatisfied with Soviet economic assistance, several Soviet client states opened trade discussions with Western countries.

In the 1980s, the Soviet Union needed considerable sums of hard currency to pay for food and capital goods imports and to support client states. What the country could not earn from exports or gold sales it borrowed through its banks in London, Frankfurt, Vienna, Paris, and Luxembourg. Large grain imports pushed the Soviet debt quite high in 1981. Better harvests and lower import requirements redressed this imbalance in subsequent years. By late 1985, however, a decrease in oil revenues nearly returned the Soviet debt to its 1981 level. At the end of that same year the Soviet Union owed US$31 billion (gross) to Western creditors, mostly commercial banks and other private sources.

In the late 1980s, the Soviet Union attempted to reduce its hard-currency debt by decreasing imports from the West and increasing oil and gas exports to the West. It also sought increased participation in international markets and organizations. In 1987 the Soviet Union formally requested observer status in the General Agreement on Tariffs and Trade and in 1988 signed a normalization agreement with the European Economic Community. Structural changes in the foreign trade bureaucracy, granting direct trading rights to select enterprises, and legislation establishing joint ventures with foreigners opened up the economy to the Western technical and managerial expertise necessary to achieve the goals established by General Secretary Mikhail S. Gorbachev's program of economic restructuring (perestroika).

DEVELOPMENT OF THE STATE MONOPOLY ON FOREIGN TRADE

The government of the Soviet Union has always held a monopoly on all foreign trade activity, but only after the death of Joseph Stalin in 1953 did the government accord importance to foreign trade activities. Before that time, the Bolsheviks' ideological opposition to external economic control, their refusal to pay Russia's World War I debts, and the chaos of the Russian Civil War (1918-21) kept trade to the minimum level required for the country's industrial development. Active Soviet trade operations began only in 1921, when the government established the People's Commissariat of Foreign Trade.

The commissariat's monopoly on internal and external foreign trade was loosened, beginning in 1921, when the New Economic Policy (NEP) decentralized control of the economy. Although the commissariat remained the controlling center, the regime established other organizations to deal directly with foreign partners in the buying and selling of goods. These organizations included state import and export offices, joint stock companies, specialized import and export corporations, trusts, syndicates, cooperative organizations, and mixed-ownership companies.

The end of the NEP period, the beginning of the First Five-Year Plan (1928-32), and the forced collectivization of agriculture beginning in 1929 marked the early Stalin era. The government restructured foreign trade operations according to Decree Number 358, issued in February 1930, which eliminated the decentralized, essentially private, trading practices of the NEP period and established a system of monopoly specialization. The government then organized a number of foreign trade corporations under the People's Commissariat of Foreign Trade, each with a monopoly over a specific group of commodities.

Stalin's policy restricted trade as it attempted to build socialism in one country. Stalin feared the unpredictable movement and disruptive influence of such foreign market forces as demand and price fluctuations. Imports were restricted to factory equipment essential for the industrialization drive that began with the First Five-Year Plan.

World War II virtually halted Soviet trade and the activity of most foreign trade corporations. Trade was conducted primarily through Soviet trade representatives in Britain and Iran and the Soviet Buying Commission in the United States. After the war, Britain and other West European countries and the United States imposed drastic restrictions on trade with the Soviet Union. Thus, Soviet foreign trade corporations limited their efforts to Eastern Europe and China, establishing Soviet-owned companies in these countries and setting up joint-stock companies on very favorable terms. Comecon, founded in 1949, united the economies of Eastern Europe with that of the Soviet Union.

Soviet trade changed considerably in the post-Stalin era. Postwar industrialization and an expansion of foreign trade resulted in the proliferation of all-union foreign trade organizations (FTOs), the new name for foreign trade corporations and also known as foreign trade associations. In 1946 the People's Commissariat of Foreign Trade was reorganized into the Ministry of Foreign Trade. The Ministry of Foreign Trade, through its FTOs, retained the exclusive right to negotiate and sign contracts with foreigners and to draft foreign trade plans. The State Committee for Foreign Economic Relations (Gosudarstvennyi komitet po vneshnim ekonomicheskim sviaziam--GKES), created in 1955, managed all foreign aid programs and the export of complete factories through the FTOs subordinate to it. Certain ministries, however, had the right to deal directly with foreign partners through their own FTOs.

On January 17, 1988, Izvestiia reported the abolition of the Ministry of Foreign Trade and GKES. These two organizations were merged into the newly created Ministry of Foreign Economic Relations, which had responsibility for administering foreign trade policy and foreign aid agreements. Other legislation provided for the establishment of joint enterprises. The government retained its monopoly on foreign trade through a streamlined version of the Soviet foreign trade bureaucracy as it existed before the January 17 decree.

STRUCTURE OF THE FOREIGN TRADE BUREAUCRACY

In 1988 the foreign trade bureaucracy reflected the monopoly specification system created by the 1930 Decree Number 358. Under the authority of the Communist Party of the Soviet Union (CPSU) and the Council of Ministers, six central bodies, the Ministry of Foreign Economic Relations, and numerous FTOs together planned, regulated, monitored, and carried out all Soviet foreign economic activity.

Administration

Although the CPSU has ultimate authority over all foreign economic activity, in the late 1980s administrative control was centralized in the Council of Ministers. More specifically, the council's State Foreign Economic Commission coordinated the activities of ministries and departments in the area of economic and scientific cooperation with socialist, developing, and developed capitalist states.

Six central bodies under the Council of Ministries played important roles in foreign economic relations. The import and export of goods, services, and resources were managed by the

State Planning Committee (Gosudarstvennyi planovyi komitet--Gosplan), the State Committee for Material and Technical Supply (Gosudarstvennyi komitet po material'no-tekhnicheskomu snabzheniiu--Gossnab), and the State Committee for Science and Technology (Gosudarstvennyi komitet po nauke i tekhnike--GKNT). Gosplan formulated all import and export plans, coordinated the allocation of investment and other resources, and had final authority over all decisions concerning foreign trade, including trade levels and commodity composition. Gossnab coordinated the allocation of resources not handled by Gosplan and, as the central agency responsible for matching supplies with customers, played a major role in selecting and allocating imports. GKNT negotiated technical cooperation agreements and monitored license and patent purchases and sales in order to introduce new technology into the Soviet economy.

The State Committee on Prices (Gosudarstvennyi komitet po tsenam--Goskomtsen), the Ministry of Finance, and the State Bank (Gosudarstvennyi bank--Gosbank) held jurisdiction over the financing of foreign trade. Goskomtsen established prices for all imports and some exports. The Ministry of Finance controlled the balance of payments and monitored the impact of foreign trade on the state budget. Finally, Gosbank set the exchange rate for the ruble and managed the system of exchange within the Soviet Union. Gosbank supervised the Foreign Economic Activity Bank (Vneshnii ekonomicheskii bank--Vneshekonombank; until January 1, 1988, known as the Foreign Trade Bank), which provided international banking services for Soviet FTOs.

Operation

Until 1988 the two operative bodies involved solely and directly in foreign economic operations were GKES and the Ministry of Foreign Trade. The Ministry of Foreign Trade formulated draft import and export plans and regulated commodity trade. GKES supervised foreign aid programs and the export of complete plants. The Ministry of Foreign Trade or GKES had jurisdiction over most FTOs, which negotiated and signed commercial contracts with foreigners on behalf of individual enterprises. FTOs were generally organized by product, as had been the foreign trade corporations of the 1930s.

Some industrial ministries or other agencies, however, had their own FTOs. As of early 1987, for example, forty-eight FTOs were under the jurisdiction of the Ministry of Foreign Trade and nine under the GKES, whereas the Ministry of the Maritime Fleet, the Ministry of the Fishing Industry, and the Ministry of Trade, among others, had their own FTOs. In addition, certain other agencies had their own FTOs: the Chamber of Commerce and Industry, which handled international trade exhibitions; the State Committee for Physical Culture and Sports; the Central Union of Cooperatives; the State Committee for Publishing Houses, Printing Plants, and the Book Trade; the State Committee for Cinematography; and the State Committee for Science and Technology.

Structural Reforms, 1986 to Mid-1988

The cumbersome foreign trade bureaucracy contributed to a number of problems that hindered the efficiency and effectiveness of foreign trade. The lack of direct contact between Soviet enterprises and their foreign customers or suppliers frustrated both parties by unnecessarily delaying contract negotiations and the specification of technical details. In a May 1986 interview with Izvestiia, the general director of the Ministry of Foreign Trade's All-Union Association for the Export and Import of Technical Equipment, Boris K. Pushkin, reported that after an enterprise submitted a request for a foreign item, two to three years were required before it was included in the import plan and funds were allocated for its purchase. In the interim, the needs of the enterprise had often changed. Pushkin stressed the need to free enterprises from unnecessary petty supervision and excessive regulation.

Taking such problems into account, the Twenty-Seventh Party Congress in February-March 1986 declared that the party anticipated a step-by-step restructuring of [the country's] foreign trade in order to make exports and imports more effective. In August of the same year, the CPSU Central Committee and the Council of Ministers adopted the decree On Measures for

Improving Management of External Economic Relations,"" which outlined drastic steps to change the structure of the foreign trade bureaucracy.

Also in August 1986, the Council of Ministers' State Foreign Economic Commission became a permanent body within the council, giving more authority and visibility to the commission, the domestic activities of which previously went largely unreported. The staff was augmented, and the chairman acquired a rank equivalent to that of deputy prime minister. The new charter stated that the commission's role was "to formulate and implement the country's foreign economic strategy so as to enhance its potential contributions to acceleration, strengthen the Soviet position in the world economy, and promote structured and organized development of economic cooperation with all groups of countries."

Until 1987 the forty-eight FTOs subordinate to the Ministry of Foreign Trade administered more than 90 percent of Soviet foreign trade turnover. In 1987 the ministry lost control of 20 percent of Soviet foreign trade turnover. The government granted direct foreign trade rights to twenty-one ministries and state committees, sixty-seven industrial enterprises, and eight interbranch scientific production complexes. Exporting enterprises gained the right to retain part of their hard-currency earnings. Each ministry or enterprise was to pay for its investment imports with its own hard currency, and the heads of ministries and enterprises became personally responsible for the efficient use of hard-currency funds. These measures gave enterprises more influence in import decision making.

On January 13, 1987, the Council of Ministers adopted the resolution ""On Questions Concerning the Creation, on U.S.S.R. Territory, and the Activities of Joint Enterprises, International Associations, and Organizations with the Participation of Soviet and Foreign Organizations, Firms, and Management Bodies,"" or, more simply, a law on joint ventures. This legislation opened up enterprises inside the Soviet Union for the first time since the Bolshevik Revolution, to foreign participation. Joint ventures were to facilitate the acquisition and assimilation of Western technology, managerial know-how, and marketing abilities. Optimistic about the economic effects of their new undertaking,

Soviet officials declared that 85 to 90 percent of ""the most important types of machinery"" would meet world technical standards by 1990. The Soviet Union's vast natural resources and its lucrative, previously closed, domestic market attracted Western companies. By August 1988, more than 50 joint ventures were registered in the Soviet Union, and approximately 300 were under negotiation.

Nevertheless, numerous obstacles arose in the first eighteen months after the government adopted the joint venture law. Complaints by Western partners dealt with uncertainties concerning Soviet trade regulations, problems with the supply of goods, the dilemma of the non-convertibility of the ruble, difficulties finding qualified Soviet managers, problems in projecting production costs (as of 1989 Soviet domestic prices were administratively set and not based on market forces), and even complications finding office space in Moscow. Soviet trade officials' efforts to accommodate these complaints have included the decentralization of the foreign trade bureaucracy, the establishment of a management institute in Moscow, price reforms, and various legal reforms.

Before Western businessmen could recover from the confusion and disruption caused by this series of reforms, a second series began in early 1988. Effective January 1, 1988, the Foreign Trade Bank (Vneshnii torgovii bank--Vneshtorgbank) was renamed the Foreign Economic Activity Bank (Vneshnii ekonomicheskii bank--Vneshekonombank). The name change did not signify a major change in the bank's duties but simply more accurately reflected the nature of its operations. Vneshtorgbank had branched out from the simple management of foreign trade transactions to provide currency, credit, and accounting services as well. In a change from its previous duties, Vneshekonombank was required to administer new procedures dealing with Soviet firms that had recently acquired direct foreign trade rights.

Also on January 1, 1988, the New Enterprise Law went into effect, making enterprises economically accountable for their own business operations by 1989. According to this law, the government had the power to disband unprofitable businesses, and each ministry and its subordinate enterprises gained the responsibility for their own foreign trade activities. In addition, Gosplan, Gossnab, and GKNT relinquished some of their rights to allocate money and goods. Finally, the Ministry of Foreign Trade lost control of 15 percent more of its foreign trade turnover when fourteen additional enterprises and four other ministries acquired direct foreign trade rights.

Yet probably the most significant change in the foreign trade mechanism occurred on January 17, 1988, when Izvestiia announced the abolition of the Ministry of Foreign Trade and the GKES. The Ministry of Foreign Economic Relations, headed by Konstantin F. Katushev, former head of the GKES, assumed the duties of the two agencies. ""Thus, the state monopoly on foreign trade and its state-wide aspects remains centralized,"" reported the Soviet foreign trade monthly Vneshniaia torgovlia (Foreign Trade), ""while operational functions are continually being shifted to the business level."" In March 1988, the journal reported that approximately 20 percent of foreign trade turnover was handled by the eighty-one firms that had been granted the right to deal directly with foreigners.

Other reforms followed in April 1988, when the Central Committee and the Council of Ministers agreed on a new charter for the Chamber of Commerce and Industry. In general, the chamber monitored foreign trade conducted outside the new Ministry of Foreign Economic Relations. In addition, the chamber assisted Soviet production enterprises in locating Western partners and learning foreign trade practices.

TRADE WITH SOCIALIST COUNTRIES

In the late 1980s, the Soviet Union traded with fourteen socialist countries. The political and economic relationships between the Soviet Union and these countries determine the four groups into which these countries can be divided: members of Comecon; Yugoslavia; China; and the developing communist countries of Cambodia, Laos, and the Democratic People's Republic of Korea (North Korea).

Business with socialist countries was conducted on a bilateral, country-by-country basis in which imports balanced exports. Soviet oil exports to these countries bought machinery and equipment and industrial consumer goods, as well as political support without the expenditure of freely convertible foreign currency. In addition, Soviet aid programs, which took the form of direct loans or trade subsidies, almost exclusively involved socialist countries.

THE COUNCIL FOR MUTUAL ECONOMIC ASSISTANCE

The Soviet Union formed the Council for Mutual Economic Assistance (Comecon) in 1949, in part to discourage the countries of Eastern Europe from participating in the Marshall Plan and to counteract trade boycotts imposed after World War II by the United States and by Britain and other West European countries. Ostensibly, Comecon was organized to coordinate economic and technical cooperation between the Soviet Union and the member countries. In reality, the Soviet Union's domination over Comecon activities reflected its economic, political, and military power. In 1989 Comecon comprised ten countries: the six original members--Bulgaria, Czechoslovakia, Hungary, Poland, Romania, and the Soviet Union--plus the German Democratic Republic (East Germany, which joined in 1950), Mongolia (1962), Cuba (1972), and Vietnam (1978). Albania, although it joined in February 1949, has not participated in Comecon activities since 1961.

Since 1949 the Soviet Union has traded primarily with other Comecon members. In 1960 the Soviet Union sent 56 percent of its exports to and received 58 percent of its imports from Comecon members. From that time, the volume of this trade has steadily increased, but the proportion of Soviet trade with Comecon members decreased as the Soviet Union sought to increase trade with Western industrialized countries. In contrast to 1960, trade with Comecon members accounted for only 42 percent of Soviet exports and 43 percent of Soviet imports in 1980.

The European members of Comecon have looked to the Soviet Union for oil; in turn, they have provided machinery, equipment, agricultural goods, industrial goods, and consumer goods to the Soviet Union. Because of the peculiarities of the Comecon pricing system, throughout the 1970s and early 1980s Comecon prices for Soviet oil were lower than world oil prices. Western specialists have debated the political motivation of this implicit price subsidy to Comecon members. The cohesiveness within Comecon members seemed remarkable when in 1985 the fall in the world price left Comecon members paying above-market prices for Soviet oil.

The membership of Cuba, Mongolia, and Vietnam in Comecon has served Soviet foreign policy interests more than the economic welfare of Comecon members. In general, the more economically developed European members have supported the three less developed members by providing a large market for their exports, often at above-market prices. Most of Cuba's sugar and nickel and all of Mongolia's copper and molybdenum have been imported by the Soviet Union. In addition, the Soviet Union has established naval and air bases in Cuba and Vietnam.

Since 1985 Gorbachev has called for an increase in trade with Comecon members. At the Twenty-Seventh Party Congress in February-March 1986, both he and Prime Minister Nikolai I. Ryzhkov stressed the need to improve cooperation with the socialist countries on the basis of Comecon's Comprehensive Program for Scientific and Technical Cooperation up to the Year 2000. This program stressed the self-sufficiency of Comecon countries in five key areas: electronics, automation of production, nuclear power, biotechnology, and development of new raw materials. It also called for improvement of plan coordination, joint planning, Comecon investment strategy, production specialization, and quality of machinery and equipment exported to the Soviet Union.

Yugoslavia

In 1964 Yugoslavia negotiated a formal agreement of cooperation with Comecon. This relationship allowed Yugoslavia to maintain its nonaligned position while acquiring almost all the rights and privileges of a full Comecon member. In the 1980s, the Soviet Union's trade relationship with Yugoslavia resembled its relationship with full members of Comecon. The Soviet Union exported fuel, ferrous metals, plastics, and fertilizer to Yugoslavia. Yugoslavia's machine-tool, power-engineering, shipbuilding, and consumer goods industries supplied the Soviet Union with soft-currency goods.

In the late 1970s and early 1980s, Yugoslavia became more dependent on Soviet oil, as hostilities in the Persian Gulf cut off its supply of Iraqi oil. In addition, from 1970 well into the 1980s actual trade with the Soviet Union exceeded planned trade volumes. Thus, in 1983 the Yugoslav government informed Soviet Prime Minister Nikolai A. Tikhonov of its desire to decrease trade with the Soviet Union in the mid-to late 1980s. Because of the huge foreign currency debt accumulated by Yugoslavia from 1981 to 1985, however, the Soviet Union remained its most important trade partner in the late 1980s. In fact, for some Yugoslav products, such as shoes, the Soviet Union was the sole foreign buyer.

China

In the 1950s, the Soviet Union claimed half of China's foreign trade. The political rift that developed between the two countries in the late 1950s culminated in 1960 with the withdrawal of more than 1,000 Soviet specialists from China and an official break in trade relations in 1964. Although it had been only an observer, China stopped attending Comecon sessions in 1961. Economic relations between the Soviet Union and China resumed in 1982. Primarily as a result of Soviet political concessions and pressures on the Chinese to expand trade, trade volume between the two countries increased tenfold between 1982 and 1987.

In the 1980s, the Soviet Union proved to be an ideal trade partner for China. China's exports were not competitive on the world market, and its foreign currency reserves were severely depleted by record foreign trade deficits in 1984 and 1985. Likewise, the Soviet Union, producing dated technology that was difficult to market in more industrially advanced countries and acquiring a growing hard-currency debt, eagerly pursued the Chinese market. Each country would sell the other goods it could not market elsewhere, and each could conserve scarce hard currency by bartering. The Soviet Union possessed machinery, equipment, and technical know-how to help China develop its fuel and mineral resources and power, transportation, and metallurgical industries. China could offer a wealth of raw materials, textiles, and agricultural and industrial consumer goods.

Stepped-up economic relations reflected Soviet flexibility in overcoming various political and administrative stumbling blocks. By mid-1988 Gorbachev was speaking of reducing Soviet troops on the Chinese border, Vietnam had removed half of its troops from Cambodia, and Soviet troops had begun their withdrawal from Afghanistan. Reforms of the Soviet foreign trade complex established free trade zones in the Soviet Far East and Soviet Central Asia, simplifying border trade between the two countries. Soviet trade officials persuaded the Chinese to expand business ties beyond border trade into joint ventures, coproduction contracts, and the export of surplus Chinese labor to the Soviet Union. The Peking Restaurant in Moscow, specializing in Chinese cuisine, became the first joint venture between the Soviet Union and China. In April 1988, China's minister of foreign economic relations and trade, Zheng Toubin, stated that China would continue to expand trade with the Soviet Union ""at a rapid pace,"" thus rewarding Soviet persistence in expanding trade with China.

Cambodia, Laos, and North Korea

Soviet economic relations with non-Comecon communist states have taken the form of aid and trade. In 1987 approximately 85 percent of Soviet aid went to the communist Third World. By far the largest share of these funds was absorbed by Cuba, Mongolia, and Vietnam. The rest was left to Cambodia, Laos, and North Korea. Pledges of Soviet aid increased steadily from 1985 through 1988 and were divided evenly between direct aid and trade subsidies. Commodity exchange was characterized by the Soviet Union's providing machinery, fuel, and transportation equipment in return for Laotian ores and concentrated metals, North Korean rolled ferrous metals and labor, and Cambodian rubber.

Trade with Western Industrialized Countries

The Western industrialized countries include the countries of Western Europe, as well as Australia, Canada, Japan, New Zealand, South Africa, and the United States. Soviet trade with industrialized countries, except Finland, consisted of simple purchases paid for on a cash or credit basis, direct exchange of one good for another (Pepsi-Cola for Stolichnaya vodka, for example), or industrial cooperation agreements in which foreign firms participated in the construction or operation of plants in the Soviet Union. In the latter instances, payments were rendered in the form of the output of new plants. By contrast, trade with Finland, which does not have a convertible currency, was conducted through bilateral clearing agreements, much like Soviet trade with its Comecon partners.

In the 1970s and 1980s, the Soviet Union relied heavily on various kinds of fuel exports to earn hard currency, and Western partners regarded the Soviet Union as an extremely reliable supplier of oil and natural gas. In the 1980s, the Soviet Union gave domestic priority to gas, coal, and nuclear power in order to free more oil reserves for export. This was necessary because of higher production costs and losses of convertible currency resulting from the drop in world oil prices. The development of natural gas for domestic and export use was also stimulated by these factors. Between 1970 and 1986, natural gas exports rose from 1 percent to 15 percent of total Soviet exports to the West.

Because of the inferior quality of Soviet goods, the Soviet Union was unsuccessful in increasing its exports of manufactured goods. In 1987 only 18 percent of Soviet manufactured goods met world technical standards. As an illustration of these problems in quality, Canadian customers who had purchased Soviet Belarus tractors often found that the tractors had to be overhauled on arrival before they could be sold on the Canadian market. In 1986 less than 5 percent of Soviet exports to the West consisted of machinery. Other Soviet nonfuel exports in the 1990s included timber, exported primarily to Japan, and chemicals, the export of which grew substantially in 1984 and 1985.

In the 1980s, Soviet imports from Western industrialized countries generally exceeded exports, although trade with the West decreased overall. One-half of Soviet agricultural imports were from developed countries, and these imports made up a considerable portion of total imports from the West. Industrial equipment formed one-quarter of Soviet imports from the West, and iron and steel products, particularly steel tubes for pipeline construction, made up most of the rest. Over the course of the

1980s, high-technology items gained in importance as well. In the 1970s and 1980s, Soviet trade with the Western industrialized countries was more dynamic than was Soviet trade with other countries, as trade patterns fluctuated with political and economic changes. In the 1970s, the Soviet Union exchanged its energy and raw materials for Western capital goods, and growth in trade was substantial. Soviet exports jumped 55 percent, and imports jumped 207 percent. The Soviet Union ran a trade deficit with the West throughout this period.

In 1980 the Soviet Union exported slightly more to the West than it imported. After a temporary shortage of hard currency in 1981, the Soviet Union sought to improve its trade position with the industrialized countries by keeping imports at a steady level and by increasing exports. As a result, the Soviet Union began to run trade surpluses with most of its Western partners. Much of the income earned from fuel exports to Western Europe was used to pay off debts with the United States, Canada, and Australia, from which the Soviet Union had imported large quantities of grain.

In 1985 and 1986, trade with the West was suppressed because of heightened East-West political tensions, successful Soviet grain harvests, high Soviet oil production costs, a devalued United States dollar, and falling oil prices. Despite increases in oil and natural gas exports, the Soviet Union's primary hard-currency earners, the country was receiving less revenue from its exports to the West. The Soviet Union sold most of its oil and natural gas exports for United States dollars but bought most of its hardcurrency imports from Western Europe. The lower value of the United States dollar meant that the purchasing power of a barrel of Soviet crude oil, for example, was much lower than in the 1970s and early 1980s. In 1987 the purchasing power of a barrel of Soviet crude oil in exchange for West German goods had fallen to one-third of its purchasing power in 1984.

With the exception of grain, phosphates used in fertilizer production, and high-technology equipment, Soviet dependence on Western imports historically has been minimal. A growing hardcurrency debt of US$31 billion in 1986 led to reductions in imports from countries with hard currencies. In 1988

Gorbachev cautioned against dependence on Western technology because it required hard currency that ""we don't have."" He also warned that increased borrowing to pay for imports from the West would lead to dependence on international lending institutions.

United States

Trade between the United States and the Soviet Union averaged about 1 percent of total trade for both countries through the 1970s and 1980s. Soviet-American trade peaked in 1979 at US$4.5 billion, exactly 1 percent of total United States trade. The Soviet Union continuously ran a trade deficit with the United States in the 1970s and early 1980s, but from 1985 through 1987 the Soviet Union cut imports from the United States while maintaining its level of exports to balance trade between the two countries.

In 1987 total trade between the United States and the Soviet Union amounted to US$2 billion. The Soviet Union exported chemicals, metals (including gold), and petroleum products in addition to fur skins, alcoholic beverages, and fish products to the United States and received agricultural goods--mostly grain--and industrial equipment in return. The value of exports to the Soviet Union in 1987 amounted to US$1.5 billion, three-quarters of which consisted of agricultural products and one-quarter industrial equipment.

Competition from other parts of the world, improvements in Soviet grain production, and political disagreements between the two countries adversely affected American agricultural exports to the Soviet Union in the 1980s. In 1985 and 1986, trade was the lowest since 1973. The Soviet Union had turned to Canada and Western Europe for one-third of its grain supplies, as well as to Argentina, Eastern Europe, Australia, and China. United States government price subsidies helped to expand grain exports in 1987 and 1988.

The United States has long linked trade with the Soviet Union to its foreign policy toward the Soviet Union and, especially since the early 1980s, to Soviet human rights policies. In 1949, for example, the Coordinating Committee for Multilateral Export Controls was established by Western governments to monitor the export of sensitive high technology that would improve military effectiveness of members of the Warsaw Pact and certain other countries. The Jackson-Vanik Amendment, which was attached to the 1974 Trade Reform Act, linked the granting of most-favored-nation to the right of Soviet Jews to emigrate.

In 1987 the United States had reason to reassess its trade policy toward the Soviet Union. The Soviet Union had restructured and decentralized authority for trade under the Ministry of Foreign Trade, made improvements in human rights policies, cooperated in arms control negotiations, and shown a willingness to experiment with joint ventures. Furthermore, the United States government recognized that restrictive trade policies were hurting its own economic interests. In April 1988, Soviet and American trade delegations met in Moscow to discuss possibilities for expanded trade. Through increased trade with the United States, the Soviet Union hoped to learn Western management, marketing, and manufacturing skills. Such skills would increase the ability of the Soviet Union to export manufactured goods, and thus earn hard currency, and would improve its competitiveness on the world market. The delegations declared that Soviet-American cooperation would be expanded in the areas of food processing, energy, construction equipment, medical products, and the service sector.

Western Europe

In the mid-1980s, West European exports to the Soviet Union were marginal, less than 0.5 percent of the combined gross national product of countries of the Organization for Economic Cooperation and Development. OECD countries provided the Soviet Union with high-technology and industrial equipment, chemicals, metals, and agricultural products. In return, Western Europe received oil and natural gas from the Soviet Union.

Although oil and gas were the primary Soviet exports to Western Europe, they represented only a small percentage of Western Europe's substantial fuel imports: Soviet oil provided 3 percent and natural gas 2 percent of the energy consumed in Western Europe. The completion of the Urengoy-Uzhgorod export pipeline project increased the importance of Soviet natural gas to Western Europe in the second half of the 1980s. In 1984 France, Austria, the Federal Republic of Germany (West Germany), and Italy began receiving natural gas from western Siberia through the pipeline, for which the Soviet Union was paid in hard currency, pumping equipment, and large-diameter pipe. By 1990 the Soviet Union expected to supply 3 percent of all natural gas imported by Western Europe, including 30 percent of West Germany's gas imports.

Unlike the United States, the countries of Western Europe have not viewed trade as a tool to influence Soviet domestic and foreign policies. Western Europe rejected the trade restrictions imposed by the United States after the Soviet invasion of Afghanistan in 1979 and the declaration of martial law in Poland in 1980. From 1980 to 1982, the United States embargoed the supply of equipment for the Urengoy-Uzhgorod natural gas pipeline, but Western Europe ignored United States pleas to do the same.

Despite the poor relations between the superpowers in the early and mid-1980s, Western Europe tried to improve international relations with the Soviet Union. One major step in this direction was the normalization of relations between Comecon and the European Economic Community (EEC). After fifteen years of negotiations, the EEC approved an accord that established formal relations with Comecon effective June 25, 1988. Although it did not establish bilateral trade relations, the agreement ""set the stage"" for the exchange of information. This accord marked Comecon's official recognition of the EEC.

Japan

In 1985 trade with the Soviet Union accounted for 1.6 percent of Japanese exports and 1 percent of Japanese imports; Japan was the Soviet Union's fourth most important Western trading partner. Japan's principal exports to the Soviet Union included steel (approximately 40 percent of Japan's exports to the Soviet Union), chemicals, and textiles. The Soviet Union exported timber, nonferrous metals, rare-earth metals, and fuel to Japan. In 1986, despite a reduction in trade between the two countries, the Soviet Union had a trade deficit with

Japan. In 1987 trade dropped another 20 percent. Numerous controversies have thwarted Soviet-Japanese trade. The Toshiba affair, in which Japan was accused of shipping equipment to the Soviet Union that was prohibited by CoCom, caused Japanese-Soviet trade to decrease in 1987. In addition, the Japanese constantly prodded the Soviet Union to return the islands off the Japanese island of Hokkaido that had come under Soviet control after World War II. For its part, the Soviet Union complained of the trade imbalance and static structure of Japanese-Soviet trade.

In the late 1980s, the Soviet Union tried to increase its exports to Japan and diversify the nature of the countries' relationship. Soviet proposals have included establishing joint enterprises to exploit natural resources in Siberia and the Soviet Far East, specifically, coal in the southern Yakutiya area of Siberia and petroleum on Sakhalin; cooperating in the monetary and credit fields; jointly surveying and studying marine resources and peaceful uses of space; and establishing joint activities in other countries. The Soviet Union also proposed branching out into joint ventures in the chemical and wood chip industries, electronics, machine tools, and fish processing. The first Japanese-Soviet joint enterprise, a wood-processing plant in the Soviet Far East, began operation in March 1988. The Soviet Union provided the raw materials, and Japan supplied the technology, equipment, and managerial expertise.

Finland

In contrast to the variable trade relationships the Soviet Union has had with other West European countries, its relationship with Finland has been somewhat stable because of five-year agreements that regulated trade between the countries. The first was established in 1947, and 1986 marked the beginning of the eighth. Accounting procedures and methods of payment were agreed upon every five years as well by the Bank of Finland and Vneshtorgbank. A steady growth in trade between the two countries occurred throughout the 1970s and 1980s.

In the late 1980s, Finland was the Soviet Union's second most important trading partner among the Western nations, after West Germany. Trade with Finland, however, was based on bilateral clearing agreements rather than on exchange of hard currency used with other Western trading partners. In 1986 the Soviet Union shipped 4 percent of its exports to and received 3 percent of its imports from Finland. Finland provided the Soviet Union with ships, particularly those suited to Arctic conditions; heavy machinery; and consumer goods such as clothing, textiles, processed foodstuffs, and consumer durables. The Soviet Union exported oil, natural gas, and fuel and technology for the nuclear power industry.

The system of bilateral clearing agreements on which Soviet-Finnish trade was based required that any increase in Finnish imports from the Soviet Union be accompanied by a corresponding increase in exports to the Soviet Union in order to maintain the bilateral trade balance. At the beginning of the 1980s, Finland increased its imports of Soviet oil, which allowed it to increase its exports to the Soviet Union. This procedure accounted for the steady growth in Soviet-Finnish trade into the late 1980s. By 1988 about 90 percent of Soviet exports to Finland consisted of oil. Because the Finns imported more oil than they could consume domestically, they reexported it to other Scandinavian and West European countries. The Finns complained in late 1987 and early 1988 of a decline in Soviet ship orders and delinquent payments. The share of Finland's exports to the Soviet Union, which had previously been as high as 25 percent, dropped to 15 percent in 1988.

TRADE WITH THIRD WORLD COUNTRIES

The Third World embraces those countries the Soviet Union terms "developing countries." This category includes those countries of socialist orientation that have some sort of privileged economic affiliation with the Soviet Union, such as Afghanistan, Angola, Iraq, and Nicaragua, but excludes the developing countries ruled by Marxist-Leninist parties, such as Cambodia, Laos, and Vietnam. Soviet trade with the Third World has been marked by two characteristics. First, although the Soviet Union has generally played only a minor role in Third World trade, Soviet imports or exports have formed a large portion of the total trade of some countries. Second, the Soviet Union has concentrated its trade with the Third World in the hands of relatively few partners. For example, in 1987 India, Iran, Iraq, Syria, Argentina, Egypt, Turkey, Afghanistan, Nigeria, and Malaysia together accounted for 75 percent of Soviet imports from and 80 percent of Soviet exports to the Third World.

Although Soviet trade with the Third World increased in volume from 1965 through 1985, it remained between 13 and 15 percent of total Soviet trade for exports and 10 and 12 percent for imports. The Third World's trade with the Soviet Union, however, decreased in the 1970s and into the 1980s. These data include Cuba, since the only figures available concerning Third World trade with the Soviet Union include Cuba. As a percentage of overall Third World trade, the Soviet Union's share fell from 3.9 percent in 1970 to 2.5 percent in 1981. Deducting Soviet trade with Cuba, which has been considerable, would show an even smaller role played by the Soviet Union in Third World trade. In the late 1980s, the Soviet Union sought arrangements that would allow it to maintain a level of trade that minimized the loss of hard currency.

Balance of Trade

During the 1980s, the Soviet Union exported more to Third World countries than it imported from them. Official Soviet statistics showed a trade deficit for this period, but arms and military equipment sales, which were not reported and are thus termed "unidentifiable" exports, accounted for approximately 50 percent of total exports to the Third World throughout the 1980s. Thus, the Soviet Union's hard-currency balance of trade, including arms sales, with the Third World was positive from 1980 through 1986. In fact, the Soviet Union's positive hard-currency trade balance with the Third World exceeded its hard-currency deficit with the Western industrialized countries in 1985 and 1986. For this reason, the Soviet Union showed an overall positive hardcurrency trade balance for these years.

Until the mid-1970s, bilateral clearing agreements were the primary means by which the Soviet Union settled accounts with its Third World partners. By the early 1980s, hard-currency payments had become the preferred means of settlement.

Clearing agreements were used in less than half of all trade transactions. On occasion, the Soviet Union bartered arms for oil.

Composition of Trade

Not including arms sales, machinery accounted for 20 percent of total sales to the Third World in 1985. Soviet exports of machinery took up an even higher relative share of total sales to Algeria, Iran, Nigeria, Pakistan, the People's Democratic Republic of Yemen (South Yemen), and Turkey. From 1980 through 1984, fuel, mostly oil, made up approximately 33 percent of overall Soviet exports to the Third World, including 50 percent of its exports to Asia and 60 to 70 percent of its exports to Latin America. Since 1985 greater competition on the world market resulting from falling world oil prices and rising Soviet extraction costs has prompted the Soviet Union to try to replace its export of oil with manufactured goods.

The Soviet Union has been the largest arms exporter to the Third World for a number of years. Major arms customers were concentrated in the belt of countries that stretches from North Africa to India, close to the Soviet Union's southern border. Some 72 percent of Soviet weapons exports went to Algeria, India, Iraq, Libya, and Syria. Other important customers included Afghanistan, Angola, Ethiopia, South Yemen, and the Yemen Arab Republic (North Yemen). The Soviet Union lost arms customers in the 1980s, however, when Brazil and Egypt began to expand their arms sales to the Third World. India, which had experienced improvements in its hardcurrency balance in the 1980s, also started to buy arms from other suppliers. In an effort to retain its share of Indian arms customers, the Soviet Union continued to offer India its most sophisticated weapons at even more attractive rates.

The Soviet Union has long been an importer of Third World agricultural products. These imports increased dramatically after 1980 because of poor Soviet harvests from 1979 into the early 1980s and the United States grain embargo against the Soviet Union in 1980 and 1981. From 1980 to 1985, food and agricultural goods, half of them grain, made up 50 percent of Soviet imports from the Third World. In the first nine months of 1986, the decrease in grain purchases accounted for most of the 22 percent drop in imports from the Third World.

Africa and Latin America supplied most of the food imports other than grain. Throughout the 1980s, food imports steadily rose, but imports from individual countries fluctuated. Because of these fluctuations, the Soviet Union was often considered an unstable trade partner compared with Western customers.

Because the Soviet Union was a major producer and exporter of most of the world's minerals, its import requirements for many other commodities (nonferrous metals, in particular) were sporadic. Nonetheless, the Soviet Union was a stable importer of some minerals, particularly bauxite and phosphate rock. The Soviet Union imported up to 50 percent of its bauxite from Guinea, Guyana, India, Indonesia, and Jamaica. Phosphate rock was abundant in the Soviet Union, but because extraction costs were high most of this mineral was imported from Morocco and Syria.

A decline in Soviet imports of manufactured goods in the 1970s led Third World countries to pressure the Soviet Union to increase the import of these goods in the 1980s. In 1982 the Soviet demand for Third World manufactures began to rise. By 1984 manufactured goods, including manufactured consumer goods, made up 25 percent of Soviet imports from the Third World.

Beginning in 1973, in an effort to earn hard currency, the Soviet Union began to import oil from Third World countries for reexport to Western industrialized countries. This activity slowed from 1980 to 1982, recovered in 1983 through 1985, and continued to increase in 1986. Late that year, the Soviet Union signed an agreement with the Organization of Petroleum Exporting Countries (OPEC) that restricted the amount of oil it could buy for reexport. By 1988 this agreement had not cut total Soviet oil receipts, however, because oil was paid to the Soviet Union as compensation in arms sales.

Africa, Asia, and Latin America

During the 1980s, the geographical pattern of Soviet-Third World trade changed markedly. A decrease in trade with North

Africa and the Middle East balanced a substantial increase in trade with sub-Saharan Africa, South Asia, and Latin America.

In 1987 about 50 percent of the Soviet Union's total identified exports to the Third World went to Asia, and India was the Soviet Union's biggest trade partner. In exchange for Soviet oil and oil products, India supplied food, raw agricultural material, clothing, textiles, and machinery. India was also the Soviet Union's sole significant Third World supplier of equipment and advanced technology, e.g., computers and copiers, much of which was produced by Indian subsidiaries of Western multinational corporations. Malaysia, another important partner of the Soviet Union in Asia, was an important supplier of rubber, palm oil, and tin.

From 1980 to 1983, Soviet exports to Africa increased slightly to 30 percent of its Third World exports and decreased thereafter. Imports from Africa fluctuated from 1980 to 1985 but remained at about 25 percent. Nigeria was the Soviet Union's only important trade partner in sub-Saharan Africa, receiving Soviet machinery and exporting cocoa.

Exports to Latin America grew during the 1980s and reached 8 percent in 1985. Latin America's share of Soviet Third World imports was high (40 percent in 1982) because of large imports of Argentine grain. As the Soviet Union's main grain supplier, Argentina was the Soviet Union's most significant import partner in the Third World in 1980, 1981, and 1983. In 1986 the Soviet Union renewed its grain agreement with Argentina for another five years. However, because of a US$11 billion trade deficit with Argentina that the Soviet Union had amassed from 1980 through 1985 and the successful Soviet harvest of 1986, the Soviet Union cut its grain imports from Argentina drastically. In 1986 they were at a six-year low.

Countries of Socialist Orientation

The countries of socialist orientation can be categorized into two groups: those that had observer status in Comecon and those that were not observers but had privileged affiliations with Comecon member countries. The Soviet Union's trade with the Third World has always been heavily skewed toward countries of socialist orientation. Soviet aid provided most of the foreign capital for these countries and influenced their domestic economic development significantly. The Soviet Union often profited more politically than economically from this trade: most Soviet surpluses were not repaid but became clearing credit, longterm cooperation credit, or short-term commercial credit.

In 1986 the countries that had observer status in Comecon were Afghanistan, Angola, Ethiopia, Mozambique, Nicaragua, and South Yemen. These countries were all characterized by political instability, low GNP, and low export potential. The share of exports to this group rose from 14 percent of total Soviet identified exports to the Third World in 1980 to 28 percent in the first nine months of 1986. Afghanistan, a recipient of Soviet machinery and military equipment, was the Soviet Union's most significant partner in this group. By contrast, trade with Mozambique and South Yemen was negligible.

Countries that had privileged affiliations with Comecon countries were Algeria, Benin, Burma, Congo, Guinea (until 1984), Iraq, Madagascar, Nicaragua (1979-85), Nigeria, Syria, and Tanzania and, at times, Guinea-Bissau, Mali, Seychelles, and Zimbabwe. Throughout the 1980s, Soviet exports to these countries oscillated, for example, from 27 percent in 1981 to 15 percent in 1983. This fluctuation, as well as fluctuations in imports, was primarily a result of changes in trade with Iraq, a major Soviet arms-for-oil trading partner in the Third World.

Trade with the Organization of Petroleum Exporting Countries

The Organization of Petroleum Exporting Countries (OPEC), particularly Iraq and Algeria, absorbed the largest share of the Soviet Union's "unidentified" exports. Although Soviet statistics usually showed a very low or negative trade balance with these countries, the balance was probably high because of arms sales. In the 1980s, some OPEC countries, particularly Iran and Iraq, together with Syria, which was not a member of OPEC, exchanged oil for Soviet arms and military equipment. Oil from these countries was resold to the West for hard currency. In the late 1980s, the Soviet Union attempted to increase its exports of nonmilitary goods to these countries. In May 1986, the Soviet Union and Iraq agreed to increase Soviet nonmilitary equipment sales, and in August 1986 an attempt was made to revive Iraqi gas sales.

GORBACHEV'S ECONOMIC REFORMS

When Gorbachev delivered his report on the CPSU's economic policy on June 12, 1985, he noted that growth in exports, particularly machinery and equipment, was slow because the poor quality of Soviet goods prohibited them from being competitive on the world market. In the next three years, Gorbachev introduced many changes that would enable the foreign trade complex to better support his economic policy of acceleration. By May 1988, the structure of the Soviet foreign trade complex had been changed, and operations had been dramatically overhauled.

The price reform called for by the Twenty-Seventh Party Congress was an important step in improving Soviet international economic involvement. Soviet officials admitted that pricing was "economically unsubstantiated" and "unrealistic." They understood that although a fully convertible ruble would not be possible for some time, prices that more accurately reflected production costs, supply and demand, and world market prices were essential for developing a convertible currency. The non-convertible ruble and the Soviet pricing system discouraged Western businessmen who could not accurately project production costs nor easily convert their ruble profits.

The new joint venture law, passed on January 13, 1987, opened up the Soviet economy to foreign participation, particularly in manufacturing. It was believed that the experience gained in such ventures would facilitate integration into the world economy. Specifically, through upgraded production processes, the Soviet Union could export more competitive manufactured goods and decrease its dependency on energy and raw materials to earn hard currency.

In August 1987, the Soviet Union formally requested observer status in the General Agreement on Tariffs and Trade (GATT). The Soviet Union also expressed its desire to join other international economic organizations and establish contacts with other regional groups. A major step in this direction occurred in 1988 when the Soviet Union signed a normalization agreement with the EEC. The Soviet government, however, professed no interest in joining the World Bank or the International Monetary Fund (IMF). Although Soviet officials claimed that the international monetary system "was not managed properly," it is more likely that IMF and World Bank regulations were the obstacles: both institutions required that members' currencies be freely convertible and that members provide accurate information concerning gold sales and economic performance.

Gorbachev transformed the role of foreign trade in the Soviet economy. Whereas imports previously were regarded exclusively as a vehicle to compensate for difficulties in the short term, Soviet economists under Gorbachev declared that imports should be regarded as alternatives to domestic investment and that exports should serve to gauge the technical level of domestic production. Foreign economic ties were to support growth in production beyond the capacities of the domestic economy. The Soviet Union could thus take a place in the world market that was commensurate with its scientific and technical progress and political weight.

7

Management

The term "management" characterizes the process of and/ or the personnel leading and directing all or part of an organization (often a business) through the deployment and manipulation of resources (human, financial, material, intellectual or intangible).

According to the Oxford English Dictionary, the word "manage" comes from the Italian maneggiare (to handle-especially a horse), which in turn derives from the Latin manus (hand).

Management has to do with power by position, whereas leadership involves power by influence.

MEANING AND SCOPE

Mary Parker Follett (1868-1933), who wrote on the topic in the early twentieth-century, defined management as "the art of getting things done through people". One can also think of management functionally, as the action of measuring a quantity on a regular basis and of adjusting some initial plan; or as the actions taken to reach one's intended goal. This applies even in situations where planning does not take place. From this perspective, Frenchman Henri Fayol considers management consists of five functions:

MAIN FUNCTIONS

Planning

Planning is the (psychological) process of creating and refining a plan, or integrating it with other plans. The term is also used to describe the formal procedures used in such an endeavour, such as the creation of documents, diagrams, or meetings to discuss the important issues to be addressed, the objectives to be met, and the strategy to be followed. Beyond this, planning has a different meaning depending on the political or economic context in which it is used.

IN PUBLIC POLICY

Planning refers to the practice and profession associated with land use planning, urban planning or spatial planning. In many countries, the operation of town and country planning system is often referred to as 'planning' and the professionals which operate the system are known as 'planners'. It is a process which is decided in advance what is to be done in the coming future.

Objectives for Non-profit-making Organizations

In the case of non-profit organizations the objectives may be less than clear. Keith Blois suggested five main reasons for the differences from `commercial' organizations:

1. Ambiguous Goals [more actors and groups of actors are involved]
2. Lack of Agreement in Means-End Relationships [even where there is consensus on the goal there may be disagreement on how to get there]
3. Environmental Turbulence [non-profit organizations seem to be exposed more to turbulence than commercial ones]
4. Unmeasurable Outputs [unfortunately, by definition, non-profit organizations do not have the classically convenient simplicity of `bottom-line profit']
5. The Effects of Management Intervention are Unknown [the lack of precision caused by factors 1-4 is problem enough, but the `culture' seems to add further barriers to managing these organizations]

Even so, Kotler and Andreasen suggested some possible objectives for such organizations:

1. Surplus Maximization [equivalent to profit maximization]
2. Revenue Maximization [as for profit-making organizations]
3. Usage Maximization [maximizing the numbers of users and their usage]
4. Usage Targeting [matching the capacity available]
5. Full Cost Recovery [breaking even]
6. Partial Cost Recovery [minimizing the subsidy]
7. Budget Maximization [maximizing what is offered]
8. Producer Satisfaction Maximization [satisfying the wants of staff]

In Organizations

Planning is also a management function, concerned with defining goals for future organizational performance and deciding on the tasks and resources to be used in order to attain those goals. To meet the goals, managers will invest significant resources for training and incentives to motivate employees.

THE MARKETING PLANNING PROCESS

In most organizations `strategic planning' is an annual process, typically covering just the year ahead. Occasionally, a few organizations may look at a practical plan which stretches three or more years ahead. To be most effective, the plan has to be formalized, usually in written form, as a formal `marketing plan'. The essence of the process is that it moves from the general to the specific; from the overall objectives of the organization down to the individual action plan for a part of one marketing programme. It is also an iterative process, so that the draft output of each stage is checked to see what impact it has on the earlier stages-and is amended accordingly.

The Corporate Plan

The starting point for the marketing plan, and the context within which it is set, is the corporate plan. In most marketing-oriented organizations the contents of the corporate plan will closely match those of the marketing plan itself; but it will also include the plans for the disposition of the other internal resources of the organization. Thus, the corporate plan is likely to contain three main components: The first category is intimately involved with the customers. In marketing terms, although there are many other factors to take into account, the most important definition of where the company 'is' revolves around where it is in the market (and hence where it is with its consumers). The same is largely true of the second stage as well; since, no matter how much its managers may wish otherwise, where the company can realistically expect to go is totally in the hands of its customers. It is only at the third stage that the 4 Ps come into play as vehicles for moving the company to reach its objectives.

Corporate Objectives

The overall objectives of commercial organizations are conventionally supposed to be financial. However, other aims are also possible. Many companies choose long-term growth (which may be quite different to revenue maximization in the short term). Almost all have an implicit, and very powerful, aim of survival. One of the best known `alternatives', that of `satisficing' (rather than profit maximization), came from Herbert Simon: "In one way or another, they [alternative theories] incorporate the notions of bounded rationality: the need to search for decision alternatives, the replacement of optimization [profit-based objectives] by targets and satisficing [minimal] goals, and mechanisms of learning and adaptation."

Pfeffer and Salancik said that: "We prefer to view organizations as coalitions... altering their purposes and domains to accommodate new interests, sloughing off parts of themselves to avoid some interests, and when necessary, becoming involved in activities far afield from their stated central purposes. Organizations are social instruments of tremendous power and energy, and the critical issue becomes who will control this energy and for what purpose."

If we accept the traditional assumption, as to the financial basis of the objectives behind the corporate plan, these objectives are ideally meant to be quantified in numerical and, in particular, financial terms. In the most general terms, though, the `objectives' behind a strategy address two questions: "Where' do we want to be?' and `'When' do we expect to be there?'

Forecasting

This can be a very complcx topic but can, in general, be roughly divided into two parts.

Short-term Forecasting

This is the type of forecasting you will recognise. It is normally based upon a projection of historical trends, usually focused on sales volumes. There are many sophisticated techniques, increasingly using large amounts of computing power, but in essence all of these try to separate out the four main components:

1. Long term trends probably represent the most important information you are trying to extract from the mass of data before you.
2. Medium term cycles are supposed to result from regular economic ups and downs (from boom to bust) which used to be encapsulated in a 5 year 'business cycle' which, unfortunately, became unpredictable in the 1980s. The much quoted 'Kondratieff Cycles' are much longer, if they exist at all, being of the order of 25-50 years; and hence do not normally enter into shorter term forecasts.
3. Seasonal is the pattern within a single year, a pattern which most suppliers who are affected by it know well.
4. Random fluctuations, which do not fit regular patterns, afflict all products and services, and make computer analysis a very difficult proposition.

The end result of all these patterns superimposed may appear very confusing indeed. Despite all the sophistication on offer, therefore, by far the best advice is to keep it as simple as possible. The human eye is much better at resolving the complications shown above than the most powerful computer. Thus, the best approach to forecasting (and certainly the best check on any more sophisticated technique) is 'eyeballing' the sales charts! With some practise you should be able to sort out the main features of what is happening-and that is better than most computer models achieve. The evidence is that the sophistication adds little or nothing to the accuracy (though it does to the image of the forecasters, and the prices they charge). Worst of all, such unnecessary complexity hinders your understanding of what is going on under the covers of the computer (and hides the fact that most forecasts are really based on human judgement). In any case, even if historical trends are accurately analysed, there is no guarantee that the future will be the same as the past. It is much better that you surface all the assumptions, and make your own judgements in full knowledge of what is involved.

Two very simple techniques to use (if nothing else but as a check on the forecasts others are trying to sell to you);

- Eyeballing-the technique I mentioned above is the first, and best, method. It merely requires you to plot historical results graphically; and then look for the patterns. Trust your own judgement-until you are proved wrong.
- Exponential Smoothing-this is the mathematical technique which reportedly gives the best results; probably because it is so simple, and consequently easily understood. Indeed, it is a very impressive title for a simple, but useful, mathematical technique; which can quite easily be handled manually. It just allows greater weight to be given to recent periods. Instead of, for example, the average trend over the whole of the last year being calculated, the sales data for each of the months is given a weighting, depending on how recent that month was. It simply takes the previous forecast, and adds on the latest 'actual' sales figure; except that it does this in a fixed proportion, which is chosen to reflect the weighting to be given to the latest period. The general form is; $Ft+1 = Ft + aEt$ where $Ft+1$ is the new forecast you are calculating, Ft is the previous one and Et is the deviation (or 'error') of the actual performance recorded against that previous period forecast; and 'a' is the weighting to be given to the most recent events. Exponential smoothing will not, in this simple form, allow for seasonality; though more sophisticated (but less easily understood) versions can do this.

Long-term Forecasting

This tends to be qualitative (as compared with the quantitative, numeric, focus of short term forecasts). It is even more dependent on judgement; and most of the more complicated approaches to it (such as Delphi, or Jury methods) aim to reduce the risks implicit in the judgement by spreading the process over panels of experts. It does not, in the final analysis, absolve the manager from backing his or her own judgement (which is probably better informed, in terms of the specific situation, than that of the 'experts').

Of all the techniques the most useful involves developing complementary scenarios, which allow for the uncertainties involved; as well as expanding the viewpoint of all the managers involved in the process. Unfortunately, in the form most often described it can also be the most complex and sophisticated of these techniques-and in this form perhaps only the very large corporate planning team at Shell have used it really effectively. A much simplified approach, based on the version which Shell recommend for their line managers who are not part of their corporate planning group, is more practical for most organisations. In this simplified version of the form originally described by Shell the four steps to this process are:

1. Identify the important variables
2. Brainstorm to find the possible outcomes
3. Link these together in a series of alternative scenarios
4. Refine these scenarios
5. Identify the important variables-what (in the whole of the external environment, not just the marketing environment) are the most important factors which will determine the future of the organisation.
6. Brainstorm to find the possible outcomes-work through the different outcomes which different alternatives for these variables may lead to.
7. Link these together in a series of alternative scenarios-start to build six or seven scenarios ('stories' about the future of the organisation, or more importantly its market) which are able to contain these different alternatives.

8. Refine these scenarios-then work on the scenarios until they are condensed to two or three meaningful alternative (but complementary) descriptions of the future.

CORPORATE MISSION

Behind the corporate objectives, which in themselves offer the main context for the marketing plan, will lie the "corporate mission"; which in turn provides the context for these corporate objectives. This `corporate mission' can be thought of as a definition of what the organization is; of what it does: `Our business is...'.

This definition should not be too narrow, or it will constrict the development of the organization; a too rigorous concentration on the view that `We are in the business of making meat-scales', as IBM was during the early 1900s, might have limited its subsequent development into other areas. On the other hand, it should not be too wide or it will become meaningless; `We want to make a profit' is not too helpful in developing specific plans.

Abell suggested that the definition should cover three dimensions: 'customer groups' to be served, 'customer needs' to be served, and 'technologies' to be utilized.

Thus, the definition of IBM's `corporate mission' in the 1940s might well have been: `We are in the business of handling accounting information [customer need] for the larger US organizations [customer group] by means of punched cards [technology].' Fortunately, as the name itself (International Business Machines) indicates, IBM already had a wider perspective (and its corporate mission was virtually defined by its name).

Corporate Vision

Perhaps the most important factor in successful marketing is the `corporate vision'. Surprisingly, it is largely neglected by marketing textbooks; although not by the popular exponents of corporate strategy-indeed, it was perhaps the main theme of the book by Peters and Waterman, in the form of their

`Superordinate Goals'. Theodore Levitt said: "Nothing drives progress like the imagination. The idea precedes the deed."

If the organization in general, and its chief executive in particular, has a strong vision of where its future lies, then there is a good chance that the organization will achieve a strong position in its markets (and attain that future). This will be not least because its strategies will be consistent; and will be supported by its staff at all levels. In this context, all of IBM's marketing activities were underpinned by its philosophy of `customer service'; a vision originally promoted by the charismatic Watson dynasty.

Henry Mintzberg explained: "... in some cases, in addition to the mission there is the `sense of mission', that is, a feeling that the group has banded together to create something new and exciting. This is common in new organizations".

What a worthwhile vision consists of is, however, usually open to debate; hence the reason why such visions tend to be associated with strong, charismatic leaders. But the vision must be relevant. The message for the marketer is that, to be most effective, the marketing strategies must be converted into a powerful long-term vision; if such a vision does not already exist.

Marketing Audit

The first formal step in the marketing planning process is that of conducting the marketing audit. Ideally, at the time of producing the marketing plan, this should only involve bringing together the source material which has already been collected throughout the year-as part of the normal work of the marketing department.

The emphasis at this stage is on obtaining a complete and accurate picture. In a single organization, however, it is likely that only a few aspects will be sufficiently important to have any significant impact on the marketing plan; but all may need to be reviewed to determine just which 'are' the few.

In this context some factors related to the customer, which should be included in the material collected for the audit, may be:

- Who are the customers?
- What are their key characteristics?
- What differentiates them from other members of the population?
- What are their needs and wants?
- What do they expect the `product' to do?
- What are their special requirements and perceptions?
- What do they think of the organization and its products or services?
- What are their attitudes?
- are their buying intentions?

A `traditional'-albeit product-based-format for a `brand reference book' (or, indeed, a `marketing facts book') was suggested by Godley more than three decades ago:

1. *Financial Data:* Facts for this section will come from management accounting, costing and finance sections.
2. *Product Data:* From production, research and development.
3. *Sales and Distribution Data:* Sales, packaging, distribution sections.
4. Advertising, sales promotion, merchandising data-Information from these departments.
5. *Market Data and Miscellany:* From market research, who would in most cases act as a source for this information.

His sources of data, however, assume the resources of a very large organization. In most organizations they would be obtained from a much smaller set of people (and not a few of them would be generated by the marketing manager alone). It is apparent that a marketing audit can be a complex process, but the aim is simple: 'it is only to identify those existing (external and internal) factors which will have a significant impact on the future plans of the company'. It is clear that the basic material to be input to the marketing audit should be comprehensive. Accordingly, the best approach is to accumulate this material continuously, as and when it becomes available; since this avoids the otherwise heavy workload involved in collecting it as part of the regular, typically annual, planning process itself-when time is usually at a premium. Even so, the first task of this `annual' process should be to check that the material held in the current `facts book' or `facts files' actually 'is' comprehensive and accurate, and can form a sound basis for the marketing audit itself.

The structure of the facts book will be designed to match the specific needs of the organization, but one simple format-suggested by Malcolm McDonald-may be applicable in many cases. This splits the material into three groups:

1. 'Review of the marketing environment'. A study of the organization's markets, customers, competitors and the overall economic, political, cultural and technical environment; covering developing trends, as well as the current situation.
2. 'Review of the detailed marketing activity'. A study of the company's marketing mix; in terms of the 4 Ps-product, price, promotion and place.
3. 'Review of the marketing system'. A study of the marketing organization, marketing research systems and the current marketing objectives and strategies.

The last of these is too frequently ignored. The marketing system itself needs to be regularly questioned, because the validity of the whole marketing plan is reliant upon the accuracy of the input from this system, and `garbage in, garbage out' applies with a vengeance.

An Summative Analysis

The analysis of this material will, no doubt, require significant effort. In the first instance it is a matter of selection, of sorting the wheat from the chaff. What is important, and will need to be taken into account in the marketing plan that will eventually emerge from the overall process, will be different for each product or service in each situation. One of the most important skills to be learned in marketing is that of being able to concentrate on just what is important.

It is important to say not just what happened but why. The process of marketing planning encompasses all of the marketing skills. However, a number of these may be particularly relevant at this stage:

- *'Positioning':* The starting point of the marketing plan must be the consumer. It is a matter of definition that his or her needs should drive the whole marketing process. The techniques of positioning and segmentation therefore usually offer the best starting point for what has to be achieved by the whole planning process.
- *'Portfolio Planning':* In addition, the coordinated planning of the individual products and services can contribute towards the balanced portfolio.
- *'80:20 Rule':* To achieve the maximum impact, the marketing plan must be clear, concise and simple. It needs to concentrate on the 20 per cent of products or services, and on the 20 per cent of customers, which will account for 80 per cent of the volume and 80 per cent of the `profit'.
- *'4 Ps':* The 4 Ps can sometimes divert attention from the customer, but the framework they offer can be very useful in building the action plans.

MARKETING OBJECTIVES

It is only at this stage (of deciding the marketing objectives) that the active part of the marketing planning process begins'.

This next stage in marketing planning is indeed the key to the whole marketing process. The marketing objectives state just where the company intends to be; at some specific time in the future. James Quinn succinctly defined objectives in general as: "Goals (or objectives) state 'what' is to be achieved and 'when' results are to be accomplished, but they do not state 'how' the results are to be achieved".

They typically relate to what products (or services) will be where in what markets (and must be realistically based on customer behaviour in those markets). They are essentially about the match between those 'products' and 'markets'. Objectives for pricing, distribution, advertising and so on are at a lower level, and should not be confused with marketing objectives. They are part of the marketing strategy needed to achieve marketing objectives.

To be most effective, objectives should be capable of measurement and therefore 'quantifiable'. This measurement may be in terms of sales volume, money value, market share, percentage penetration of distribution outlets and so on. An example of such a measurable marketing objective might be `to enter the market with product Y and capture 10 per cent of the market by value within one year'. As it is quantified it can, within limits, be unequivocally monitored; and corrective action taken as necessary.

The marketing objectives must usually be based, above all, on the organization's financial objectives; converting these financial measurements into the related marketing measurements.

It is conventionally assumed that marketing objectives will be designed to maximize volume or profit (or to optimize the utilization of resources in the non-profit sector), by creating demand or rejuvenating existing demand, say; although the various sub-objectives may indicate many different routes to achieving such optimization. However, as Kotler suggested (in the earlier edition of his book), there may be a number of other objectives:

Synchromarketing: The aim may be to `redistribute' existing sales (which are already at optimum levels) so that they occur at times, or in places, which the supplier prefers. Thus, for example, organizations which have highly seasonal sales (which make inefficient use of resources) may want to increase non-seasonal sales. Walls achieved this by balancing its summer sales of ice-cream with pies and sausages, demand for which peaks in winter. The suppliers of central-heating oil offer special deals for those customers willing to restock their tanks in summer.

Demarketing: Demand may sometimes exceed supply. In these circumstances the emphasis will be on rationing scarce supplies. Occasionally the supplier, rather than bring on-stream expensive new plant, may seek to persuade customers to buy less (or be less dissatisfied with the scarcity). Some suppliers of electrical energy (electricity generators in Europe and the USA) have heavily advertised energy conservation measures to achieve this end (otherwise, the cost of meeting the peak winter loads would be very high-and unprofitable).

Counter-marketing: In what is usually a public-sector activity (but is occasionally undertaken by the private sector, where some uses of a product are damaging the corporate image), there may be an objective of stopping consumption completely. The anti-tobacco and anti-drug campaigns are the most obvious examples; but McDonald's campaigns to stop its customers dropping litter, or the brewers' campaigns to stop drinking and driving, fall into this category.

Emergent Strategy

In this case, the intended strategy, decided upon traditionally or incrementally, is overtaken by events in two main ways. One, which will probably be recognised by the organisation, is that of unrealised strategy; where it proves impossible to implement the chosen strategy in practice.

Less obvious is the emergent strategy which is decided by events in the external environment; and, thus, forced upon the organisation. This may not necessarily be recognised, in its totality, by the organisation-since many of its implications may be hidden. As markets become more complex, however, such emergent strategies are becoming more common.

Many organizations see both these processes in terms of failure-they have been forced, usually by unpredictable events, to abandon their own strategy. There is, accordingly, a tendency for these unwelcome facts to be ignored until they are so obvious that they cannot be avoided. This is a major error. Such deviations must be recognised (probably through one or other form of environmental analysis coupled with networking) as soon as possible-so that the organisation can react in good time.

A much more powerful approach is, though, to be proactive; so seize upon these deviations as the basis for future developments. What needs to be recognised is that emergent strategies are the most powerful of all. They must, by definition, be dierctly derived from the needs of the market-where even successful deliberate strategies may not ideally match market needs but may achieve their targets by sheer force (especially where conviction marketing lies behind them). Emergent strategies are, thus, likely to be vigorous ones. There are two main approaches to capitalising on such emergent strategies. The first of these, favoured in the West, is the umbrella strategy. This is a form of very positive delegation, in that the overall strategies, the umbrella, are very general in nature-and allow the lower level managers, who are closest to the external environment, the freedom to react to these changes.

A much more direct, and hence even more powerful, approach is that favoured by the Japanese corporations. They integrate emergent strategies with their own. Indeed it is arguable that, in terms of marketing, to a large extent they use emergent strategies instead of their own deliberate strategies. This is evidenced as much by an attitude of mind as by any other feature. They deliberately go out to look for symptoms of such emergent trends which can be detected in the performance of their own products. More than that, though, they often deliberately launch a range of products rather than a single one to see which is most successful. It is almost as if they deliberately seek out the emergent strategies by offering the best environment for them to develop-the very reverse of the Western approach which seeks to avoid them! The Japanese then go on to build on these emergent strategies with a number of very effective tools-most of which are designed to overcome the major problem which accompanies emergent strategies, that they emerge on the scene much later than deliberate ones (and are likely to be visible to all the competitors at the same time) so that time is the essence. Thus, time management techniques (including parallel development along with flexible manufacturing and JIT) which have been developed by the Japanese offer them a significant competitive advantage in handling such emergent strategies.

Marketing Strategies

There are numerous definitions of what strategy is, but again James Quinn again gave a succinct general definition: "A strategy is a 'pattern' or 'plan' that 'integrates' an organization's 'major' goals, policies and action sequences into a 'cohesive' whole"

He went on to explain his view of the role of `policies', with which strategy is most often confused: "Policies are rules or guidelines that express the 'limits' within which action should occur.

Simplifying somewhat, marketing strategies can be seen as the means, or `game plan', by which marketing objectives will be achieved and, in the framework that we have chosen to use, are generally concerned with the 4 Ps. Examples are:

Product

- developing new products, repositioning or relaunching existing ones and scrapping old ones
- adding new features and benefits
- balancing product portfolios
- changing the design or packaging

Price

- setting the price to skim or to penetrate
- pricing for different market segments
- deciding how to meet competitive pricing

Promotion

- specifying the advertising platform and media
- deciding the public relations brief
- organizing the salesforce to cover new products and services or markets

Place

- choosing the channels
- deciding levels of customer service

In principle, these strategies describe how the objectives will be achieved. The 4 Ps are a useful framework for deciding how the company's resources will be manipulated (strategically) to achieve the objectives. It should be noted, however, that they are not the only framework, and may divert attention from the real issues. The focus of the strategies must be the objectives to be achieved-not the process of planning itself. Only if it fits the needs of these objectives should you choose, as we have done, to use the framework of the 4 Ps.

The strategy statement can take the form of a purely verbal description of the strategic options which have been chosen. Alternatively, and perhaps more positively, it might include a structured list of the major options chosen.

One aspect of strategy which is often overlooked is that of 'timing'. Exactly when it is the best time for each element of the strategy to be implemented is often critical. Taking the right action at the wrong time can sometimes be almost as bad as taking the wrong action at the right time. Timing is, therefore, an essential part of any plan; and should normally appear as a schedule of planned activities.

Having completed this crucial stage of the planning process, you will need to re-check the feasibility of your objectives and strategies in terms of the market share, sales, costs, profits and so on which these demand in practice. As in the rest of the marketing discipline, you will need to employ judgement, experience, market research or anything else which helps you to look at your conclusions from all possible angles.

Detailed Plans and Programmes

At this stage, you will need to develop your overall marketing strategies into detailed plans and programmes. Although these detailed plans may cover each of the 4 Ps, the focus will vary, depending upon your organization's specific strategies. A product-oriented company will focus its plans for the 4 Ps around each of its products. A market or geographically oriented company will concentrate on each market or geographical area. Each will base its plans upon the detailed needs of its customers, and on the strategies chosen to satisfy these needs.

Again, the most important element is, indeed, that of the detailed plans; which spell out exactly what programmes and individual activities will take place over the period of the plan (usually over the next year). Without these specified-and preferably quantified-activities the plan cannot be monitored, even in terms of success in meeting its objectives.

It is these programmes and activities which will then constitute the `marketing' of the organization over the period. As a result, these detailed marketing programmes are the most important, practical outcome of the whole planning process. These plans should therefore be:

- *Clear:* They should be an unambiguous statement of 'exactly' what is to be done.
- *Quantified:* The predicted outcome of each activity should be, as far as possible, quantified; so that its performance can be monitored.
- *Focused:* The temptation to proliferate activities beyond the numbers which can be realistically controlled should be avoided. The 80:20 Rule applies in this context too.
- *Realistic:* They should be achievable.
- *Agreed:* Those who are to implement them should be committed to them, and agree that they are achievable.

The resulting plans should become a working document which will guide the campaigns taking place throughout the organization over the period of the plan. If the marketing plan is to work, every exception to it (throughout the year) must be questioned; and the lessons learned, to be incorporated in the next year's plan.

ORGANIZING

Organizing is the act of rearranging following one or mores. It can also be seeing as the opposite of messing up. One organized opposite could be disordered, since ordered is almost synonymous. The difference between ordered and organized is that something is only ordered as long as it is both organized and standardized.

Organizing Metal Movable Type

Examples: Anything is commonly considered organized when it looks like everything has a correct order of placement.

But it's only ultimately organized if any element has no difference on time taken to find it. In that sense, organizing can also be defined as the act to place different objects in sequential arrangement for better searching.

Organizations are groups of people frequently trying to organize some specific subject, such as political issues. So, even while organizing can be viewed as a simple definition, it can get as complex as organizing the world's information.

History

Historically, humans have always tried to organize ourselves. Be it on religion, through books and spoken word, or in science, through journals and studies, or in many other ways. Writing ideas in a book, not to talk to someone, but to specific catalog is also an attempt to organize information.

Science books are notable by their organization attempt of a specific subject. Encyclopedias, instead, usually try to organize any subject into one place, for faster indexing and seeking of meanings.

Recently there was the advent of computers and in the last decade, a huge Internet usage world wide. Notably, the Internet growth is directly related to the advent of websites to search the internet, which also means organizing the internet, since nobody would know how to get anywhere without either guessing, hints or those websites.

Applications

Organizing, in companies point of view, is the management function that usually follows after planning. And it involves the assignment of tasks, the grouping of tasks into departments and the assignment of authority and allocation of resources across the organization.

LEADING

The word leadership can refer to:

1. the process of leading
2. the concept of leading

3. those entities that perform one or more acts of leading.

The various meanings can lead to some confusion.

TERMINOLOGY, USAGE AND CONCEPTUAL SCOPE

House defines "leadership" organizationally and narrowly as "the ability of an individual to influence, motivate, and enable others to contribute toward the effectiveness and success of the organizations of which they are members" (House, R. J. 2004: page 15). Compare the discussions on group leadership and ad hoc leadership below. One can also characterize leadership by the period of the authority, as in "During the 1940s Russia was under Stalinist leadership". In formal hierarchies the term can also serve to describe the position or relationships which allow and legitimize the exercising of what one might term "leadership behavior".

In some languages the term for a leader and the term for the principle of leadership have very different meanings. Furthermore, note the different connotations of a synonym of the word "leader" adopted from the German: the word Führer, and its accompanying ideas on the Führerprinzip.

In would-be controlling groups such as the military, political parties, ruling élites, and other belief-based enterprises like religions or businesses, the idea of leadership can become a Holy Grail and people can come to expect transformational change stemming from the leader; such entities may encourage their followers and believers to worship leadership, to respect it, and to strive (whether realistically or not) to become proficient in it. Ideally, one cannot buy or sell leadership in the military (or elsewhere); instead, leaders must ratify their position of command in the hearts and minds of their soldiers in order to obtain the best from them. Followers in such a situation may become uncritically obedient. Personal strategies that one can use to guard against the unrealistic expectations associated with belief in leaders include:

- maintaining a questioning and skeptical attitude
- bolstering confidence in one's own decision-making abilities

CATEGORIES AND TYPES OF LEADERSHIP

One can categorize the exercise of leadership as either actual or potential:

- actual-giving guidance or direction, as in the phrase "the emperor has provided satisfactory leadership".
- potential-the capacity or ability to lead, as in the phrase "she could have exercised effective leadership"; or in the concept "born to lead".

In both cases, as a result of the constancy of change some people detect within the late 20th and early 21st centuries, the act of learning appears fundamental to certain types of leading and leadership. When learning and leadership coalescee, one could characterize this as "learnership".

Leadership can have a formal aspect (as in most political or business leadership) or an informal one (as in most friendships). Speaking of "leadership" (the abstract term) rather than of "leading" (the action) usually implies that the entities doing the leading have some "leadership skills" or competencies. Several types of entities may provide or exhibit leadership, actual or potential, including:

- a person in a position or office of authority, such as a President or a chairperson
- a person in a position or office associated with expertise, skill, or experience, such as a team leader, a ship's captain, a chief engineer, a chief, or a parent
- a group or person in the vanguard of some trend or movement, as in fashion trend-setters
- a group of respected people, (called a "reference group" by sociologists) such as business commentators or union spokespersons.
- a product that influences other product offerings in a competitive marketplace

Leadership can come from an individual, a collective group of leaders, or even from the disincarnate-if not mystical-characteristics of a celebrity figurehead (compare hero). Yet other usages have a "leadership" which does little active leading, but to which followers show great (often traditional) respect (compare the courtesy title reverend). Followers often endow the leader with status or prestige. Aside from the prestige-role sometimes granted to inspirational leaders, a more mundane usage of the word "leadership" can designate current front-runners that exercise influence over competitors, for example, a corporation or a product can hold a position of "market leadership" without any implication of permanence or of merited respect.

Note that the ability to influence others does form an integral part of the "leadership" of some but not all front-runners. A front-runner in a sprint may "lead" the race, but does not have a position of "leadership" if he does not have the potential to influence others in some way. Thus one can make an important distinction between "being in the lead" and the process of leadership. Leadership implies a relationship of power-the power to guide others.

THE PSYCHOLOGY OF LEADERSHIP

Analyzing the inspirational leader (one who can instill passion and direction into a group of individuals) requires an understanding of how the psychology of a group can affect the members of the group.

Different approaches to group dynamics (for example: Arthur F Carmazzi's ideas on "directive communication"; and Sigal Barsade's theory of "the ripple effect", see leadership as a product of awareness and command of the reactions and influences of a group on the emotions of the individual.

According to Arthur F Carmazzi, leadership does not involve changing the mindset of the group, but the cultivation of an environment that brings out the best (inspires) the individuals in that group... Each individual has various environments that bring out different facets from their own identity, and emotionally charged perceptions drive each facet within each environment. To lead, Carmazzi says, one must build a platform through education and awareness where individuals fill each others needs. Leaders accomplish this by knowing why people may react favorably to a situation in environment A, but get frustrated or disillusioned in environment B.

When leaders change their actions in accordance with their awareness of what those actions really mean, they affect the emotional and perceptive affects on a group. By taking control of the "standard" reactions to the actions of the group, a leader can in effect change the psychology of the group and change the culture of an organization.

LEADERSHIP ASSOCIATED WITH POSITIONS OF AUTHORITY

In On Heroes, Hero-Worship, and the Heroic in History, Thomas Carlyle demonstrated the concept of leadership associated with a position of authority (auctoritas in Latin). In praising Oliver Cromwell's use of power to bring King Charles I to trial and eventual beheading, he wrote the following: "Let us remark, meanwhile, how indispensable everywhere a King is, in all movements of men. It is strikingly shown, in this very War, what becomes of men when they cannot find a Chief Man, and their enemies can."

From this viewpoint, leadership emerges when an entity as "leader" contrives to receive deference from other entities who become "followers". And as the passage from Carlyle demonstrates, the process of getting deference can become competitive in that the emerging "leader" draws "followers" from the factions of the prior or alternative "leaders".

In representative democracies the people retain sovereignty (popular sovereignty) but delegate day-to-day administration and leadership to elected officials. In the United States, for example, the Constitution provides an example of recycling authority.

In the Constitutional Convention of 1787, the American Founders rejected the idea of a monarch. But they still proposed leadership by people in positions of authority, with the authority split into three powers: in this case the legislative, the executive, and the judiciary. Under the American theory, the authority of the leadership derives from the power of the voters as conveyed through the electoral college. Many individuals share authority, including the many legislators in the Senate and the House of Representatives.

Leadership Cycles

If a group or an organization wants or expects identifiable leadership, it will require processes for appointing/acquiring and replacing leaders.

Traditional closed groups rely on bloodlines or seniority to select leaders and/or leadership candidates: monarchies, tribal chiefdoms, oligarchies and aristocratic societies rely on (and often define their institutions by) such methods.

Competence or perceived competence provides a possible basis for selecting leadership elites from a broader pool of potential talent. Political lobbying may prove necessary in electoral systems, but immediately demonstrated skill and character may secure leadership in smaller groups such as gangs.

Many organizations and groups aim to identify, foster and promote what they see as leadership potential or ability-especially among younger members of society.

The issues of succession planning or of legitimation become important at times when leadership (particularly individual leadership) might or must change due to term-expiry, accident or senescence.

Leadership as a Phase in Human Life-cycles

Some cultures, especially those with a reverence for age and wisdom, see leadership as a standard part of the life-cycle of a person. Just as a youth becomes initiated into adulthood, so an adult may gain initiation as a leader. Such societies may require special reinforcement of the respect and kudos due to such senior members in order to maintain their position. If aged adults can no longer hunt or fight or play a full part in physical labor, for example, those adults' positions in society must rest on respect and implied wisdom and teaching roles, whether or not they show identified "leadership traits".

Titles Emphasizing Authority

At certain stages in their development, the hierarchies of social ranks implied different degrees or ranks of leadership in society. Thus a knight led fewer men in general than did a duke; a baronet might in theory control less land than an earl. See peerage for a systematization of this hierarchy, and order of precedence for links to various systems.

In the course of the 19th and 20th centuries, several political operators took non-traditional paths to become dominant in their societies. They or their systems often expressed a belief in strong individual leadership, but existing titles and labels ("King", "Emperor", "President" and so on) often seemed inappropriate, insufficient or downright inaccurate in some circumstances. The formal or informal titles or descriptions they or their flunkeys employed express and foster a general veneration for leadership of the inspired and autocratic variety. The definite article when used as part of the title (in languages which use definite articles) emphasizes the existence of a sole "true" leader. Cases include:

- Caudillos in Spanish-speaking countries, notably Spain's Francisco Franco, Chile's Augusto Pinochet or the Dominican Republic's Rafael Trujillo
- Conducator in Romania-Nicolae Ceausescu
- II Duce in Italy-Benito Mussolini
- Der Führer in Germany-Adolf Hitler
- The Dear Leader in North Korea-Kim Jong-il
- The Great Helmsman in China-Mao Zedong
- The Great Leader in North Korea-Kim Il-sung
- Vozd in Serbia-Karadjordje
- Poglavnik in Croatia-Ante Pavelic
- Vozhd in the Soviet Union-Joseph Stalin

The different etymologies of these titles suggest various images of leadership: that of a "driver" (Führer, Vozhd), of a "head" (Caudillo, Poglavnik), or of someone followed (Duce, Conducator).

Such titles, and even the personal names associated with them, may also appear with reference--often jocular--to heirs and would-be imitators. Thus people may continue to speak of little Hitlers in a workplace or refer to a non-collegial prime minister ironically as The Great Helmsman. Compare the way in which the personal family name Caesar and the adopted by-name Augustus became effectively titles or designations for successive heads of the Roman Empire.

The whole structure of military hierarchies and the idea and the titles of an officer corps tend to reinforce the importance attached to leadership and to the chain of command in the military. Thus (for example) other ranks defer to Lieutenants who defer to Majors who defer to Colonels who defer to Generals who defer to Marshals. Similar elaborate structures of hierarchical leadership titles can occur in Christian churches (Deacon-Priest-Bishop-Archbishop-Cardinal) or in commercial enterprises (team leader-supervisor-line manager/middle manager-staff manager/senior manager-vice president etc).

Informal, often spontaneously-generated titles or descriptions can provide informative insights. The use of "boss" in work-places and crime-syndicates may suggest a relatively loose hierarchy, while dubbing someone "chief" can express either instantaneous readiness to follow of an acknowledgment of collegiality.

Some titles can outstay their use. "Divine Augustus" fell prey to religious changes in the later Roman Empire. "Master" (or "Massa") has fallen out of general use in the American South, and "Baas" has new connotations in the new South Africa since the late 20th century.

Other honorifics can also change in accordance with social circumstances. Britons whose remote ancestors paid due deference to the local "lord" will now find that title more concentrated in the areas of politics and the law. Their American cousins have virtually confined the word "lord" to religious usage. Various symbolic attributes-often varying according to the cultural milieu-mark out authority-figures and help make them seem special and revered.

LEADERSHIP AMONGST PRIMATES

Richard Wrangham and Dale Peterson, in Demonic Males: Apes and the Origins of Human Violence present empirical evidence that only humans and chimpanzees, among all the animals living on earth, share a similar tendency for a cluster of behaviors: violence, territoriality, and competition for uniting behind the one chief male of the land. (Note the status of chimpanzees as humans' closest species-relatives: humans inherited 98% of their genes from the ancestors of the chimpanzees.

By comparison, bonobos, the second-closest species-relatives of man, do not unite behind the chief male of the land. The bonobos show deference to an alpha or top-ranking female that, with the support of her coalition of other females, can prove as strong as the strongest male in the land. Thus, if leadership amounts to getting the greatest number of followers, then among the bonobos, a female almost always exerts the strongest and most effective leadership.

Some have argued that, since the bonobo pattern inverts the dominant pattern among chimpanzees and men with regard to whether a female can get more followers than a male, humans and chimpanzees both likely inherited gender-bias against women from the ancestors of the chimpanzees; gender-bias features as a genetic condition of men. And the bias against women having leadership as a position of authority occurs in most cultures in the world. As of 2002, Sweden had the highest percentage of women in the legislature: but only 43%. And the United States, Andorra, Israel, Sierra Leone, and Ireland tied for 57th place with less than 15% of the legislature women. Admittedly, those percentages significantly outclass the occurrence of female chimpanzees becoming alpha of the community by getting the most followers, but similar trends exist in manifesting a general gender-bias across cultures against females gaining leadership as a position of authority over followers.

An alternative explanation suggests that those individuals best suited to lead the a group will somehow rise to the occasion and that followers (for some reason) will accept them as leaders or as proto-leaders. In this scenario, the traits of the leaders (such as gender, aggressiveness, etc.) will depend on the requirements of a given situation, and ongoing leadership may become extrapolated from a series of such situations.

In cultural anthropology, much speculation on the origins of human leadership relates to the perceived increasing need for dispute resolution in increasingly densely-populated and increasingly complex societies.

LEADERSHIP AS A VANGUARD

Sometimes followership can occur without intentional leadership. Despite (or because of) its mythical origin, the image of swarms of lemmings which follow the first lemming off a cliff appears frequently in characterizing followers. The animal kingdom also provides the actual model of the bellwether function in a mob of sheep. And human society also offers many examples of emulation. The fashion industry, for example, depends on it. Fashion marketers design clothing for celebrities, then offer less expensive variations/imitations for those who emulate the celebrities.

Unintentional leadership can also occur from more proactive forms followership. For example, in organizations which punish both leadership inaction and mistakes, and in which a predicament has no good solution, a common tendency involves declaring oneself a follower of someone else-metaphorically passing the buck.

Another example of followership without intentional leadership comes with the market leadership of a pioneering company, or the price leadership of a monopolist. Other companies will emulate a successful strategy, product, or price, but originators may certainly not desire this-in fact they often do all they can legally do to prevent such direct competition.

The term "leadership" sometimes applies (confusingly) to a winning position in a race. One can speak of a front-runner in a sprint or of the "leader" in an election or poll as in a position of leadership. But such "leadership" does not involve any influence processes, and the "leader" will have followers who may not willingly choose to function as followers. Once again: one can make an important distinction between "in the lead" and the process of leadership. Once again, leadership implies a relationship of power-the power to guide others. Leading from the front, in a military sense, may imply foolhardiness and unnecessary self-exposure to danger: these do not necessarily make for successful long-term leadership strategies.

SCOPE OF LEADERSHIP

One can govern oneself, or one can govern the whole earth. In between, we may find leaders who operate primarily within:

- families
- bands
- tribes
- states and nations
- empires

Intertwined with such categories, and overlapping them, we find (for example) religious leaders (potentially with their own internal hierarchies), work-place leaders (executives, officers, senior/upper managers, middle managers, staff-managers, line-managers, team-leaders, supervisors...) and leaders of voluntary associations.

Some anthropological ideas envisage a widespread (but by no means universal) pattern of progression in the organisation of society in ever-larger groups, with the needs and practices of leadership changing accordingly. Thus simple dispute resolution may become legalistic dispensation of justice before developing into proactive legislative activity. Some leadership careers parallel this sort of progression: today's school-board chairperson may become tomorrow's city councillor, then take in (say) a mayordom before graduating to nationwide politics. Compare the cursus honorum in ancient Rome.

Orthogonality and Leadership

Those who sing the praises of leadership or of certain types of leadership may encounter problems in implementing consistent leadership structures. For example, a pyramidical structure in which authority consistently emanates from the summit can stifle initiative and leave no path for grooming future leaders in the ranks of subordinate levels. Similarly, a belief in universal direct democracy may become unwieldy, and a system consisting of nothing but representative leaders may well become stymied in committees. Thus many leadership systems promote different rules for different levels of leadership. Hereditary autocrats meet in the United Nations on equal representative terms with elected governments in a collegial leadership. Or individual local democracies may assign some of their powers to temporary dictators in emergencies, as in ancient Rome. Hierarchies intermingle with equality of opportunity at different levels.

Support-structures for Leadership

Though advocates of the "big man" school of visionary leadership would have us believe that charisma and personality alone can work miracles, most leaders operate within a structure of supporters and executive agents who carry out and monitor the expressed or filtered-down will of the leader. This undercutting of the importance of leadership may serve as a reminder of the existence of the follower: compare followership. A more or less formal bureaucracy (in the Weberian sense) can throw up a colorless nonentity as an entirely effective leader: this phenomenon may occur (for example) in a politburo environment. Bureaucratic organizations can also raise incompetent people to levels of leadership.

In modern dynamic environments formal bureaucratic organizations have started to become less common because of their inability to deal with fast-changing circumstances. Most modern business organizations (and some government departments) encourage what they see as "leadership skills" and reward identified potential leaders with promotions. According to B. Nanus, the forces that shape today's leading-edge organizations and their implications provide the key to visionary leadership. To underline his point we can examine the success-story of Bill Gates: in brief he built Microsoft from the start as a twenty-first-century organization, and he allegedly runs it with a highly-developed sense of visionary leadership.

In a potential down-side to this sort of development, a big-picture grand-vision leader may foster another sort of hierarchy: a fetish of leadership amongst subordinate sub-leaders, encouraged to seize resources for their own sub-empires and to apply to the supreme leader only for ultimate arbitration.

Some leaders build coalitions and alliances: political parties abound with this type of leader. Still others depend on rapport with the masses: they labor on the shop-floor or stand in the front-line of battle, leading by example.

Determining what Makes "Effective Leadership"

In comparing various leadership styles in many cultures, academic studies have examined the patterns in which leadership emerges and then fades, sometimes by natural succession according to established rules and sometimes by the imposition of brute force. The simplest way to measure the effectiveness of leadership involves evaluating the size of the following that the leader can muster. By this standard, Adolf Hitler became a very effective leader for a period-even if through delusional promises and coercive techniques. However, this approach may measure power rather than leadership. To measure leadership more specifically, one may assess the extent of influence on the followers, that is, the amount of leading. This may involve testing the results of leadership activities against a goal, vision, or objective.

James MacGregor Burns introduced a normative element: an effective Burnsian leader will unite followers in a shared vision that will improve an organization and society at large. Burns calls leadership that delivers "true" value, integrity, and trust transformational leadership. He distinguishes such leadership from "mere" transactional leadership that builds power by doing whatever will get more followers. But problems arise in quantifying the transformational quality of leadership-evaluation of that quality seems more difficult to quantify than merely counting the followers that the straw man of transactional leadership James MacGregor Burns has set as a primary standard for effectiveness. Thus transformational leadership requires an evaluation of quality, independent of the market demand that exhibits in the number of followers.

Current assessments of transformational and transactional leadership commonly make use of the Multifactor Leadership Questionnaire (MLQ), developed by Bass and Avolio in 1990 and revised in 1995. It measures five dimensions of transformational leadership:

1. idealized influence-attributions
2. idealized influence-behaviors
3. inspirational motivation
4. individualized consideration
5. intellectual stimulation

The three dimensions of transactional leadership measured by the MLQ cover:

1. contingent reward
2. management by exception (active)
3. management by exception (passive)

The functional leadership model conceives leadership as a set of behaviours that helps a group perform a task, reach their goal, or perform their function. In this model, effective leaders encourage functional behaviors and discourage dysfunctional ones. In the path-goal model of leadership, developed jointly by Martin Evans and Robert House and based on the "Expectancy Theory of Motivation", a leader has the function of clearing the path toward the goal(s) of the group, by meeting the needs of subordinates.

Some commentators use the metaphor of an orchestral conductor to describe the quality of the leadership process. An effective leader resembles an orchestra conductor in some ways. He/she has to somehow get a group of potentially diverse and talented people-many of whom have strong personalities-to work together toward a common output. Will the conductor harness and blend all the gifts his or her players possess? Will the players accept the degree of creative expression they have? Will the audience enjoy the sound they make? The conductor may have a clear determining influence on all of these questions.

Suggested Qualities of Leadership

Studies of leadership have suggested qualities that people often associate with leadership. They include:

- Guiding others through modeling (in the sense of providing a role model) and through willingness to serve others first (compare followership)
- Talent and technical/specific skill at some task at hand

- Initiative and entrepreneurial drive
- Charismatic inspiration-attractiveness to others and the ability to leverage this esteem to motivate others
- Preoccupation with a role-a dedication that consumes much of leaders' life-service to a cause
- A clear sense of purpose (or mission)-clear goals-focus-commitment
- Results orientation-directing every action towards a mission-prioritizing activities to spend time where results most accrue
- Optimism-very few pessimists become leaders
- Rejection of determinism-belief in one's ability to "make a difference"
- Ability to encourage and nurture those that report to them-delegate in such a way as people will grow
- Role models-leaders may adopt a persona that encapsulates their mission and lead by example
- Self-knowledge (in non-bureaucratic structures)
- Self-awareness-the ability to "lead" (as it were) one's own self prior to leading other selves similarly
- With regards to people and to projects, the ability to choose winners-recognizing that, unlike with skills, one cannot (in general) teach attitude. Note that "picking winners" ("choosing winners") carries implications of gamblers' luck as well as of the capacity to take risks, but "true" leaders, like gamblers but unlike "false" leaders, base their decisions on realistic insight (and usually on many other factors partially derived from "real" wisdom).
- Understanding what others say, rather than listening to how they say things-this could partly sum this quality up as "walking in someone else's shoes" (to use a common cliché).

The approach of listing leadership qualities, often termed "trait theory", assumes certain traits or characteristics will tend to lead to effective leadership. Although trait theory has an intuitive appeal, difficulties may arise in proving its tenets, and opponents frequently challenge this approach. The "strongest" versions of trait theory see these "leadership characteristics" as innate, and accordingly labels some people as "born leaders" due to their psychological makeup. On this reading of the theory, leadership development involves identifying and measuring leadership qualities, screening potential leaders from non-leaders, then training those with potential.

David McClelland, a Harvard-based researcher in the psychology of power and achievement, saw leadership skills, not so much as a set of traits, but as a pattern of motives. He claimed that successful leaders will tend to have a high need for power, a low need for affiliation, and a high level of what he called activity inhibition (one might call it self-control).

Situational leadership theory offers an alternative approach. It proceeds from the assumption that different situations call for different characteristics. According to this group of theories, no single optimal psychographic profile of a leader exists. The situational leadership model of Hersey and Blanchard, for example, suggest four leadership-styles and four levels of follower-development. For effectiveness, the model posits that the leadership-style must match the appropriate level of followership-development. In this model, leadership behaviour becomes a function not only of the characteristics of the leader, but of the characteristics of followers as well. Other situational leadership models introduce a variety of situational variables. These determinants include:

- the nature of the task (structured or routine)
- organizational policies, climate, and culture
- the preferences of the leader's superiors
- the expectations of peers
- the reciprocal responses of followers

The contingency model of Vroom and Yetton uses other situational variables, including:

- the nature of the problem
- the requirements for accuracy

- the acceptance of an initiative
- time-constraints
- cost constraints

However one determines leadership behaviour, one can categorize it into various leadership styles. Many ways of doing this exist. For example, the Managerial Grid Model, a behavioral leadership-model developed by Robert Blake and Jane Mouton in 1964, suggests five different leadership styles, based on leaders' strength of concern for people and their concern for goal achievement.

Kurt Lewin, Ronald Lipitt, and R. K. White identified three leadership styles: authoritarian, democratic, and laissez-faire, based on the amount of influence and power exercised by the leader.

The Fiedler contingency model bases the leader's effectiveness on what Fred Fiedler called situational contingency. This results from the interaction of leadership style and situational favourableness (later called "situational control").

Leadership Styles

In 1994 House and Podsakoff attempted to summarize the behaviors and approaches of "outstanding leaders" that they obtained from some more modern theories and research findings. These leadership behaviors and approaches do not constitute specific styles, but cumulatively they probably characterize the most effective style of today's leaders/managers. The listed leadership "styles" cover:

1. *Vision:* Outstanding leaders articulate an ideological vision congruent with the deeply-held values of followers, a vision that describes a better future to which the followers have an alleged moral right.
2. *Passion and Self-sacrifice:* Leaders display a passion for, and have a strong conviction of, what they regard as the moral correctness of their vision. They engage in outstanding or extraordinary behavior and make extraordinary self-sacrifices in the interest of their vision and mission.

3. *Confidence, Determination, and Persistence:* Outstanding leaders display a high degree of faith in themselves and in the attainment of the vision they articulate. Theoretically, such leaders need to have a very high degree of self-confidence and moral conviction because their mission usually challenges the status quo and, therefore, may offend those who have a stake in preserving the established order.
4. *Image-building:* House and Podsakoff regard outstanding leaders as self-conscious about their own image. They recognize the desirability of followers perceiving them as competent, credible, and trustworthy.
5. *Role-modeling:* Leader-image-building sets the stage for effective role-modeling because followers identify with the values of role models whom they perceived in positive terms.
6. *External Representation:* Outstanding leaders act as spokespersons for their respective organizations and symbolically represent those organizations to external constituencies.
7. Expectations of and confidence in followers. Outstanding leaders communicate expectations of high performance from their followers and strong confidence in their followers' ability to meet such expectations.
8. *Selective Motive-arousal:* Outstanding leaders selectively arouse those motives of followers that the outstanding leaders see as of special relevance to the successful accomplishment of the vision and mission.
9. *Frame Alignment:* To persuade followers to accept and implement change, outstanding leaders engage in "frame alignment". This refers to the linkage of individual and leader interpretive orientations such that some set of followers' interests, values, and beliefs, as well as the leader's activities, goals, and ideology, becomes congruent and complementary.
10. *Inspirational Communication:* Outstanding leaders often, but not always, communicate their message in an inspirational manner using vivid stories, slogans, symbols, and ceremonies.

Even though these ten leadership behaviors and approaches do not really equate to specific styles, evidence has started to accumulate that a leader's style can make a difference. Style becomes the key to the formulation and implementation of strategy and plays an important role in work-group members' activity and in team citizenship. Little doubt exists that the way (style) in which leaders influence work-group members can make a difference in their own and their people's performance.

Leadership and Vision

Many definitions of leadership involve an element of vision-except in cases of involuntary leadership and often in cases of traditional leadership. A vision provides direction to the influence process. A leader (or group of leaders) can have one or more visions of the future to aid them to move a group successfully towards this goal. A vision, for effectiveness, should allegedly:

- appear as a simple, yet vibrant, image in the mind of the leader
- describe a future state, credible and preferable to the present state
- act as a bridge between the current state and a future optimum state
- appear desirable enough to energize followers
- succeed in speaking to followers at an emotional or spiritual level (logical appeals by themselves seldom muster a following)

For leadership to occur, according to this theory, some people ("leaders") must communicate the vision to others ("followers") in such a way that the followers adopt the vision as their own. Leaders must not just see the vision themselves, they must have the ability to get others to see it also. Numerous techniques aid in this process, including: narratives, metaphors, symbolic actions, leading by example, incentives, and penalties.

Stacey (1992) has suggested that the emphasis on vision puts an unrealistic burden on the leader. Such emphasis appears to perpetuate the myth that an organization must depend on a single, uncommonly talented individual to decide what to do. Stacey claims that this fosters a culture of dependency and conformity in which followers take no proactive incentives and do not think independently.

Leadership's Relation with Management

Some commentators link leadership closely with the idea of management. Some regard the two as synonymous, and others consider management a subset of leadership. If one accepts this premise, one can view leadership as:

- centralized or decentralized
- broad or focused
- decision-oriented or morale-centred
- intrinsic or derived from some authority

Any of the bipolar labels traditionally ascribed to management style could also apply to leadership style. Hersey and Blanchard use this approach: they claim that management merely consists of leadership applied to business situations; or in other words: management forms a sub-set of the broader process of leadership. They put it this way: "Leadership occurs any time one attempts to influence the behavior of an individual or group, regardless of the reason.... Management is a kind of leadership in which the achievement of organizational goals is paramount." (Hersey, P. and Blanchard, K.: 1982: page 3)

However, a clear distinction between management and leadership may nevertheless prove useful. This would allow for a reciprocal relationship between leadership and management, implying that an effective manager should possess leadership skills, and an effective leader should demonstrate management skills. One clear distinction could provide the following definition:

- Management involves power by position.
- Leadership involves power by influence.

Abraham Zaleznik (1977), for example, delineated differences between leadership and management. He saw leaders as inspiring visionaries, concerned about substance;

while managers he views as planners who have concerns with process. Warren Bennis (1989) further explicated a dichotomy between managers and leaders. He drew twelve distinctions between the two groups:

- Managers administer, leaders innovate
- Managers ask how and when, leaders ask what and why
- Managers focus on systems, leaders focus on people
- Managers do things right, leaders do the right things
- Managers maintain, leaders develop
- Managers rely on control, leaders inspire trust
- Managers have a short-term perspective, leaders have a longer-term perspective
- Managers accept the status-quo, leaders challenge the status quo
- Managers have an eye on the bottom line, leaders have an eye on the horizon
- Managers imitate, leaders originate
- Managers emulate the classic good soldier, leaders are their own person
- Managers copy, leaders show originality

Paul Birch (1999) also sees a distinction between leadership and management. He observed that, as a broad generalization, managers concerned themselves with tasks while leaders concerned themselves with people. Birch does not suggest that leaders do not focus on "the task." Indeed, the things that characterise a great leader include the fact that they achieve. The difference lies in the leader realising that the achievement of the task comes about through the goodwill and support of others, while the manager may not.

This goodwill and support originates in the leader seeing people as people, not as another resource for deployment in support of "the task". The manager often has the role of organizing resources to get something done. People form one of these resources, and many of the worst managers treat people as just another interchangeable item. A leader has the role of causing others to follow a path he/she has laid out or a vision he/she has articulated in order to achieve a task. Often, people see the task as subordinate to the vision. For instance, an organization might have the overall task of generating profit, but a good leader may see profit as a by-product that flows from whatever aspect of their vision differentiates their company from the competition.

Leadership does not only manifest itself as purely a business phenomenon. Many people can think of an inspiring leader they have encountered who has nothing whatever to do with business: a politician, an officer in the armed forces, a Scout or Guide leader, a teacher, etc. Similarly, management does not occur only as a purely business phenomenon. Again, we can think of examples of people that we have met who fill the management niche in non-business organisations. Non-business organizations should find it easier to articulate a non-money-driven inspiring vision that will support true leadership. However, often this does not occur.

Differences in the mix of leadership and management can define various management styles. Some management styles tend to de-emphasize leadership. Included in this group one could include participatory management, democratic management, and collaborative management styles. Other management styles, such as authoritarian management, micro-management, and top-down management, depend more on a leader to provide direction. Note, however, that just because an organisation has no single leader giving it direction, does not mean it necessarily has weak leadership. In many cases group leadership (multiple leaders) can prove effective. Having a single leader (as in dictatorship) allows for quick and decisive decision-making when needed as well as when not needed. Group decision-making sometimes earns the derisive label "committee-itis" because of the longer times required to make decisions, but group leadership can bring more expertise, experience, and perspectives through a democratic process.

Patricia Pitcher (1994) has challenged the bifurcation into leaders and managers. She used a factor analysis technique on data collected over 8 years, and concluded that three types of leaders exist, each with very different psychological profiles.

She characterises one group as imaginative, inspiring, visionary, entrepreneurial, intuitive, daring, and emotional, and calls them "artists". In a second grouping she places "craftsmen" as well-balanced, steady, reasonable, sensible, predictable, and trustworthy. Finally she identifies "technocrats" as cerebral, detail-oriented, fastidious, uncompromising, and hard-headed. She speculates that no one profile offers a preferred leadership style. She claims that if we want to build, we should find an "artist leader"; if we want to solidify our position, we should find a "craftsman leader"; and if we have an ugly job that needs to get done (like downsizing), we should find a "technocratic leader." Pitcher also observed that a balanced leader exhibiting all three sets of traits occurs extremely rarely: she found none in her study.

Leadership by a Group

In contrast to individual leadership, some organizations have adopted group leadership. In this situation, more than one person provides direction to the group as a whole. Some organizations have taken this approach in hopes of increasing creativity, reducing costs, or downsizing. Others may see the traditional leadership of a boss as costing too much in team performance. In some situations, the maintenance of the boss becomes too expensive-either by draining the resources of the group as a whole, or by impeding the creativity within the team, even unintentionally.

A common example of group leadership involves cross-functional teams. A team of people with diverse skills and from all parts of an organization assembles to lead a project. A team structure can involve sharing power equally on all issues, but more commonly uses rotating leadership. The team member(s) best able to handle any given phase of the project become(s) the temporary leader(s).

For example, the Orpheus orchestra has performed for over thirty years without a conductor--that is, without a sole leader. As a team of over 25 members, it has drawn discriminating audiences, and has produced over 60 recordings for Deutsche Grammophon in successful competition with other world-class orchestras.

Rather than an autocratic or charismatic conductor deciding the overall conception of a work and then dictating how each individual is to perform the individual tasks, the Orpheus team generally selects a different "core group" for each piece of music. The core group provides leadership in working out the details of the piece, and presents their ideas to the whole team. Members of the whole team then participate in refining the final conception, rehearsal, and product, including checking from various places in the auditorium how the sound balances and verifying the quality of the final recording.

At times the entire Orpheus team may follow a single leader, but whom the team follows rotates from task to task, depending on the capabilities of its members. The orchestra has developed seminars and training sessions for adapting the Orpheus Process to business.

Co-leadership

As a compromise between individual leadership and an open group, leadership structures of two or three people or entities occur commonly. Ancient Rome preferred two consuls to a single king, and the Roman Empire grew to accommodate two Emperors-those of the East and of the West-simultaneously. The Middle Ages saw leadership divided between the secular and spiritual realms-between Emperor and Pope. Some groups-often left-wing or Green in orientation-employ a co-leader structure today.

Triumvirates have long served to balance leadership ambitions-notably in Rome in the first century BC, but also as recently as in the Soviet Union troikas of the 20th century. Compare the separation of powers (legislative, judicial and executive) formalised (for example) in the constitution of the United States of America.

Divided Leadership

Whereas sometimes one can readily and definitively identify the locus of leadership, in other circumstances the situation remains obscured. Pre-modern Japan offers a classical example: the emperors provided symbolic and religious leadership, but the shoguns embodied virtually all political and administrative leadership. Similar dichotomies appear in many places and in many periods. Any constitutional monarch has a potentially confusing relationship with the day-to-day leader (typically a prime minister) who remains (at least theoretically) subordinate-socially as well as politically. Regents may stand against monarchs (and their supporters) during the minority or absence of those monarchs. Heads of state may operate at cross-purposes with heads of government. Political leaders may or may not align closely with religious leaders. And in federal-type systems, regional leadership and its potentially different systems may cross swords with national leaders. Not to mention the potentially conflicting leadership manifestations of boards of directors and of Chief Executives.

Leader Relationships with Followers

Greiner's study of the language of U.S. Presidents examined the relationship between leader and followers and observed that changes have taken place in the presidential use of words that define the leader and the community as one. Modern US presidents have an observed tendency to make more use of inclusive words like we, us and our in their inaugural speeches. The use of inclusive words may suggest an effort by these democratically selected leaders to make the community work together to solve problems collectively.

Historical Views on Leadership

Aristocratic thinkers have postulated that leadership depends on one's blue blood or genes: monarchy takes an extreme view of the same idea, and may prop up its assertions against the claims of mere aristocrats by invoking divine sanction: see the divine right of kings. Contrariwise, more democratically-inclined theorists have pointed to examples of meritocratic leaders, such as the Napoleonic marshals profiting from careers open to talent.

In the autocratic/paternalistic strain of thought, traditionalists recall the role of leadership of the Roman pater familias. Feminist thinking, on the other hand, may damn such models as patriarchal and posit against them emotionally-attuned, responsive, and consensual empathetic guidance and matriarchies.

Comparable to the Roman tradition, the views of Confucianism on "right living" relate very much to the ideal of the (male) scholar-leader and his benevolent rule, buttressed by a tradition of filial piety.

Within the context of Islam, views on the nature, scope and inheritance of leadership have played a major role in shaping sects and their history.

In the 19th century, the elaboration of anarchist thought called the whole concept of leadership into question. (Note that the Oxford English Dictionary traces the word "leadership" in English only as far back as the 19th century.) One response to this denial of élitism came with Leninism, which demanded an élite group of disciplined cadres to act as the vanguard of a socialist revolution, bringing into existence the dictatorship of the proletariat.

Other historical views of leadership have addressed the seeming contrasts between secular and religious leadership. The doctrines of Caesaro-papism have recurred and had their detractors over several centuries. Christian thinking on leadership has often emphasized stewardship of divinely-provided resources-human and material-and their deployment in accordance with a Divine plan. Compare servant leadership.

Specific theories of Leadership

In State of Exception (2005), Agamben reads Carl Schmitt's theory of sovereignty in the light of Walter Benjamin. Agamben traces Schmitt's definition of sovereignty as the power to decide the state of exception to the Roman concept of auctoritas-the power to declare justitium. Agamben writes:

"It is significative that modern specialists were so enclined to admit that auctoritas was inherent to the living person of the pater or the princeps. What was evidently an ideology or a fictio aiming to be the groundwork of auctoritas ' preeminence or, at least, specific rank compared to potestas thus became a figure of right's immanence to life. (...) Although it is evident that there can't be an eternal human type that would incarnate itself each time in Augustus, Napoleon, Hitler, but only more or less similar mechanisms {"dispositif", a term often used by Foucault}-the state of exception, justitium, the auctoritas principles, the Führertum-put in use in more or less different circumstances, in the 1930s-overall, but not only-in Germany, the power that Weber had defined as "charismatic" is related to the concept of auctoritas and elaborated in a Führertum doctrine as the original and personal power of a leader. In 1933, in a short article intending to define the fundamental concepts of national-socialism, Schmitt defines the Führung principal by the "root identity between the leader and his entourage" {"identité de souche entre le chef et son entourage"} (we shall note the use of Weberian concepts)."

James MacGregor Burns: James MacGregor Burns (1978, p. 2) wrote that a study of the definition of the word leadership revealed 130 definitions. However, several generally-accepted variations on the definition appear in the management and leadership literature.

Burns concluded by presenting five characteristics of leadership, namely:

1. Leadership is collective (p. 452). James Burns regards the notion of one-person leadership as "a contradiction in terms", because both leaders and followers must exist. Also, an organization may have multiple leaders all acting in consort with one another.
2. Leadership is dissension (p. 453). Burns claims that leadership coexists with dissent. Indeed, much of the growth of any organization centers on the management/ leadership of dissent-except in times of war.
3. Leadership is causative (p. 454). True Burnsian leadership affects the motives of individuals and groups of peoples and alters the course of the organizational history. It causes positive change.
4. Leadership is morally purposeful (p. 455). Burns sees leadership as goal-oriented, with leaders and followers pointing the way to some future state of the organization with plans about how those goals might be met.
5. Transforming leadership is elevating (p. 455). Engagement between leaders and followers takes place on a moral-but not a moralistic-plane, as both leaders and followers rise to live more principled lives.

Ronald Heifetz: Ronald Heifetz (Heifetz 1994) described the difference between a descriptive view and a prescriptive view of leadership. A descriptive view describes leadership and how it occurs, and a prescriptive view suggests how it should occur. The notion of "adaptive work" forms a central concept of Heifetz's prescriptive view. Heifetz pointed out (p. 37) that people fail to adapt to new and unsettling situations through six avoidance mechanisms:

1. blaming others
2. finding scapegoats (to the extent that this differs from blaming)
3. externalizing the enemy
4. denying that a problem exists
5. jumping to conclusions
6. finding a distracting issue

In a prescriptive view, the leader would squarely face the problem and avoid the six surface-level solutions of the non-leader. A true leader would help a community face reality and deal with the issues: finding solutions where none previously existed. Using the 1950s television character, the Lone Ranger, as an example, we see the Ranger in a weekly episode, moving from frontier town to frontier town, discovering problems wherever he goes, fixing the problems and riding off into the sunset. In this metaphor, the Ranger fixes the symptom, but not the problem. A Lone Ranger non-leader would catch fish to feed the poor while a true leader would teach the poor how to catch fish and would motivate them to do so. The true leader finds a way to help the community engage the problem and collectively find a solution.

George Terry: George Terry (Terry, G. 1960) has defined leadership as: "the activity of influencing people to strive willingly for group objectives". If we define leadership simply as "influencing others to some purpose" and we define followership as "becoming influenced by others to accept (willingly or un willingly) some purpose", then leadership and followership emerge as two sides of the same coin. In this scenario, leadership-whether successful or not-has not occurred until at least one follower joins in. Likewise, no followership exists without someone or something (not necessarily a leader) to follow. However, in this latter case, a "leader" need not exercise deliberate or even conscious leadership-that is, followers can follow someone who is not trying to lead. Some see "unconscious leadership" as a dubious concept, however. Many, using a different definition of leadership, would claim that it does not classify as leadership at all-simply because no deliberate intention to lead exists. Unconscious "leading by example" (as the phrase has it) may nevertheless exemplify such "leadership".

Robert Blake and Jane Mouton: Rachel K. McKee and Bruce Carlson's book The power to change describes "The Leadership Grid" or the "9,9 Style" of leadership developed by Drs. Robert Blake and Jane Mouton in 1964. The theory/model allows the comparison of leadership styles.

Conscious Leadership

Dr. James Farr (1918-2000) argued not for any one "correct leadership style" but for the style that each situation requires. Great leaders require the use of nearly every leadership style: one must apply the correct style to meet the situation. Farr terms this "Conscious Leadership".

"Conscious Leadership" consists of the art and science of leading change from a self-aware perspective, with clarity of purpose and an acute insight into others' perspectives and state of mind. This fully-aware state uniquely allows leaders to properly inspire motivation in others and to choose the most appropriate course of action both to solve pressing problems and to effectively achieve long-term organizational goals.

Futurist John Renesch has written extensively on conscious leadership, which he advocates for everyone-not only those in positions of authority or holding designated titles. As he wrote in early 2001:

Conscious leaders don't tolerate conditions or processes where people feel the need to compromise their values-to "sell their souls" for the task at hand. Conscious leadership includes conscious discernment, a principle that demands performance, integrity, competence and a noncalloused form of spiritual toughness. The conscious leader does not sit with his or her head in the clouds, dreaming of utopian schemes and professing New Age idealism. The conscious leader walks in the spiritual and physical domains concurrently, remaining simultaneously grounded and comfortable in both.

Renesch also writes about "The Conscious Organization" which he defines as "one which continually examines itself, committed to becoming as conscious as it can. In other words, it has very low tolerance for unconsciousness. It possesses the collective will to be vigilant, the collective commitment to continuous evolution, and the collective courage to act."

Alternatives to Leadership

Within groups, alternatives to the cult of leadership include using decision-making structures such as cooperative ventures, collegiality, consensus, anarchism and applied democracy. One can down play the ubiquitous idea of leadership by using structures such as information clearing houses or stressing functions such as administration. Note the different implications and connotations of the two phrases "coalition of the willing" and "US-led coalition". The Orpheus Chamber Orchestra, which practises a form of distributed leadership, provides a textbook example of alternative leadership.

COORDINATING

A concise and clear general definition is from (Malone and Crowston, 1991): "Coordination is the act of managing interdependencies between activities."

Coordination or Co-Ordination is "the ability to reduce all-together, in order to generate an only one all." (Alessio Bissoli, 2006)

Coordination, co-ordination is the regulation of diverse elements into an integrated and harmonious operation. Coordination means integrating or linking together different parts of an organization to accomplish a collective set of tasks.

In chemistry, a coordination compound refers usually to metal complexes of various kinds. Coordinating can also involve the organization of a group. It can be used in politics, for coherent action of different public Administration in the same country (i.e. between a State and a Federal Administration).

CONTROLLING

Some people, however, find this definition, while useful, far too narrow. The phrase "management is what managers do" occurs widely, suggesting the difficulty of defining management, the shifting nature of definitions, and the connection of managerial practices with the existence of a managerial cadre or class.

One habit of thought regards management as equivalent to "business administration", although this then excludes management in places outside commerce, as for example in charities and in the public sector. Nonetheless, university departments which teach management usually get called "business schools".

Speakers of English may also use the term "management" or "the management" as a collective word describing the managers of an organization, for example of a corporation.

Managerial Levels/hierarchy

The management of a large organisation may have three levels:

1. Senior management (or "top management" or "upper management")
2. Middle management
3. Low-level management (compare "team leadership")

Compare Harrington Emerson's distinction between "staff management" and "line management".

Historical Development

Difficulties arise in tracing the history of management. Some see it (by definition) as a late modern (in the sense of late modernity) conceptualization. On those terms it cannot have a pre-modern history, only harbingers. Others, however, detect management-like activities in the pre-modern past. Some writers trace the development of management-thought back to

Sumerian traders and to the builders of the pyramids of ancient Egypt. Slave-owners through the centuries faced the problems of exploiting/motivating a dependent but sometimes unenthusiastic or recalcitrant workforce, but many pre-industrial enterprises, given their small scale, did not feel compelled to face the issues of management systematically. However, innovations such as the spread of Hindu-Arabic numerals (5th to 15th centuries) and the codification of double-entry bookkeeping (1494) provided tools for management assessment, planning and control.

19th Century

Some argue that modern management as a discipline began as an off-shoot of economics in the 19th century. Classical economists such as Adam Smith (1723-1790) and John Stuart Mill (1806-1873) provided a theoretical background to resource-allocation, production, and pricing issues. About the same time, innovators like Eli Whitney (1765-1825), James Watt (1736-1819), and Matthew Boulton (1728-1809) developed elements of technical production such as standardization, quality-control procedures, cost-accounting, interchangeability of parts, and work-planning. Many of these aspects of management existed in the pre-1861 slave-based sector of the US economy. That environment saw 4 million people, as the contemporary usages had it, "managed" in profitable quasi-mass production.

By the late 19th century, marginal economists Alfred Marshall (1842-1924) and Léon Walras (1834-1910) and others introduced a new layer of complexity to the theoretical underpinnings of management. Joseph Wharton offered the first tertiary-level course in management in 1881.

20th Century

By about 1900 we find managers trying to place their theories on what they regarded as a thoroughly scientific basis. Examples include Henry Towne's Science of management in the 1890s, Frederick Winslow Taylor's Scientific management (1911), Frank and Lillian Gilbreth's Applied motion study (1917), and Henry L. Gantt's charts (1910s). J. Duncan wrote the first college management textbook in 1911. In 1912 Yoichi Ueno introduced Taylorism to Japan and became first management consultant of the "Japanese-management style". His son Ichiro Ueno pioneered Japanese quality-assurance.

The first comprehensive theories of management appeared around 1920. People like Henri Fayol (1841-1925) and Alexander Church described the various branches of management and their inter-relationships. In the early 20th century, people like Ordway Tead (1891-1973), Walter Scott and J. Mooney applied the principles of psychology to management, while other writers, such as Elton Mayo (1880-1949), Mary Parker Follett (1868-1933), Chester Barnard (1886-1961), Max Weber (1864-1920), Rensis Likert (1903-1981), and Chris Argyris (1923-) approached the phenomenon of management from a sociological perspective.

Peter Drucker (1909-2005) wrote one of the earliest books on applied management: Concept of the Corporation (published in 1946). It resulted from Alfred Sloan (chairman of General Motors until 1956) commissioning a study of the organisation. Drucker went on to write 39 books, many in the same vein.

H. Dodge, Ronald Fisher (1890-1962), and Thornton C. Fry introduced statistical techniques into management-studies. In the 1940s, Patrick Blackett combined these statistical theories with microeconomic theory and gave birth to the science of operations research. Operations research, sometimes known as "management science", attempts to take a scientific approach to solving management problems, particularly in the areas of logistics and operations.

Some of the more recent developments include the theory of constraints, management by objectives, reengineering, and various information-technology-driven theories such as agile software development, as well as group management theories such as Cog's Ladder.

As the general recognition of managers as a class solidified during the 20th century and gave perceived practitioners of the art/science of management a certain amount of prestige, so the way opened for popularised systems of management ideas to peddle their wares. In this context many management fads may have had more to do with pop psychology than with scientific theories of management.

Towards the end of the 20th century, business management came to consist of six separate branches, namely:

- Human resource management
- Operations management or production management
- Strategic management
- Marketing management
- Financial management
- Information technology management responsible for management information systems

21st Century

In the 21st century observers find it increasingly difficult to subdivide management into functional categories in this way. More and more processes simultaneously involve several categories. Instead, one tends to think in terms of the various processes, tasks, and objects subject to management. A list of some of the areas of management appears later in this article.

Branches of management theory also exist relating to nonprofits and to government: such as public administration, public management, and educational management. Further, management programs related to civil-society organizations have also spawned programs in nonprofit management and social entrepreneurship. Note that many of the assumptions made by management have come under attack from business ethics viewpoints, critical management studies, and anti-corporate activism.

As one consequence, workplace democracy has become both more common, and more advocated, in some places distributing all management functions among the workers, each of whom takes on a portion of the work. However, these models predate any current political issue, and may occur more naturally than does a command hierarchy. All management to some degree embraces democratic principles in that in the long term workers must give majority support to management; otherwise they leave to find other work, or go on strike. Hence management has started to become less based on the conceptualisation of classical military command-and-control, and more about facilitation and support of collaborative activity, utilizing principles such as those of human interaction management to deal with the complexities of human interaction. Indeed, the concept of Ubiquitous command-and-control posits such a transformation for 21st century military management.

Nature of the Work

In for-profit work, management has as its primary function the satisfaction of a range of stakeholders. This typically involves making a profit (for the shareholders), creating valued products at a reasonable cost (for customers), and providing rewarding employment opportunities (for employees). In nonprofit management, add the importance of keeping the faith of donors. In most models of management/governance, shareholders vote for the board of directors, and the board then hires senior management. Some organizations have experimented with other methods (such as employee-voting models) of selecting or reviewing managers; but this occurs only very rarely.

In the public sector of countries constituted as representative democracies, voters elect politicians to public office. Such politicians hire many managers and administrators, and in some countries like the United States political appointees lose their jobs on the election of a new president/governor/mayor. Some 2500 people serve at the pleasure of the United States Chief Executive, including all of the top US government executives. Public, private, and voluntary sectors place different demands on managers, but all must retain the faith of those who select them (if they wish to retain their jobs), retain the faith of those people that fund the organization, and retain the faith of those who work for the organization. If they fail to convince employees of the advantages of staying rather than leaving, they may tip the organization into a downward spiral of hiring, training, firing, and recruiting. Management also has the task of innovating and of improving the functioning of organizations.

MANAGEMENT CONSULTING

Management consulting (sometimes also called strategy consulting) refers to both the practice of helping companies to improve performance through analysis of existing business problems and development of future plans, as well as to the firms that specialize in this sort of consulting. Management consulting may involve the identification and cross-fertilization of best practices, analytical techniques, change management and coaching skills, technology implementations, strategy development or even the simple advantage of an outsider's perspective. Management consultants generally bring formal frameworks or methodologies to identify problems or suggest more effective or efficient ways of performing business tasks.

Management Consulting is becoming more prevalent in non-business related fields as well. As the need for professional and specialized advice grows, other industries such as government, quasi-government and not-for-profit agencies are turning to the same managerial principles that have helped the private sector for years. There is a relatively unclear line between management consulting and other consulting practices, such as Information technology consulting.

History

Management consulting grew with the rise of management as a unique field of study. The first management consulting firm was Arthur D. Little, founded in the late 1890s by the MIT professor of the same name. Though Arthur D. Little later became a general management consultancy, it originally specialized in technical research. Booz Allen Hamilton was founded by Edwin G. Booz, a graduate of the Kellogg School of Management at Northwestern University, in 1914 as a management consultancy and the first to serve both industry and government clients. The first pure management and strategy consulting company was McKinsey & Company. McKinsey was founded in Chicago during 1926 by James O. McKinsey, but the modern McKinsey was shaped by Marvin Bower, who believed that management consultancies should adhere to the same high professional standards as lawyers and doctors. McKinsey is credited with being the first to hire newly minted MBAs from top schools to staff its projects vs. hiring older industry personnel. Andrew T. Kearney, an original McKinsey partner broke off and started A.T. Kearney in 1937.

After World War II, a number of new management consulting firms formed, most notably Boston Consulting Group, founded in 1963, which brought a rigorous analytical approach to the study of management and strategy. Work done at Booz Allen, McKinsey, BCG, and the Harvard Business School during the 1960s and 70s developed the tools and approaches that would define the new field of strategic management, setting the groundwork for many consulting firms to follow.

Another major player of more recent fame is Bain & Company, whose innovative focus on shareholder wealth (including its successful private equity business) set it apart from its older brethren. Also significant was the development of consulting arms by both accounting firms (such as Accenture of the now defunct Arthur Andersen) and global IT services companies (such as IBM). Though not as focused on strategy or the executive agenda, these consulting businesses were well-funded and often arrived on client sites in force.

The current trend in the market is a clear segmentation of management consulting firms. McKinsey, Bain, and BCG retain their strong strategy focus, with pure strategy houses such as OC&C Strategy Consultants, and Parthenon competing effectively in this high end market. Many other generalist management consultancies such as Accenture are broadening their offering increasing into high volume, lower margin work such as system integration.

CURRENT STATE OF THE INDUSTRY

Management consulting has grown quickly, with growth rates of the industry exceeding 20% in the 1980s and 1990s. As a business service, consulting remains highly cyclical and linked to overall economic conditions. The consulting industry shrank during the 2001-2003 period, but had been experiencing slowly increasing growth since. In 2004, revenues were up 3% over the previous year, yielding a market size of just under $125 billion.

Currently, there are three main types of consulting firms. First, there are large, diversified organizations, such as Accenture and IBM Global Services that offer a range of services, including information technology consulting, in addition to a management consulting practice. Second are the large management and strategic consulting specialists that offer purely management consulting but are not specialized in any specific industry, such as Bain & Company, BCG, and McKinsey & Company. Finally, there are boutique firms, often quite small, which have focused areas of consulting expertise in specific industries or technologies.

Added to these approaches are corporations that set up their own internal consulting groups, hiring internal management consultants either from within the corporation or from external firms whose employees have tired of the road warrior lifestyle. Corporations such as SunLife, IBM, Fidelity, Siemens, Chevron Texaco, Metlife and Bristol Myers Squibb have found these groups to be particularly helpful. Many of these corporations have interal groups of as many as 25 to 30 full-time consultants.

The internal consultant approach is chosen for three reasons. First, the corporation does not want to pay the large fees typically associated with external consulting firms. Second, they want to keep certain corporate information private. Finally, they want a group that more closely works with, and monitors, consulting firm relationships. Often, the internal consultant has less ramp up time on a project due to familiarity with the corporation, and is able to guide a project through to implementation-a step that would be too costly if an external consultant was used.

Internal consulting groups are often formed around a number of practice areas. The more common areas are: organizational development, process management, information technology, design services, training and development. There are three potential problems. First, the internal consultant may not bring objectivity to the consulting relationship that an external firm can. Second, when the external consulting industry is strong it is increasingly difficult to find the required high calibre of consultant provided by consulting firms. Finally, when financial times get tough, often the internal consulting group is the first to face layoffs.

Despite these problems there is a clear advantage. External consultants may pose more conflicts of interest and bias in favor of one client company over another. This is especially true in economies that are experiencing high degrees of consolidation, which results in industry and product overlap among client companies.

DIFFERENT APPROACHES

Management consulting has become the primary source for innovation in the practice of management, forming a bridge between academia, firms, and thought leaders in other fields. As a result, management consulting firms use a variety of tools and techniques to approach business problems.

Criticism

Management consultants are often criticized for overuse of buzzwords, reliance on management fads, and a failure to develop executable plans that can be followed through. A number of highly critical books about management consulting argue that the mismatch between management consulting advice and the ability of business executives to actually create the change suggested results in substantial damages to existing businesses, see, for example Dangerous Company by James O'Shea.

Further criticisms include: analysis reports only, junior consultants charging senior rates, reselling similar reports to multiple clients as "custom work", lack of innovation, overbilling for days not worked, speed at cost of quality, unresponsive large firms & lack of (small) client focus, lack of clarity of deliverables in contracts, and more.

8

Foreign Exchange Management

The Foreign Exchange Regulation Act of 1973 (FERA) was repealed on 1st June, 2000. It was replaced by the Foreign Exchange Management Act (FEMA), which was passed in the winter session of Parliament in 1999. Enacted in 1973, in the backdrop of acute shortage of Foreign Exchange in the country, FERA had a controversial 27 year stint during which many bosses of the Indian Corporate world found themselves at the mercy of the Enforcement Directorate (E.D.). Any offense under FERA was a criminal offense liable to imprisonment, whereas FEMA seeks to make offenses relating to foreign exchange civil offenses.

FEMA, which has replaced FERA, had become the need of the hour since FERA had become incompatible with the pro-liberalisation policies of the Government of India. FEMA has brought a new management regime of Foreign Exchange consistent with the emerging frame work of the World Trade Organisation (WTO). It is another matter that enactment of FEMA also brought with it Prevention of Money Laundering Act, 2002 which came into effect recently from 1st July, 2005 and the heat of which is yet to be felt as "Enforcement Directorate" would be invesitigating the cases under PMLA too.

Unlike other laws where everything is permitted unless specifically prohibited, under FERA nothing was permitted unless specifically permitted. Hence the tenor and tone of the Act was very drastic. It provided for imprisonment of even a very minor offence. Under FERA, a person was presumed guilty unless he proved himself innocent whereas under other laws, a person is presumed innocent unless he is proven guilty.

OBJECTIVES AND EXTENT OF FEMA

The object of the Act is to consolidate and amend the law relating to foreign exchange with the objective of facilitating external trade and payments and for promoting the orderly development and maintenance of foreign exchange market in India.

FEMA extends to the whole of India. It applies to all branches, offices and agencies outside India owned or controlled by a person who is a resident of India and also to any contravention there under committed outside India by any person to whom this Act applies.

Except with the general or special permission of the Reserve Bank of India, no person can:

- deal in or transfer any foreign exchange or foreign security to any person not being an authorized person;
- make any payment to or for the credit of any person resident outside India in any manner;
- receive otherwise through an authorized person, any payment by order or on behalf of any person resident outside India in any manner;
- reasonable restrictions for current account transactions as may be prescribed.

Any person may sell or draw foreign exchange to or from an authorized person for a capital account transaction. The Reserve Bank may, in consultation with the Central Government, specify:

- any class or classes of capital account transactions which are permissible;
- the limit up to which foreign exchange shall be admissible for such transactions

However, the Reserve Bank cannot impose any restriction on the drawing of foreign exchange for payments due on account of amortization of loans or for depreciation of direct investments in the ordinary course of business.

The Reserve Bank can, by regulations, prohibit, restrict or regulate the following:

- transfer or issue of any foreign security by a person resident in India;
- transfer or issue of any security by a person resident outside India;
- transfer or issue of any security or foreign security by any branch, office or agency in India of a person resident outside India;
- any borrowing or lending in foreign exchange in whatever form or by whatever name called;
- any borrowing or tending in rupees in whatever form or by whatever name called between a person resident in India and a person resident outside India;
- deposits between persons resident in India and persons resident outside India;
- export, import or holding of currency or currency notes;
- transfer of immovable property outside India, other than a lease not exceeding five years, by a person resident in India;
- acquisition or transfer of immovable property in India, other than a lease not exceeding five years, by a person resident outside India;
- giving of a guarantee or surety in respect of any debt, obligation or other liability incurred
  (i) by a person resident in India and owed to a person resident outside India or
  (ii) by a person resident outside India.

A person, resident in India may hold, own, transfer or invest in foreign currency, foreign security or any immovable property situated outside India if such currency, security or property was acquired, held or owned by such person when he was resident outside India or inherited from a person who was resident outside India. A person resident outside India may hold, own, transfer or invest in Indian currency, security or any immovable property situated in India if such currency, security or property was acquired, held or owned by such person when he was resident in India or inherited from a person who was resident in India. The Reserve Bank may, by regulation, prohibit, restrict, or regulate establishment in India of a branch, office or other place of business by a person resident outside India, for carrying on any activity relating to such branch, office or other place of business. Every exporter of goods and services must:

- furnish to the Reserve Bank or to such other authority a declaration in such form and in such manner as may be specified, containing truc and correct material particulars, including the amount representing the full export value or, if the full export value of the goods is not ascertainable at the time of export, the value which the exporter, having regard to the prevailing market conditions, expects to receive on the sale of the goods in a market outside India;
- furnish to the Reserve Bank such other information as may be required by the Reserve Bank for the purpose of ensuring the realization of the export proceeds by such exporter.

The Reserve Bank may, for the purpose of ensuring that the full export value of the goods or such reduced value of the goods as the Reserve Bank determines, having regard to the prevailing market-conditions, is received without any delay, direct any exporter to comply with such requirements as it deems fit.

Where any amount of foreign exchange is due or has accrued to any person resident in India, such person shall take all reasonable steps to realize and repatriate to India such foreign exchange within such period and in such manner as may be specified by the Reserve Bank.

CONTRAVENTIONS AND PENALTIES

If any person contravenes any provision of this Act, or contravenes any rule, regulation, notification, direction or order issued in exercise of the powers under this Act, or contravenes any condition subject to which an authorization is issued by the Reserve Bank, he shall, upon adjudication, be liable to a penalty up to thrice the sum involved in such contravention where such amount is quantifiable, or up to two lakh rupees where the amount is not quantifiable, and where such contravention is a continuing one, further penalty which may extend to five thousand rupees for every day after the first day during which the contravention continues.

Any Adjudicating Authority adjudging any contravention may, if he thinks fit in addition to any penalty which he may impose for such contravention direct that any currency, security or any other money or property in respect of which the contravention has taken place shall be confiscated to the Central Government and further direct that the foreign exchange holdings, if any, of the persons committing the contraventions or any part thereof, shall be brought back into India or shall be retained outside India in accordance with the directions made in this behalf.

"Property" in respect of which contravention has taken place, shall include deposits in a bank, where the said property is converted into such deposits, Indian currency, where the said property is converted into that currency; and any other property which has resulted out of the conversion of that property.

If any person fails to make full payment of the penalty imposed on him within a period of ninety days from the date on which the notice for payment of such penalty is served on him, he shall be liable to civil imprisonment.

INVESTIGATION

The Directorate of Enforcement investigate to prevent leakage of foreign exchange which generally occurs through the following malpractices:

- Remittances of Indians abroad otherwise than through normal banking channels, i.e. through compensatory payments.
- Acquisition of foreign currency illegally by person in India.
- Non-repatriation of the proceeds of the exported goods.
- Unauthorised maintenance of accounts in foreign countries.

- Under-invoicing of exports and over-invoicing of imports and any other type of invoice manipulation.
- Siphoning off of foreign exchange against fictitious and bogus imports.
- Illegal acquisition of foreign exchange through Hawala.
- Secreting of commission abroad.

Organisational setup and Functions of Enforcement Directorate

Directorate of Enforcement has to detect cases of violation and also perform substantially adjudicatory functions to curb above malpractices. The Enforcement Directorate, with its Headquarters at New Delhi has seven zonal offices at Bombay, Calcutta, Delhi, Jalandhar, Madras, Ahmedabad and Bangalore. The zonal offices are headed by the Deputy Directors. The Directorate has nine sub-zonal offices at Agra, Srinagar, Jaipur, Varanasi, Trivandrum, Calicut, Hyderabad, Guwahati and Goa, which are headed by the Assistant Directors. The Directorate has also a Unit at Madurai, which is headed by a Chief Enforcement Officer. Besides, there are three Special Directors of Enforcement and one Additional Director of Enforcement.

The main functions of the Directorate are as under:

- To collect and develop intelligence relating to violation of the provisions of Foreign Exchange Regulation Act and while working out the same, depending upon the circumstances of the case:
- To conduct searches of suspected persons, conveyances and premises for seizing incriminating materials (including Indian and foreign currencies involved) and/ or.
- To enquire into and investigate suspected violations of provisions of the Foreign Exchange Management Act.
- To adjudicate cases of violations of Foreign Exchange Management Act for levying penalties departmentally and also for confiscating the amounts involved in contravent ions;
- To realise the penalties imposed in departmental adjudication.

PROCEDURAL PROVISIONS

For enforcing the provisions of various sections of FEMA, 1999, the officers of Enforcement Directorate of the level of Assistant Director and above will have to undertake the following functions:

- Collection and development of intelligence/information.
- Keeping surveillance over suspects.
- Searches of persons/vehicles as per provisions of Income-tax Act, 1961.
- Searches of premises as per provisions of Income-tax Act, 1961.
- Summoning of persons for giving evidence and producing of documents as per provisions of Income-tax Act, 1961.
- Power to examine persons as per provisions of Income-tax Act, 1961.
- Power to call for any information/document as per provisions of Income-tax Act, 1961.
- Power to seize documents etc. as per provisions of Income-tax Act, 1961.
- Custody of documents as per Income-tax Act, 1961.
- Adjudication and appeals-Officers of and above the rank of Dy Director of Enforcement, are empowered to adjudicate cases of contravention of the provisions of the Act; these proceedings which are quasi-judicial in nature, start with the issuance of show cause notice; in the event of cause shown by the Notice-not being found satisfactory, further proceedings are held, vis. personal hearing, in which the notice has a further right to present his defence, either in person or through any authorised representative; on conclusion of these proceedings, the adjudicating authority has to examine and consider the evidence on record, in its entirety and in case the charges not being found proved, the notice is acquitted, and in the event of charges being found substantiated, such penalty, as is considered appropriate as per provisions of section 13 of the Act can be imposed, besides confiscation of amounts involved in these contraventions.

9

Insurance in India

Insurance is a federal subject in India and has history dating back till 1818. Life and general insurance in India is still a nascent sector with huge potential for various global players with the life insurance premiums accounting to 2.5% of the country's GDP while general insurance premiums to 0.65% of India's GDP.

The Insurance sector in India has gone through a number of phases and changes, particularly in the recent years when the Govt. of India in 1999 opened up the insurance sector by allowing private companies to solicit insurance and also allowing FDI up to 26%.

Ever since, the Indian insurance sector is considered as a booming market with every other global insurance company wanting to have a lion's share. Currently, the largest life insurance company in India is still owned by the government.

HISTORY OF INSURANCE IN INDIA

Insurance in India has its history dating back till 1818, when Oriental Life Insurance Company started was started by Europeans in Kolkata to cater to the needs of European community. Pre-independent era in India saw discrimination among the life of foreigners and Indians with higher premiums being charged for the latter. It was only in the year 1870, Bombay Mutual Life Assurance Society, the first Indian insurance company covered Indian lives at normal rates.

At the dawn of the twentieth century, insurance companies started mushrooming up. In the year 1912, the Life Insurance

Companies Act, and the Provident Fund Act were passed to regulate the insurance business.

The Life Insurance Companies Act, 1912 made it necessary that the premium rate tables and periodical valuations of companies should be certified by an actuary. However, the disparage still existed as discrimination between Indian and foreign companies.

Related Acts

The insurance sector went through a full circle of phases from being unregulated to completely regulated and then currently being partly deregulated. It is governed by a number of acts, with the first one being the Insurance Act, 1938.

The Insurance Act, 1938

The Insurance Act, 1938 was the first legislation governing all forms of insurance to provide strict state control over insurance business.

Life Insurance Corporation Act, 1956

Even though the first legislation was enacted in 1938, it was only in 19th of January, 1956, that life insurance in India was completely nationalized, through the Life Insurance Corporation Act, 1956. There were 245 insurance companies of both Indian and foreign origin in 1956. Nationalization was accomplished by the govt. acquisition of the management of the companies. The Life Insurance Corporation of India was created on 1st September, 1956, as a result and has grown to be the largest insurance company in India as of 2006.

General Insurance Business (Nationalisation) Act, 1972

The General Insurance Business (Nationalisation) Act, 1972 was enacted to nationalise the 100 odd general insurance companies and subsequently merging them into four companies. All the companies were amalgamated into National Insurance, New India Assurance, Oriental Insurance, United India Insurance which were headquartered in each of the four metropolitan cities.

Insurance Regulatory and Development Authority (IRDA) Act, 1999

Till 1999, there were not any private insurance companies in the Indian insurance sector. The Govt. of India, then introduced the Insurance Regulatory and Development Authority Act in 1999, thereby de-regulating the insurance sector and allowing private companies into the insurance. Further, foreign investment was also allowed and capped at 26% holding in the Indian insurance companies.

10

Capital Management

In economics, capital or capital goods or real capital refers to durable produced goods for use as a factor of production. Steam shovels (equipment) and office buildings (structures) are examples.

Real capital, such as physical capital, may be acquired with money or financial capital. That is a link to other usages of 'capital'. In finance and accounting, capital generally refers to financial wealth, especially that used to start or maintain a business.

Problems of aggregating capital are treated in the capital controversy and economic capital.

CAPITAL IN NARROW AND BROAD USES

In classical economics, capital is one of three factors of production. The others are land and labor. Goods with the following features are capital:

- It can be used in the production of other goods (this is what makes it a factor of production).
- It was produced, in contrast to "land," which refers to naturally occurring resources such as geographical locations and minerals.
- It is not used up immediately in the process of production, unlike raw materials or intermediate goods.

These distinctions of convenience carried over to neoclassical economics with little change in formal analysis for an extended period. Illustrations typically described capital as physical items, such as tools, buildings, and vehicles that are used in the production process.

Since at least the 1960s economists have increasingly focused on broader forms of capital. For example, investment in skills and education can be viewed as building up human capital or knowledge capital, and investments in intellectual property can be viewed as building up intellectual capital. These terms lead to certain questions and controversies discussed in those articles. Human development theory describes human capital as being composed of distinct social, imitative and creative elements:

- Social capital is the value of network trusting relationships between individuals in an economy.
- Individual capital which is inherent in persons, protected by societies, and trades labor for trust or money. Close parallel concepts are 'talent', 'ingenuity', 'leadership', 'trained bodies', or 'innate skills' that cannot reliably be reproduced by using any combination of any of the others above. In traditional economic analysis individual capital is more usually called labour.

Further classifications of capital that have been used in various theoretical or applied uses include:

- Financial capital which represents obligations, and is liquidated as money for trade, and owned by legal entities. It is in the form of capital assets, traded in financial markets. Its market value is not based on the historical accumulation of money invested but on the perception by the market of its expected revenues and of the risk entailed.
- Natural capital which is inherent in ecologies and protected by communities to support life, e.g. a river which provides farms with water.
- Infrastructural capital is non-natural support systems (e.g. clothing, shelter, roads, personal computers) that minimize need for new social trust, instruction, and natural resources. (Almost all of this is manufactured, leading to the older term manufactured capital, but some arises from interactions with natural capital, and

so it makes more sense to describe it in terms of its appreciation/depreciation process, rather than its origin: much of natural capital grows back, infrastructural capital must be built and installed.)

In part as a result, separate literatures have developed to describe both natural capital and social capital. Such terms reflect a wide consensus that nature and society both function in such a similar manner as traditional industrial infrastructural capital, that it is entirely appropriate to refer to them as different types of capital in themselves. In particular, they can be used in the production of other goods, are not used up immediately in the process of production, and can be enhanced (if not created) by human effort. There is also a literature of intellectual capital and intellectual property law. However, this increasingly distinguishes means of capital investment, and collection of potential rewards for patent, copyright (creative or individual capital), and trademark (social trust or social capital) instruments.

CAPITAL IN CLASSICAL ECONOMICS AND BEYOND

Within classical economics, David Ricardo distinguished fixed capital from circulating capital, including raw materials and intermediate products. For an enterprise, both were kinds of capital.

Karl Marx adds a distinction that is often confused with Ricardo's. In Marxian theory, variable capital refers to a capitalist's investment in labor-power, seen as the only source of surplus-value. It is called "variable" since the amount of value it can produce varies from the amount it consumes, i.e., it creates new value. On the other hand, constant capital refers to investment in non-human factors of production, such as plant and machinery, which Marx takes to contribute only its own replacement value to the commodities it is used to produce. It is constant, in that the amount of value committed in the original investment, and the amount retrieved in the form of commodities produced, remains constant.

Investment or capital accumulation in classical economic theory is the production of increased capital. In order to invest, goods must be produced which are not to be immediately consumed, but instead used to produce other goods as a means of production. Investment is closely related to saving, though it is not the same. As Keynes pointed out, saving involves not spending all of one's income on current goods or services, while investment refers to spending on a specific type of goods, i.e., capital goods.

The Austrian economist Eugen von Böhm-Bawerk maintained that capital intensity was measured by the roundaboutness of production processes. Since capital is defined by him as being goods of higher-order, or goods used to produce consumer goods, and derived their value from them, being future goods.

CAPITALISM

Capitalism generally refers to an economic system in which the means of production are mostly privately owned and operated for profit and in which distribution, production and pricing of goods and services are determined in a largely free market. It is usually considered to involve the right of individuals and groups of individuals acting as "legal persons" or corporations to trade capital goods, labor and money. The term also refers to several theories that developed in the context of the Industrial Revolution and the Cold War meant to explain, justify, or critique the private ownership of capital; to explain the operation of capitalistic markets; and to guide the application or elimination of government regulation of property and markets.

Capitalist economic practices became institutionalized in Europe between the 16th and 19th centuries, although some features of capitalist organization existed in the ancient world. Capitalism has emerged as the Western world's dominant economic system since the decline of feudalism, which eroded traditional political and religious restraints on capitalist exchange. Since the Industrial Revolution, capitalism gradually spread from Europe, particularly from Britain, across political and cultural frontiers. In the 19th and 20th centuries, capitalism provided the main, but not exclusive, means of industrialization throughout much of the world.

The concept of capitalism has limited analytic value, given the great variety of historical cases over which it is applied, varying in time, geography, politics and culture. Some economists have specified a variety of different types of capitalism, depending on specifics of concentration of economic power and wealth, and methods of capital accumulation (Scott 2005). During the last century capitalism has been contrasted with centrally planned economies. Most developed countries are usually regarded as capitalist, but some are also often called mixed economies due to government ownership and regulation of production, trade, commerce, taxation, money-supply, and physical infrastructure.

Perspectives on the Characteristics of Capitalism

The concept of capitalism has evolved over time, with later thinkers often building on the analyses of earlier thinkers. Moreover, the component concepts used in defining capitalism-such as private ownership, markets, and investment-have evolved along with changes in theory, in law, and in practice. The following subsections describe several schools of thought in which the thinkers involved do not necessarily agree on all analytic points, but participate in a common general approach to understanding what capitalism is.

CLASSICAL POLITICAL ECONOMY

The "classical" tradition in economic thought emerged in Britain in the late 18th century. The classical political economists Adam Smith, David Ricardo, Jean-Baptiste Say, and John Stuart Mill published analyses of the production, distribution, and exchange of goods in a capitalist economy that have since formed the basis of study for most contemporary economists. Contributions to this tradition are also found in the earlier work of David Hume and the Physiocrats like Richard Cantillon.

Adam Smith's attack on mercantilism and his reasoning for "the system of natural liberty" in The Wealth of Nations (1776), are usually taken as the beginning of classical political economy. Smith devised a set of concepts that remain strongly associated with capitalism today, particularly his theory of the "invisible hand" of the market, through which the pursuit of individual interest produces a collective good for society. He criticized monopolies, tariffs, duties, and other state enforced restrictions of his time and believed that the market is the most fair and efficient arbitrator of resources. This view was shared by David Ricardo, second most important of the classical political economists and one of the most influential economists of modern times. In The Principles of Political Economy and Taxation (1817) he developed the law of comparative advantage, which explains why it is profitable for two parties to trade, even if one of the trading partners is more efficient in every type of economic production. This principle supports the economic case for free trade. Ricardo was a supporter of Say's Law and held the view that full employment is the normal equilibrium for a competitive economy. He also argued that inflation is closely related to changes in quantity of money and credit and was a proponent of the law of diminishing returns, which states that each additional unit of input yields less and less additional output.

The values of classical political economy are strongly associated with the classical liberal doctrine of minimal government intervention in the economy. Liberal capitalist thought has generally assumed a clear division between the economy and other realms of social activity, such as the state.

MARXIAN POLITICAL ECONOMY

Karl Marx considered capitalism to be a historically specific mode of production (the way in which the productive property is owned and controlled, combined with the corresponding social relations between individuals based on their connection with the process of production) in which capital has become the dominant mode of production (Burnham). The capitalist stage of development or "bourgeois society," for Marx, represented the most advanced form of social organization to date.

Following Adam Smith, Marx distinguished the use value of commodities from their exchange value in the market. Capital, according to Marx, is created with the purchase of commodities for the purpose of creating new commodities with an exchange value higher than the sum of the original purchases. For Marx, the use of labor power had itself become a commodity under capitalism; the exchange value of labor power, as reflected in the wage, is less than the value it produces for the capitalist. This difference in values, he argues, constitutes surplus value, which the capitalists extract and accumulate. In his book Capital, Marx argues that the capitalist mode of production is distinguished by how the owners of capital extract this surplus from workers-all prior societies had extracted surplus labor, but capitalism was new in doing so via the sale-value of produced commodities.

For Marx, this cycle of the extraction of the surplus value by the owners of capital or the bourgeoisie becomes the basis of class struggle. However, this argument is intertwined with Marx's labor theory of value asserting that labor is the source of all value, and thus of profit. This theory is contested by most current economists, including some contemporary Marxian economists (Scott 2005). One line of subsequent Marxian thinking sees the centrally-planned economic systems of existing "communist" societies that were still based on exploitation of labor as "state capitalism." Some 20th century Marxian economists consider capitalism to be a social formation where capitalist class processes dominate, but are not exclusive (Resnick & Wolff). Capitalist class processes, to these thinkers, are simply those in which surplus labour takes the form of surplus value, usable as capital; other tendencies for utilization of labor nonetheless exist simultaneously in existing societies where capitalist processes are predominant.

WEBERIAN POLITICAL SOCIOLOGY

In some social sciences, the understanding of the defining characteristics of capitalism have been strongly influenced by 19th century German social theorist Max Weber. Weber considered market exchange, rather than production, as the defining feature of capitalism; capitalist enterprises, in contrast to their counterparts in prior modes of economic activity, was their rationalization of production, directed toward maximizing efficiency and productivity. According to Weber, workers in pre-capitalist economic institutions understood work in term of a personal relationship between master and journeyman in a guild, or between lord and peasant in a manor.

In his book The Protestant Ethic and the Spirit of Capitalism (1904-1905), Weber sought to trace how capitalism transformed traditional modes of economic activity. For Weber, the 'spirit' of rational calculation eroded traditional restraints on capitalist exchange, and fostered the development of modern capitalism. This 'spirit' was gradually codified by law; rendering wage-laborers legally 'free' to sell work; encouraging the development of technology aimed at the organization of production on the basis of rational principles; and clarifying the separation of the public and private lives of workers, especially between the home and the workplace. Therefore, unlike Marx, Weber did not see capitalism as primarily the consequence of changes in the means of production. Instead, for Weber the origins of capitalism rested chiefly in the rise of a new entrepreneurial 'spirit' in the political and cultural realm. In the Protestant Ethic, Weber suggested that the origins of this 'spirit' was related to the rise of Protestantism, particularly Calvinism.

Capitalism, for Weber, is the most advanced economic system ever developed over the course of human history. Weber associated capitalism with the advance of the business corporation, public credit, and the further advance of bureaucracy of the modern world. Although Weber defended capitalism against its socialist critics of the period, he saw its rationalizing tendencies as a possible threat to traditional cultural values and institutions, and a possible 'iron cage' constraining human freedom.

THE GERMAN HISTORICAL SCHOOL AND THE AUSTRIAN SCHOOL

From the perspective of the German Historical School, capitalism is primarily identified in terms of the organization of production for markets. Although this perspective shares similar theoretical roots with that of Weber, its emphasis on markets and money lends it different focus (Burnham). For followers of the German Historical School, the key shift from traditional modes of economic activity to capitalism involved the shift from medieval restrictions on credit and money to the modern monetary economy combined with an emphasis on the profit motive.

Ludwig von Mises

In the late 19th century the German historical school of economics diverged with the emerging Austrian School of economics, led at the time by Carl Menger. Later generations of followers of the Austrian School continued to be influential in Western economic thought through much of the 20th century. The Austrian economist Joseph Schumpeter, a forerunner of the Austrian School of economics, emphasized the "creative destruction" of capitalism-the fact that market economies undergo constant change. At any moment of time, posits Schumpeter, there are rising industries and declining industries. Schumpeter, and many contemporary economists influenced by his work, argue that resources should flow from the declining to the expanding industries for an economy to grow, but they recognized that sometimes resources are slow to withdraw from the declining industries because of various forms of institutional resistance to change.

The Austrian economists Ludwig von Mises and Friedrich Hayek were among the leading defenders of market capitalism against 20th century proponents of socialist planned economies. Mises and Hayek argued that only market capitalism could manage a complex, modern economy. Since a modern economy produces such a large array of distinct goods and services, and consists of such a large array of consumers and enterprises, asserted Mises and Hayek, the information problems facing any other form of economic organization other than market capitalism would exceed its capacity to handle information. Thinkers within Supply-side economics built on the work of the Austrian School, and particular emphasize Say's Law: "supply creates its own demand." Capitalism, to this school, is defined by lack of state restraint on the decisions of producers.

Austrian economics has been a major influence on the ideology of libertarianism, which considers laissez-faire capitalism to be the ideal economic system.

Keynesian Economics

In his 1936 The General Theory of Employment, Interest, and Money, the British economist John Maynard Keynes argued that capitalism suffered a basic problem in its ability to recover from periods of slowdowns in investment. Keynes argued that a capitalist economy could remain in an indefinite equilibrium despite high unemployment. Essentially rejecting Say's law, he argued that some people may have a liquidity preference which would see them rather hold money than buy new goods or services, which therefore raised the prospect that the Great Depression would not end without what he termed in the General Theory "a somewhat comprehensive socialization of investment."

Keynesian economics challenged the notion that laissez-faire capitalist economics could operate well on their own, without state intervention used to promote aggregate demand, fighting high unemployment and deflation of the sort seen during the 1930s. He and his followers recommended "pump-priming" the economy to avoid recession: cutting taxes, increasing government borrowing, and spending during an economic down-turn. This was to be accompanied by trying to control wages nationally partly through the use of inflation to cut real wages and to deter people from holding money. The premises of Keynes's work have, however, since been challenged by neoclassical and supply-side economics and the Austrian School.

Another challenge to Keynesian thinking came from his colleague Piero Sraffa, and subsequently from the Neo-Ricardian school that followed Sraffa. In Sraffa's highly-technical analysis, capitalism is defined by an entire system of social relations among both producers and consumers, but with a primary emphasis on the demands of production. According to Sraffa, the tendency of capital to seek its highest rate of profit causes a dynamic instability in social and economic relations.

NEOCLASSICAL ECONOMICS AND THE CHICAGO SCHOOL

Today, most academic research on capitalism in the English-speaking world draws on neoclassical economic thought. It favors extensive market coordination and relatively neutral patterns of governmental market regulation aimed at maintaining property rights, rather than privileging particular social actors; deregulated labor markets; corporate governance dominated by financial owners of firms; and financial systems depending chiefly on capital market-based financing rather than state financing.

The Chicago School of economics is best known for its free market advocacy and monetarist ideas. According to Milton Friedman and monetarists, market economies are inherently stable if left to themselves and depressions result only from government intervention. Friedman, for example, argued that the Great Depression was result of a contraction of the money supply, controlled by the Federal Reserve, and not by the lack of investment as Keynes had argued. Ben Bernanke, Chairman of the Federal Reserve, later acknowledged that Friedman was right to blame Federal Reserve for the Great Depression.

Neoclassical economists, which today are the majority of economists, consider value to be subjective, varying from person to person and for the same person at different times, and thus reject the labor theory of value. Marginalism is the theory that economic value results from marginal utility and marginal cost (the marginal concepts). These economists see capitalists as earning profits by forgoing current consumption, by taking risks, and by organizing production.

Historical Perspective

Private ownership of some means of production has existed at least since the invention of agriculture. However, in feudal society much of this property was considered to be inalienable and so capital markets were not established. Some writers see medieval guilds as forerunners of the modern capitalist concern (especially through using apprentices as a kind of paid laborer); but economic activity was bound by customs and controls which, along with the rule of the aristocracy which would expropriate wealth through arbitrary fines, taxes and enforced loans, meant that profits were difficult to accumulate. By the 18th century, however, these barriers to profit were overcome and capitalism became the dominant economic system of much of the world.

In the period between the late 15th century and the late 18th century the institution of private property was brought into existence in the full, legal meaning of the term. Important contribution to the theory of property is found in the work of

John Locke, who argued that the right to private property is one of natural rights. Since the Industrial Revolution much of Europe underwent a thoroughgoing economic transformation associated with the rise of capitalism and levels of wealth and economic output in the Western world have risen dramatically.

Over the course of the past five hundred years, capital has been accumulated by a variety of different methods, in a variety of scales, and associated with a great deal of variation in the concentration of economic power and wealth (Scott 2005). Much of the history of the past five hundred years is concerned with the development of capitalism in its various forms, its defense and its rejection, particularly by socialists.

MERCANTILISM

Earliest stages of modern capitalism, arising in the period between the 16th and 18th centuries, are commonly described as merchant capitalism and mercantilism (Burnham; EB). This period was associated with geographic discoveries by merchant overseas traders, especially from England and the Low Countries; the European colonization of the Americas; and the rapid growth in overseas trade. The associated rise of a bourgeoisie class eclipsed the prior feudal system.

Mercantilism was a system of trade for profit, although commodities were still largely produced by non-capitalist production methods (Scott 2005). Noting the various pre-capitalist features of mercantilism, Karl Polanyi argued that capitalism did not emerge until the establishment of free trade in Britain in the 1830s.

Under mercantilism, European merchants, backed by state controls, subsidies, and monopolies, made most of their profits from the buying and selling of goods. In the words of Francis Bacon, the purpose of mercantilism was "the opening and well-balancing of trade; the cherishing of manufacturers; the banishing of idleness; the repressing of waste and excess by sumptuary laws; the improvement and husbanding of the soil; the regulation of prices..." Similar practices of economic regimentation had begun earlier in the medieval towns. However, under mercantilism, given the contemporaneous rise of the absolutism, the state superseded the local guilds as the regulator of the economy.

Among the major tenets of mercantilist theory was bullionism, a doctrine stressing the importance of accumulating precious metals. Mercantilists argued that a state should export more goods than it imported so that foreigners would have to pay the difference in precious metals. Mercantilists asserted that only raw materials that could not be extracted at home should be imported; and promoted government subsides, such as the granting of monopolies and protective tariffs, were necessary to encourage home production of manufactured goods.

Proponents of mercantilism emphasized state power and overseas conquest as the principal aim of economic policy. If a state could not supply its own raw materials, according to the mercantilists, it should acquire colonies from which they could be extracted. Colonies constituted not only sources of supply for raw materials but also markets for finished products. Because it was not in the interests of the state to allow competition, held the mercantilists, colonies should be prevented from engaging in manufacturing and trading with foreign powers.

Industrial Capitalism and Laissez-faire

Mercantilism declined in Great Britain in the mid-18th century, when a new group of economic theorists, led by Adam Smith, challenged fundamental mercantilist doctrines as the belief that the amount of the world's wealth remained constant and that a state could only increase its wealth at the expense of another state. However, in more undeveloped economies, such as Prussia and Russia, with their much younger manufacturing bases, mercantilism continued to find favor after other states had turned to newer doctrines.

The mid-18th century gave rise to industrial capitalism, made possible by the accumulation of vast amounts of capital under the merchant phase of capitalism and its investment in machinery. Industrial capitalism, which Marx dated from the last third of the 18th century, marked the development of the factory system of manufacturing, characterized by a complex division of labor between and within work process and the routinization of work tasks; and finally established the global domination of the capitalist mode of production (Burnham).

During the resulting Industrial Revolution, the industrialist replaced the merchant as a dominant actor in the capitalist system and affected the decline of the traditional handicraft skills of artisans, guilds, and journeymen. Also during this period, capitalism marked the transformation of relations between the British landowning gentry and peasants, giving rise to the production of cash crops for the market rather than for subsistence on a feudal manor. The surplus generated by the rise of commercial agriculture encouraged increased mechanization of agriculture.

The rise of industrial capitalism was also associated with the decline of mercantilism. Mid-to late-nineteenth-century Britain is widely regarded as the classic case of laissez-faire capitalism (Burnham). Laissez-faire gained favor over mercantilism in Britain in the 1840s with the repeal of the Corn Laws and the Navigation Acts. In line with the teachings of the classical political economists, led by Adam Smith and David Ricardo, Britain embraced liberalism, encouraging competition and the development of a market economy.

FINANCE CAPITALISM AND MONOPOLY CAPITALISM

In the late 19th century, the control and direction of large areas of industry came into the hands of financiers. This period has been defined as "finance capitalism," characterized by the subordination of process of production to the accumulation of money profits in a financial system. Major features of capitalism in this period included the establishment of huge industrial cartels or monopolies; the ownership and management of industry by financiers divorced from the production process; and the development of a complex system of banking, an equity market, and corporate holdings of capital through stock ownership. Increasingly, large industries and land became the subject of profit and loss by financial speculators.

Late 19th and early 20th century capitalism has also been described as an era of "monopoly capitalism," marked by the movement from the laissez-faire phase of capitalism to the concentration of capital into large monopolistic or oligopolistic holdings by banks and financiers, and characterized by the growth of large corporations and a division of labor separating shareholders, owners, and managers (Scott 2005).

By the last quarter of the 19th century, the emergence of large industrial trusts had provoked legislation in the U.S. to reduce the monopolistic tendencies of the period. Gradually, the U.S. federal government played a larger and larger role in passing antitrust laws and regulation of industrial standards for key industries of special public concern. By the end of the 19th century, economic depressions and boom and bust business cycles had become a recurring problem. In particular, the Long Depression of the 1870s and 1880s and the Great Depression of the 1930s affected almost the entire capitalist world, and generated discussion about capitalism's long-term survival prospects. During 1930s, Marxist commentators often posited the possibility of capitalism's decline or demise, often in alleged contrast to the ability of the Soviet Union to avoid suffering the effects of the global depression.

Capitalism following the Great Depression

The economic recovery of the world's leading capitalist economies in the period following the end of the Great Depression and the Second World War-a period of unusually rapid growth by historical standards-eased discussion of capitalism's eventual decline or demise (Engerman 2001).

In the period following the global depression of the 1930s, the state played an increasingly prominent role in the capitalistic system throughout much of the world. In 1929, for example, total U.S. government expenditures (federal, state, and local) amounted to less than one-tenth of GNP; from the 1970s they amounted to around one-third (EB). Similar increases were seen in all industrialized capitalist economies, some of which, such as France, have reached even higher ratios of government expenditures to GNP than the United States. These economies have since been widely described as "mixed economies."

During the postwar boom, a broad array of new analytical tools in the social sciences were developed to explain the social and economic trends of the period, including the concepts of post-industrial society and welfare statism (Burnham). The phase of capitalism from the beginning of the postwar period through the 1970s has sometimes been described as "state capitalism", especially by Marxian thinkers.

The long postwar boom ended in the 1970s, amid the economic crises experienced following the 1973 oil crisis. The "stagflation" of the 1970s led many economic commentators politicians to embrace neoliberal policy prescriptions inspired by the laissez-faire capitalism and classical liberalism of the 19th century, particularly under the influence of Friedrich Hayek and Milton Friedman. In particular, monetarism, a theoretical alternative to Keynesianism that is more compatible with laissez-faire, gained increasing support in the capitalist world, especially under the leadership of Ronald Reagan in the U.S. and Margaret Thatcher in the UK in the 1980s.

GLOBALIZATION

Although overseas trade has been associated with the development of capitalism for over five hundred years, some thinkers argue that a number of trends associated with globalization have acted to increase the mobility of people and capital since the last quarter of the 20th century, combining to circumscribe the room to maneuver of states in choosing non-capitalist models of development. Today, these trends have bolstered the argument that capitalism should now be viewed as a truly world system (Burnham). However, other thinkers argue that globalization, even in its quantitative degree, is no greater now than during earlier periods of capitalist trade.

After the abandonment of the Bretton Woods system and the strict state control of foreign exchange rates, the total value of transactions in foreign exchange was estimated to be at least twenty times greater than that of all foreign movements of goods and services (EB). The internationalization of finance, which some see as beyond the reach of state control, combined with the growing ease with which large corporations have been able to relocate their operations to low-wage states, has posed the question of the 'eclipse' of state sovereignty, arising from the growing 'globalization' of capital.

Economic growth in the last half-century has been relatively strong. Life expectancy has almost doubled in the developing world since the postwar years and is starting to close the gap on the developed world where the improvement has been smaller. Infant mortality has decreased in every developing region of the world. Income inequality for the world as a whole is diminishing. Many other variables such as per capita food supplies, literacy, child labor, and access to clean water have also improved.

POLITICAL ADVOCACY

Proponents of Capitalism

Many theorists and policymakers in predominantly capitalist nations have emphasized capitalism's ability to promote economic growth, as measured by Gross Domestic Product (GDP), capacity utilization or standard of living. This argument was central, for example, to Adam Smith's advocacy of letting a free market control production and price, and allocate resources. Many theorists have noted that this increase in global GDP over time conincides with the emergence of the modern world capitalist system. While the measurements are not identical, proponents argue that increasing GDP (per capita) is empirically shown to bring about improved standards of living, such as better availability of food, housing, clothing, health care, reduction of working hours, and freedom from work for children and the elderly. Proponents also believe that a capitalist economy offers far more opportunities for individuals to raise their income through new professions or business ventures than do other economic forms. To their thinking, this potential is much greater than in either traditional feudal or tribal societies or in socialist societies.

Milton Friedman has argued that the "economic freedom" of competitive capitalism is a requisite of political freedom. Friedman argued that centralized control of economic activity is always accompanied by political repression. In his view, transactions in a market economy are voluntary, and the wide diversity that voluntary activity permits is a fundamental threat to repressive political leaders and greatly diminish power to coerce. Friedman's view was also shared by Friedrich Hayek and John Maynard Keynes, both of whom believed that capitalism is vital for freedom to survive and thrive.

Austrian School economists have argued that capitalism can organize itself into a complex system without an external guidance or planning mechanism. Friedrich Hayek coined the term "catallaxy" to describe what he considered the phenomenon of self-organization underpinning capitalism. From this perspective, in process of self-organization, the profit motive has an important role. From transactions between buyers and sellers price systems emerge, and prices serve as a signal as to the urgent and unfilled wants of people. The promise of profits gives entrepreneurs incentive to use their knowledge and resources to satisfy those wants. Thus the activities of millions of people, each seeking his own interest, are coordinated.

This decentralized system of coordination is viewed by some supporters of capitalism as one of its greatest strengths. They argue that it permits many solutions to be tried, and that real-world competition generally finds a good solution to emerging challenges. In contrast, they argue, central planning often selects inappropriate solutions as a result of faulty forecasting. However, in all existing modern economies, the state conducts some degree of centralized economic planning (using such tools as allowing the country's central bank to set base interest rates), ostensibly as an attempt to improve efficiency, attenuate cyclical volatility, and further particular social goals. Proponents who follow the Austrian School argue that even this limited control creates inefficiencies because we cannot predict the long-term activity of the economy. Milton Friedman, for example, has argued that the Great depression was caused by the erroneous policy by the Federal reserve.

CRITICS OF CAPITALISM

Capitalism has met with strong opposition throughout its history, largely from the left, but also from the right; and from religious elements. Many 19th century conservatives were among the most strident critics of capitalism, seeing market exchange and commodity production as threats to cultural and religious traditions.

Prominent leftist critics have included socialists like Karl Marx, Frantz Fanon, Vladimir Lenin, Mao Zedong, Leon Trotsky and anarchists including Pierre-Joseph Proudhon, Mikhail

Bakunin, Peter Kropotkin, Murray Bookchin, Noam Chomsky, and others. Movements like the Luddites, Narodniks, Shakers, Utopian Socialists and others have opposed capitalism for various reasons. Marxism has influenced the creation of social democratic and labour parties, which seek change through existing democratic channels instead of revolution. These parties believe that capitalism should be heavily regulated instead of abolished. Many aspects of capitalism have come under attack from the relatively recent anti-globalization movement.

Some religions criticize or outright oppose specific elements of capitalism. Some traditions of Judaism, Christianity, and Islam forbid lending money at interest, although methods of Islamic banking have been developed. Christianity has been a source of both praise and criticism for capitalism, particularly its materialist aspects. The first socialists drew many of their principles from Christian values, against the "bourgeois" values of profiteering, greed, selfishness and hoarding. Many Christians do not oppose capitalism entirely, but support a mixed economy in order to ensure adequate labour standards and relations, as well as economic justice. There are many Protestant denominations (particularly in the United States) who have reconciled with-or are ardently in favour of-capitalism, particularly in opposition to secular socialism.

Some problems claimed to be associated with capitalism include: unfair and inefficient distribution of wealth and power; a tendency toward market monopoly or oligopoly (and government by oligarchy); imperialism, various forms of economic exploitation; and phenomena such as social alienation, inequality, unemployment, and economic instability. Near the start of the 20th century, Vladimir Lenin claimed that state use of military power to defend capitalist interests abroad was an inevitable corollary of monopoly capitalism. Some environmentalists claim that capitalism requires continual economic growth, and will inevitably deplete the finite natural resources of the earth, and other resources utilized broadly. Some environmentalists, such as Murray Bookchin, have argued that capitalist production passes on environmental costs to all of society, and is unable to consider its impact upon ecosystems and the biosphere at large.

Some labor historians and other scholars have also argued that unfree labor-the use of a labor force comprised or slaves, indentured servants, criminal convicts, political prisoners and/ or other coerced persons-is compatible with capitalist relations. However, this view is controversial and is at odds with both conventional theorists of capitalism, and many of the critics named above.

DEMOCRACY, THE STATE AND LEGAL FRAMEWORKS

The relationship between the state, its formal mechanisms, and capitalist societies has been debated in many fields of social and political theory, with active discussion since the 19th century. Hernando de Soto is a contemporary economist who has argued that an important characteristic of capitalism is the functioning state protection of property rights in a formal property system where ownership and transactions are clearly recorded. According to de Soto, this is the process by which physical assets are transformed into capital, which in turn may be used in many more ways and much more efficiently in the market economy. A number of Marxian economists have argued that the Enclosure Acts in England, and similar legislation elsewhere, were an integral part of capitalist primitive accumulation and that specific legal frameworks of private land ownership have been integral to the development of capitalism.

New institutional economics, a field pioneered by Douglass North, stresses the need of capitalism for a legal framework to function optimally, and focuses on the relationship between the historical development of capitalism and the creation and maintenance of political and economic institutions. In new institutional economics and other fields focusing on public policy, economists seek to judge when and whether governmental intervention (such as taxes, welfare, and government regulation) can result in potential gains in efficiency. According to Gregory Mankiw, a New Keynesian economist, governmental intervention can improve on market outcomes under conditions of "market failure," or situations in which the market on its own does not allocate resources efficiently. Almost all nations have some kind of market regulations, although the desirable degree is debated.

The relationship between democracy and capitalism is a contentious area in theory and popular political movements. The extension of universal adult male suffrage in 19th century Britain occurred along with the development of industrial capitalism, and democracy become widespread at the same time as capitalism, leading many theorists to posit a causal relationship between them, or that each affects the other. However, in the 20th century, according to some authors, capitalism also accompanied a variety of political formations quite distinct from liberal democracies, including fascist regimes, monarchies, and single-party states (Burnham). While some thinkers argue that capitalist development more-or-less inevitably eventually leads to the emergence of democracy, others dispute this claim. Research on the democratic peace theory further argue that capitalist democracies rarely make war with one another and have little internal violence.

Some commentators argue that though economic growth under capitalism has led to democratization in the past, it may not do so in the future. Under this line of thinking, authoritarian regimes have been able to manage economic growth without making concessions to greater political freedom.

In response to criticism of the system, some proponents of capitalism have argued that its advantages are supported by empirical research. For example, advocates of different Index of Economic Freedom point to a statistical correlation between nations with more economic freedom (as defined by the Indices) and higher scores on variables such as income and life expectancy, including the poor in these nations. Some peer-reviewed studies find evidence for causation.

CORPORATE ECONOMY

Historically, corporatism or corporativism (Italian corporativismo) refers to a political or economic system in which power is given to civic assemblies that represent economic, industrial, agrarian, and professional groups. These civic assemblies, known as corporations (not necessarily the same as contemporary business corporations) are unelected bodies with an internal hierarchy; their purpose is to exert control over their respective areas of social or economic life. Thus, for example, a steel corporation would be a cartel composed of all the business leaders in the steel industry, coming together to discuss a common policy on prices and wages. When much political and economic power rests in the hands of such groups, then a corporatist system is in place.

The word "corporatism" is derived from the Latin word for body, corpus. This original meaning was not connected with the specific notion of a business corporation, but rather a general reference to anything collected as a body. Its usage reflects medieval European concepts of a whole society in which the various components each play a part in the life of the society, just as the various parts of the body serve specific roles in the life of a body. According to various theorists, corporatism was an attempt to create a "modern" version of feudalism by merging the "corporate" interests with those of the state.

Political scientists may also use the term corporatism to describe a practice whereby an authoritarian state, through the process of licensing and regulating officially-incorporated social, religious, economic, or popular organizations, effectively co-opts their leadership or circumscribes their ability to challenge state authority by establishing the state as the source of their legitimacy. This usage is particularly common in the area of East Asian studies, and is sometimes also referred to as state corporatism.

In Italian Fascism, this non-elected form of state 'officializing' of every interest into the state was professed to better circumvent the marginalization of singular interests as would happen by the unilateral end condition inherent in the democratic voting process. Which would better instead recognize or 'incorporate' every divergent interest as it stands alone into the state "organically", thus being the inspiration behind their use of the term Totalitarian, perceivable to them as not meaning a coercive system but described distinctly as without coercion in the 1932 Doctrine of Fascism as thus;

"...(The state) is not simply a mechanism which limits the sphere of the supposed liberties of the individual..." & "...Neither has the Fascist conception of authority anything in common with that of a police ridden State..." but rather clearly connoting "...Far from crushing the individual, the Fascist State multiplies his energies, just as in a regiment a soldier is not diminished but multiplied by the number of his fellow soldiers..."

This prospect in Italian Fascist Corporativism claimed to be the direct heir of Georges Sorel's Anarcho-syndicalism. Wherein each interest was to form as its own entity with separate organizing parameters according to their own standards, only however within the corporative model of Italian Fascism each was supposed to be incorporated through the auspices & organizing ability of a statist construct. This was by their reasoning the only possible way to achieve such a function, i.e. when resolved in the capability of an indissolvable state.

Contemporary popular usage of the term is more pejorative, especially when used as the shorter form corporatism (corporativism usually implies only the Italian construct indicating public rather than private organizing), emphasizing the role of business corporations in government decision-making at the expense of the public. The power of business to affect government legislation through lobbying and other avenues of influence in order to promote their interests is usually seen as detrimental to those of the public. In this respect, corporatism may be characterized as an extreme form of regulatory capture, and is also termed corporatocracy. If there is substantial military-corporate collaboration it is often called militarism or the military-industrial complex.

Some contemporary political scientists and sociologists use the term neo-corporatism to describe a process of bargaining between labor, capital, and government identified as occurring in some small, open economies (particularly in Europe) as a means of distinguishing their observations from popular pejorative usage and to highlight ties to classical theories.

ORIGINS OF CLASSICAL THEORIES

Corporatism is a form of class collaboration put forward as an alternative to class conflict, and was first proposed in Pope Leo XIII's 1891 encyclical Rerum Novarum, which influenced Catholic trade unions that organised in the early twentieth century to counter the influence of trade unions founded on a socialist ideology. Theoretical underpinnings came from the medieval traditions of guilds and craft-based economics; and later, syndicalism. Corporatism was encouraged by Pope Pius XI in his 1931 encyclical Quadragesimo Anno.

Gabriele D'Annunzio and anarcho-syndicalist Alceste de Ambris incorporated principles of corporative philosophy in their Charter of Carnaro.

One early and important theorist of corporatism was Adam Müller, an advisor to Prince Metternich in what is now eastern Germany and Austria. Müller propounded his views as an antidote to the twin "dangers" of the egalitarianism of the French Revolution and the laissez-faire economics of Adam Smith. In Germany and elsewhere there was a distinct aversion among rulers to unrestricted capitalism, owing to the feudalist and aristocratic tradition of giving state privileges to the wealthy and powerful.

Under fascism in Italy, business owners, employees, tradespeople, professionals, and other economic classes were organized into 22 guilds, or associations, known as "corporations" according to their industries, and these groups were given representation in a legislative body known as the Camera dei Fasci e delle Corporazioni.

Similar ideas were also ventilated in other European countries at the time. For instance, Austria under the Dollfuß dictatorship had a constitution modelled on that of Italy; but there were also conservative philosophers and/or economists advocating the corporate state, for example Othmar Spann. In Portugal, a similar ideal, but based on bottom-up individual moral renewal, inspired Salazar to work towards corporatism. He wrote the Portuguese Constitution of 1933, which is credited as the first corporatist constitution in the world.

NEO-CORPORATISM

In the recent literature of political science and sociology, corporatism (or neo-corporatism) lacks negative connotation. In the writings of Philippe Schmitter, Gerhard Lehmbruch, and their followers, "neo-corporatism" refers to social arrangements dominated by tri-partite bargaining between unions, the private sector (capital), and government. Such bargaining is oriented toward (a) dividing the productivity gains created in the economy "fairly" among the social partners and (b) gaining wage restraint in recessionary or inflationary periods.

Most political economists believe that such neo-corporatist arrangements are only possible in societies in which labor is highly organized and various labor unions are hierarchically organized in a single labor federation. Such "encompassing" unions bargain on behalf of all workers, and they have a strong incentive to balance the employment cost of high wages against the real income consequences of small wage gains. Many of the small, open European economies, such as Finland, Sweden, Austria, Norway, Ireland, and the Netherlands fit this classification. In the work of some scholars, such as Peter J. Katzenstein, neo-corporatist arrangements enable small open economies to effectively manage their relationship with the global economy. The adjustment to trade shocks occurs through a bargaining process in which the costs of adjustment are distributed evenly ("fairly") among the social partners.

Examples of modern neocorporatism include the ILO Conference, the Economic and Social Committee of the European Union, the collective agreement arrangements of the Scandinavian countries, the Dutch Poldermodel system of consensus, and the Republic of Ireland's system of Social Partnership. In Australia, the Labor Party governments of 1983-96 fostered a set of policies known as The Accord, under which the Australian Council of Trade Unions agreed to hold back demands for pay increases, the compensation being increased expenditure on the "social wage", Prime Minister Paul Keating's name for broad-based welfare programs. In Singapore, the National Wages Council and other state-created entities form a tripartite arrangement between the major trade unions (NTUC), employers, and the Government that coordinates the national economy. In Italy, the Carlo Azeglio Ciampi administration inaugurated in July 23' 1993 a concertation (Italian: concertazione) policy of peaceful agreement on salary rates between government, the three main trade unions and the Confindustria employers' federation. Before that, salary augmentations were always conquered by strikes.

In 2001 the Silvio Berlusconi administration put an end to concertation. Coincidentally, he was a billionaire.

Most theorists agree that traditional neo-corporatism is undergoing a crisis. In many classically corporatist countries, traditional bargaining is on the retreat. This crisis is often attributed to globalization, with increasing labour mobility and competition from developing countries. However, this claim is not undisputed with nations like Singapore still strongly following neo-corporatist models.

STATE CORPORATISM

While classical corporatism and its intellectual successor, neo-corporatism (and their critics) emphasize the role of corporate bodies in influencing government decision-making, corporatism used in the context of the study of autocratic states, particularly within East Asian studies, usually refers instead to a process by which the state uses officially-recognized organizations as a tool for restricting public participation in the political process and limiting the power of civil society.

Under such a system, as described by Jonathan Unger and Anita Chan in their essay China, Corporatism, and the East Asian Model, at the national level the state recognizes one and only one organization (say, a national labour union, a business association, a farmers' association) as the sole representative of the sectoral interests of the individuals, enterprises or institutions that comprise that organization's assigned constituency. The state determines which organizations will be recognized as legitimate and forms an unequal partnership of sorts with such organizations. The associations sometimes even get channelled into the policy-making processes and often help implement state policy on the government's behalf.

By establishing itself as the arbitrator of legitimacy and assigning responsibility for a particular constituency with one sole organization, the state limits the number of players with which it must negotiate its policies and co-opts their leadership into policing their own members. This arrangement is not limited to economic organizations such as business groups or trade unions; examples can also include social or religious groups. Examples abound, but one such would be the People's

Republic of China's Islamic Association of China, in which the state actively intervenes in the appointment of imams and controls the educational contents of their seminaries, which must be approved by the government to operate and which feature courses on "patriotic reeducation". Another example is the phenomenon known as "Japan, Inc.", in which major industrial conglomerates and their dependent workforces were consciously manipulated by the Japanese MITI to maximize postwar economic growth. In December 2005, Andrei Illarionov, former economic adviser to Vladimir Putin, claimed that Russia had become a corporativist state.

CRITICISM OF CORPORATISM

Corporatism or neo-corporatism is often used popularly as a pejorative term in reference to perceived tendencies in politics for legislators and administrations to be influenced or dominated by the interests of business enterprises, employers' organizations, and industry trade groups. The influence of other types of corporations, such as labor unions, is perceived to be relatively minor. In this view, government decisions are seen as being influenced strongly by which sorts of policies will lead to greater profits for favored companies.

Corporatism is also used to describe a condition of corporate-dominated globalization. Points enumerated by users of the term in this sense include the prevalence of very large, multinational corporations that freely move operations around the world in response to corporate, rather than public, needs; the push by the corporate world to introduce legislation and treaties which would restrict the abilities of individual nations to restrict corporate activity; and similar measures to allow corporations to sue nations over "restrictive" policies, such as a nation's environmental regulations that would restrict corporate activities.

In the United States, corporations representing many different sectors are involved in attempts to influence legislation through lobbying including many non-business groups, unions, membership organizations, and non-profits. While these groups have no official membership in any legislative body, they can often wield considerable power over law-makers. In recent times, the profusion of lobby groups and the increase in campaign contributions has led to widespread controversy and the McCain-Feingold Act. Many critics of free market theories, such as George Orwell, have argued that corporatism (in the sense of an economic system dominated by massive corporations) is the natural result of free market capitalism.

Critics of capitalism often argue that any form of capitalism would eventually devolve into corporatism, due to the concentration of wealth in fewer and fewer hands. A permutation of this term is corporate globalism. John Ralston Saul argues that most Western societies are best described as corporatist states, run by a small elite of professional and interest groups, that exclude political participation from the citizenry.

Other critics say that they are pro-capitalist, but anti-corporatist. They support capitalism but only when corporate power is separated from state power. These critics can be from both the right and the left.

In the United States Republican President Ronald Reagan echoed Republican President Herbert Hoover and other scholars who claimed that Franklin D. Roosevelt's New Deal programs represented a move in the direction of a corporatist state. In particular these critics focussed on the National Recovery Administration. In 1935 Herbert Hoover described some of the New Deal measures as "Fascist regimentation." In his 1951 memoirs [v 3, p 420] he used the phrases "early Roosevelt fascist measures", and "this stuff was pure fascism", and "a remaking of Mussolini's corporate state".

These claims continue to be aired in right-wing publications. These authors also discuss modern American corporatism.

Other critics argue that corporatist arrangements exclude some groups, notably the unemployed, and are thus responsible for high unemployment. This argument is the basis of the book Logic of Collective Action by Harvard economist Mancur Olson.

CORPORATISM AND FASCISM

Some critics equate too much corporate power and influence with fascism. Often they cite a quote claimed to be from Mussolini: "Fascism should more properly be called corporatism because it is the merger of state and corporate power." Several variations of the alleged quote exist. However the veracity of this quote is highly doubtful since the most common cited texts for the quote do not contain anything like this alleged quote.. Despite this, the alleged quote has entered into modern discourse, and it appears on thousands of web pages, and in books, and even a conspiracy theory advertisement in the Washington Post.. However, the alleged quote contradicts almost everything else written by Mussolini on the subject of the relationship between corporations and the Fascist State.

In one 1935 English translation of what Mussolini wrote, the term "corporative state" is used, but this has a different meaning from modern uses of the terms used to discuss business corporations. In that same translation, the phrase "national Corporate State of Fascism," refers to syndicalist corporatism. The dubious quote is sometimes claimed to more accurately summarize what Mussolini did and not what he said. However many scholars of fascism reject this claim.

There is a very old argument about who controlled whom in the fascist states of Italy and Germany at various points in the timeline of power. It is agreed that the army, the wealthy, and the big corporations ended up with much more say in decision making than other elements of the corporative state. There was a power struggle between the fascist parties/leaders and the army, wealthy, and big corporations. It waxed and waned as to who had more power at any given time. Scholars have used the term "Mussolini's corporate state" in many different ways.

NATURAL ECONOMY

Natural economy refers to a type of economy in which money is not used in the transfer of resources among people.

Belgian economic historian Henri Pirenne noted that:

"German economists have invented the term Naturalwirtschaft, natural economy, to describe the period prior to the invention of money. (...) The writers who describe this period as one of natural economy obviously do not intend the term to be understood in any absolute sense. They are well aware that ever since its invention, money has been in continuous use among all the civilised people of the West, and that the Roman Empire handed it on without interruption to its succession states. Thus when the early Middle Ages are described as a period of natural economy, all that is meant is that the part played by money was then so small as to be almost negligible. Undoubtedly there is a good deal of truth in this contention; but at the same time we must be on our guard against exaggeration" (Henri Pirenne, Economic and social history of medieval Europe. London: Routledge & Kegan Paul, 1936, p. 103-104).

The term is also used by Karl Marx in his economic writings such as Grundrisse and Capital. Marx comments as follows:

Natural economy, money-economy, and credit-economy have (...) been placed in opposition to one another as being the three characteristic economic forms of movement in social production. In the first place these three forms do not represent equivalent phases of development. The so-called credit-economy is merely a form of the money-economy, since both terms express functions or modes of exchange among the producers themselves. In developed capitalist production, the money-economy appears only as the basis of the credit-economy. The money-economy and credit-economy thus correspond only to different stages in the development of capitalist production, but they are by no means independent forms of exchange vis-à-vis natural economy. With the same justification one might contrapose as equivalents the very different forms of natural economy to those two economies. In the second place, since it is not the economy, i.e., the process of production itself that is emphasised as the distinguishing mark of the two categories, money-economy and credit-economy, but rather the mode of exchange-corresponding to that economy-between the various agents of production, or producers, the same should apply to the first category. Hence exchange economy instead of natural economy.

11

Market Economy

A market economy (also called a free market economy, free enterprise economy) is an economic system in which the production and distribution of goods and services takes place through the mechanism of free markets guided by a free price system rather than by the state in a planned economy. In a market economy businesses and consumers decide what they will produce and purchase, as opposed to a planned economy where the government decides what is to be produced and in what quantities.

A market economy has no central coordinator guiding its operation, yet theoretically self-organization emerges amidst the complex interplay of supply and demand and price regarding a multitude of goods and services. Supporters of a market economy generally hold that individuals pursuing their self-interest through trade has the incidental effect of bringing about a spontaneous order that is effective in supplying the greatest abundance of goods for society and in the most efficient manner. Adam Smith says that the individual who:

"intends only his own gain is led by an invisible hand to promote an end which was no part of his intention. Nor is it always the worse for society that it was no part of it. By pursuing his own interest [an individual] frequently promotes that of the society more effectually than when he really intends to promote it. I have never known much good done by those who affected to trade for the [common] good." (Wealth of Nations)

The economists' model of a free market is one in which there is no governmental intervention or other coercion. The theoretical model of a large-scale free market economy does not occur legally, however the underground economy may be seen as an actualized free market economy.

FREE MARKET ECONOMY

In order for an economy to be considered a true free market, the factors of labor, goods, services, and capital, must be free from government restrictions and trading barriers so they are able to move freely across borders. The United States has restrictions on the attainment of monopoly, but also grants monopoly rights in some cases. Less market restrictions are found in other countries, such as in Hong Kong and Singapore, according to the Index of Economic Freedom.

Free markets are also conflated with anarchy as many people believe that free market implies an absence of government. Only a few free market scholars advocate the elimination of government; most have believed government had a role to play, albeit a limited one (notably Adam Smith and Milton Friedman). Even anarcho-capitalists believe in the rule of law (either natural or contract) being defended by voluntarily-funded institutions.

Most free market scholars believe that governments should be limited to at least: operating a court system for the settlement of disputes, maintaining stable currency (combating inflation), protecting market competition and consumers, and protecting the country through national defense. These scholars debate and disagree with each other on whether or not governments are necessary to have government funded roads, schools, post offices, libraries, police stations, and fire stations, as some free market scholars believe the market can solve their externalities.

Although no country has ever had within its border an economy in which all markets were absolutely free, the term is typically not used in an absolute sense. Many states which are said to have a capitalist system have a high level of market freedom, even if it is less than some would prefer.

Decision Making

Generally market economies are bottom up in decisionmaking as consumers input information to producers through prices paid when purchasing products on the market. For a brief time during the 20th century even self described capitalist states engaged in top down market command where the government and or producers attempted to command and direct resources to valued uses. All states today have some form of control over the market that removes the free and unrestricted direction of resources from consumers and prices such as tariffs, and corporate subsidies. Milton Friedman and many other microeconomists, believe that these forms of intervention provide incentives for resources to be sent, and sometimes wasted, producing products society may not value as much as a product that is, as a result of these restrictions, not being produced in many ways.

However, the term "market economy" is not exclusive to traditional capitalist ownership where a corporation hires workers as a labor commodity to produce material wealth and boost shareholder profits. Market mechanisms have been utilized in a handful of socialist states, such as Yugoslavia and even Cuba to a very limited extent. China's government is still run by the Communist Party, but its economy involves considerable private enterprise and market forces in both private and public sectors. It is also possible to envision an economic system based on cooperative, democratic worker ownership and market allocation of final goods and services; the labor-managed market economy is one of several proposed forms of market socialism

MARKET EXTERNALITIES

Examples of market failures, or externalities, include negative externalities, monopolies, lack of provision of public goods, and social disparities such as extreme poverty. Market failures are the result of the market not receiving enough or appropriate information through signals such as prices. For example there is currently no way for the market to understand the cost or harm pollution causes to society. These failures are the reason some have thought that limited government intervention is necessary.

Milton Friedman believes that many market failures can be solved not through government regulation of current information but through information disclosure. Information disclosure would be a requirement of government law but would not actually seriously regulate how businesses operate. Instead the disclosure of information would allow the market to react to their behavior by allowing consumers to vote with their dollars given better information about the companies they do business with.

Friedman also argues for pollution permits to solve pollution externalities. By selling permits to the public, the public is now able to demonstrate a price for the harm or benefit caused by pollution. He believes that this type of government "regulation" allows better flowing information rather than the masking of current information to the market. If people really do value clean air, the information will be felt in the market and companies will react more quickly to be environmentally friendly.

Friedman believes governments may have a role in fixing market externalities but only if the government is helping solve information transmission problems not masking current information.'

GOVERNMENT INTERVENTION

It is possible for a market economy to have government intervention in the economy. The key difference between market economies and planned economies lies not with the degree of government influence but whether that influence is used to coercively preclude private decision. In a market economy, if the government wants more steel, it collects taxes and then buys the steel at market prices. In a planned economy, a government which wants more steel simply orders it to be produced and sets the price by decree. An economy where both central planning and market mechanisms of production and distribution are present is known as a mixed economy. Germany's social market economy was one of the better functioning mixed economies, as microeconomists note that it had relativily free prices compared to other more socialist countries like the United Kingdom for much of the later 20th century.

The proper role for government in a market economy remains controversial. Most supporters of a market economy believe that government has a legitimate role in defining and enforcing the basic rules of the market. More controversial is the question of how strong a role the government should have in both guiding the economy and addressing the inequalities the market produces. For example, there is no universal agreement on issues such as protectionist tariffs, federal control of interest rates, and welfare programs.

Milton Friedman, along with many microeconomists, believes that too much government intervention and regulation can result in hampering or stopping the transmission of information necessary to allow the market to operate, what results, he believes, are very serious government externalities that can lead to inflation, deflation, recesions, and depressions. Milton Friedman believes that the Great Depression was the result of a government created externalities and thus was responsible for the causes of the Great Depression.

MARKET FREEDOM

Friedrich von Hayek and Milton Friedman stated that economic freedom is a necessary condition for the creation and sustainability of civil and political freedoms. They believe that this economic freedom can only be achieved in a market oriented economy, specifically a free market economy. They do believe, however, that sufficient economic freedom can be achieved in economies with functioning markets through prices and private property rights. They believe that the more economic freedom that is available the more civil and political freedoms a society will enjoy.

Friedman states: "economic freedom is simply a requisite for political freedom. By enabling people to cooperate with one another without coercion or central direction it reduces the area over which political power is exercised." Friedman, Milton and Rose Friedman, Free to Choose: A Personal Statement, Harcort Brace Janovich, 1980, p. 2-3

Studies by the Canadian "conservative" free market oriented Fraser Institute, the American "conservative" free market oriented Heritage Foundation, and the Wall Street Journal state that there is a relationship between economic freedom and political and civil freedoms to the extent claimed by Friedrich von Hayek. They agree with Hayek that those countries which restrict economic freedom ultimately restrict civil and political freedoms.

MARKETS AND COMMUNIST STATES

In the 1980s, most of the planned economies in the world attempted to transform themselves into market economies, for various reasons and with varying degrees of success. In the Soviet Union, this process was known as perestroika while in China the creation of a "socialist market economy" was one element of Chinese economic reform.

Despite being the largest country whose ruling party refers to itself as communist, the People's Republic of China runs Special Economic Zones dedicated to capitalist enterprise, which are free from central government control. This is contrary to the communist theory proposed by Marx and Engels and later adapted by Lenin, Stalin, and Mao. After opening up trade to the world under Deng Xiaoping, the People's Republic of China runs some of the most economically free regions in the world, including Hong Kong, which is regarded by the Hoover Institute and the Wall Street Journal as the world's freest economy.

These Special Economic Zones have few restrictions upon businesses, industries, imports and exports, including the elimination of duties, and a free price system. Since the opening of the Free Trade Zones China has maintained a growth rate of over 8%, and originally saw growth rates around 12%. These Special Economic Zones are different from the State Capitalism, as practiced in the Soviet Union, because the SEZs allow for capitalists to build and expand their industries and private property, free from the control of the central government. SEZ's operate under market economy rather than the state capitalist top down command economy approach.

According to China.org "After opening Shenzhen and other three coastal cities in South China as special economic regions and then dozens of economic and technological development zones in the 1980s, the country introduced free trade zones in the early 1990s in 15 coast cities, including Shanghai, Guangzhou, Shenzhen and Tianjin."

In addition, China has recently declared private property to be a right and as also allowed the opening of foreign capitalist enterprises such as Wal-Mart to operate shopping centers in the Special Economic Zones.

Several other countries ruled by Communist Parties, such as Vietnam, have also made pro-market reforms in the last few decades.

The government is not in charge in this kind of economy.

CRITICISM OF MARKET ECONOMY

There are a variety of critics of market as an organizing principle of an economy. These critics range from those who reject markets entirely, in favor of a planned economy, such as that advocated by socialism, to those who merely wish to see them regulated to various degrees, and they range from those who believe that greed is inherently immoral to those who raise practical objections. One prominent practical objection is the claim that markets wreak havoc through their externalities (things that the market price does not take into account), for example through environmental pollution. Another is the claim that through the creation of monopolies, markets sow the seeds of their own destruction.

Some proponents of market economies believe that governments should not diminish market freedom because they disagree on what is a market externality and what are government created externalities, and disagree over what the appropriate level of intervention is necessary to solve market created externalities. Others believe that government should intervene to prevent market failure while preserving the general character of a market economy. In the model of a social market economy the state intervenes where the market does not fulfill the demands of political demands. John Rawls is a prominent proponent of this idea.

THE GLOBAL ECONOMY

The rise of technology has allowed our environment to be characterized as a global one. "The global economy gave business the ability to market products and services all over the globe.

It has also allowed them to develop partnerships and alliances throughout the world, which has become essential for success in today's business." Prior to Globalization, the United States dominated the global economy. In recent years, however, the U.S. share of the global economy has shrunk to approximately 25% and will continue that trend as the economies of many Newly industrialized countries continue to pick up steam.

Advantages

There are numerous adavantages to the shift to a global economy. A major one being the possibility to increase benefits from economies of scale. The breaking down of global barriers allows companies to benefit from the largest and cheapest workforces, raw materials and technology. For example, "many North American publishers actually write and produce much of their software in countries such as India." Other advantages that companies benefit from include: the opportunity for smaller companies to expand globally quicker, having more choices when recruiting a workforce and lastly the opportunity to target a larger customer base (which translates to greater earning potential). A global economy would also help in promoting international cooperation and peace. If countries are dependent upon one another's economic success then armed conflict would be less likely. For instance, India and Pakistan are often in dispute over land territory such as Kashmir. It is likely that these two countries will not enter into combat for the severe negative effects on their economies. Essentially it would be mutually assured destruction (MAD) on a financial level.

Disadvantages

One disadvantage of a global economy is the increased need for transportation due to less local production. Increased transportation leads to increased emissions of greenhouse gases.

Another disadvantage of a shift towards a global economy is the argued loss of domestic jobs. Certain labour-intensive industries (like textile and even parts of the software development industry) tend to shift their production from developed countries to developing countries where wages are lower. This shift, it is argued, not only increases the unemployment rate in the developed countries, but in some cases leads to exploitation of third world workers, in particular, children. In contrast, many economists believe that the loss of domestic jobs is a temporary state, which will be offset by other industries if the barriers of trade are kept low.

Other disadvantages include: increased instability as was seen during the Asian crisis; the inability to create globally uniform regulations and legislation, which leads to phenomena like tax havens.

ECONOMIES OF SCALE

Economies of scale represent a particularly important source of increasing returns. Economies of Scale are unit cost reductions associated with a large scale of output. In many cases international trade results in a country specializing in the production of a certain good, and if economies of scale results, then the output of that good expands and therefore the unit cost will decrease.

To fully realize the benefits of economies of scale, the good in that area must be a substantial proportion of the total world demand. This is because in many cases the world market is only able to support a limited number of firms in a certain country.

The world market determines their level of support by the product demand and also by the number of other countries in the world that are producing the same product. A recent example of this would be the EU banana dispute and the European Union has been forced by the WTO to decrease their levels of subsidies going to their former colonies. By decreasing the EU funding the WTO is trying to create a more level playing field for the rest of the banana growing regions so that true economies of scale can emerge.

The Global Economy

This increase in globalization has created many new opportunities, such as niche markets, and requires everyone to keep up with globalization in order to stay competitive. As David Shane points out in his article entitled "Youth must learn skills to succeed in Global Economy", "Technology and trade separate the economy into two camps--those with the skill to participate in the global economy and those who lack them." Shane indicates that advances in technology are giving developing countries the ability to compete directly with developed countries in terms of education and skills. With the ever increasing Global Economy and widespread use of the internet, people and businesses are realizing that they are often competing with people around the world for contracts and business deals.

The Global Economy has created an environment in which many large corporations are becoming transnational firms. This trend has developed in to a worldwide 'race-to-the-bottom' where companies are so focused on staying competitive that they often outsource production to developing countries with the lowest labour, environmental and economic standards. While these business practices allow companies to save money, leading to larger returns for investors and more affordable products for their clients, while at the same time balancing the world economy, it also serves as a motivation for governments in developing nations to keep their legislation lax when it comes to labour and environmental laws.

These transnational corporations often lobby their government in order to gain access into these developing countries. Still, many developed countries have protectionist policies that do not enable developing countries to export their goods into developed markets. Trade barriers more often hamper economic development in the Global South, as compared to the North. New technologies like the internet may speed up the reduction of trade barriers.

The expanding Global Economy and the reduction of trade barriers will create harder competition for the previously protected companies in developing countries, but maybe also new possibilities in Global markets for new emerging companies like Haier (China) and the Tata Group (India). In 2006 the global economy continued to expand so that most individual, corporate and government borrowers are making good on their obligations, which in turn has kept financial markets in clover.

PLANTATION ECONOMY

A plantation economy is an economy which is based on agricultural mass production, usually of a few staple products grown on large farms called plantations. Plantation economies are usually dependent on outside forces, due to the fact that the products being harvested en masse are cash crops to be exported.

Throughout history, countries with plantation economies have usually been in South America, the Caribbean, and Africa, and usually during the historical period of colonization, though Fordlândia is a 20th century example. Plantation economies are also historically associated with slavery, particularly in the United States. Plantation economies usually benefit the large countries to which they are exporting; they usually take the raw materials grown on the plantation and return manufactured goods, making a profit. Throughout most of history, the countries receiving the crops have usually been in Western Europe.

Tobacco Plantations in Colonial Virginia

Tobacco production was labor intensive and required thousands of slaves to produce millions of pounds that were exported. The period covered by this article ranges from 1700 to the end of the American Civil War (1865).

The wealth and Influence of Virginia planters depended on one crop, and that crop was tobacco. The production of tobacco spread down the James, York.

Tobacco and Virginia Economy

Over the years tobacco contributed greatly to Virginia's economy. In the year 1758 Virginia exported 70,000 hogsheads of tobacco. The production of tobacco in colonial times required much toil. The plants had to be grown from seeds in a cold frame, set out, weeded, tasseled, harvested, and cured. All of this work was done by man and beast. Each acre produced about 5,000 plants that required hand care over and over again. But, with slave labor, profits exceeded any other plant that could be grown.

Slave Statistics

In the year 1860, one out of every four families in Virginia owned slaves. The figures cited here are from the 1860 census. There were over 100 plantation owners that owned over 100 slaves.

- Number of slaves in the Lower South: 2,312,352 (47% of total population).
- Number of slaves in the Upper South: 1,208,758 (29% of total population).
- Number of slaves in the Border States: 432,586 (13% of total population).

Less than one-third of all Southern families owned slaves at the peak of slavery prior to the Civil War. In Mississippi and South Carolina it approached one half. The total number of slave owners was 385,000 (including, in Louisiana, some free Negroes). On a typical plantation (more than 20 slaves) the capital value of the slaves was greater than the capital value of the land and implements.

Tobacco Plantation Owners

Many of the wealthy and influential men in Colonial Virginia were tobacco plantation owners. A number of America's first presidents owned slaves. They owned numerous plantations, each with large numbers of slaves.

Thomas Jefferson

In 1776 Thomas Jefferson took a census of the slaves in his "family." He documented, in his "Farm Book", 117 slaves who lived on his plantation. He continued to acquire slaves at Monticello until the total was 140. Some were thought to be his own children.

George Washington

A planter's wealth was measured by the number of slaves he owned, and George Washington was a wealthy man. Without adequate tobacco farming, George Washtington would have been under financed to campaign against the English. Tobacco planters found that slave labor produced the greatest tobacco profits.

In Virginia, the black population increased from about 25% of the population in 1660 to more than 40% by 1760. Of the 277 slaves belonging to Washington in his own right or by marriage, 179 were 12 years old or older, eighteen of whom were "Passed labor." George Washington's father (Poppa George) owned the Popes Creek plantation. Slaves sold for 30-35 pounds. When his father died in 1743 he owned 64 slaves who were distributed across several estates.

Robert "King" Carter

By the year 1700, Robert "King" Carter was the richest man in the Virginia colony. He owned nearly 300,000 acres (1,200 km^2) scattered across the Northern Neck of Virginia. His tobacco plantations were tilled by about 1500 African slaves. The tobacco produced by "King" Carter was stored in his own warehouses, and he purchased tobacco from other planters as well.

He owned the ships that transported the tobacco to Europe where family members profited from its sale. The same ships were also stocked with trading goods, and sailed down to Africa, where the goods were traded for slaves that were brought back to Virginia.

James Madison

President James Madison was also a slave holder all of his adult life. Slavery remained a moral dilemma for him. Financial difficulties late in life led Madison to sell some slaves and he decided against freeing his slaves upon his death in order to provide for his wife's later years.

SUGAR PLANTATIONS

The system of Sugar plantations in the Caribbean islands and Brazil was a system that had to be followed to an exact science in order to profit from the production.

The slaves working the sugar plantation were caught in an unceasing rhythm of arduous labor year after year. Sugarcane is harvested about 18 months after planting and the plantations usually divided their land for efficiency. One plot was lying fallow, one plot was growing cane, and the final plot was being harvested. During the May-December rainy season, slaves planted, fertilized with animal dung, and weeded.

From January to June, they harvested the cane by chopping the plants off close to the ground, stripping the leaves, then cutting them into shorter strips to be bundled off to be sent to the mill. In the mill, the cane was crushed using a three roller mill. The juice from the crushing of the cane was then boiled or clarified until it crystallized into sugar. Some plantations also went a step further and distilled the molasses (the liquid left after the sugar is boiled or clarified) to make rum. The sugar was then shipped back to Europe and for the slave labor the routine started all over again.

SOCIAL MARKET ECONOMY

The social market economy was the main economic model used in Western and Northern Europe during the Cold War era. It originated in West Germany, and it is known as Soziale Marktwirtschaft in German.

In West Germany, the social market model was created and implemented by the Christian Democrat Ludwig Erhard, Minister of Economics under Konrad Adenauer's chancellorship and German Chancellor in his own right from 1963 to 1966. Erhard once told Friedrich Hayek that the free market economy did not need to be made social but was social in its origin.

The social market economy seeks a middle path between socialism and capitalism (i.e. a mixed economy) and aims at maintaining a balance between a high rate of economic growth, low inflation, low levels of unemployment, good working conditions, social welfare, and public services, by using state intervention. Important figures in the development of the concept include Franz Oppenheimer, Walter Eucken, Wilhelm Röpke, Franz Böhm and Alfred Müller-Armack (who originally coined the term Soziale Marktwirtschaft).

An important part of social market economies is the tripartite talks between labour unions, employers' organizations (the social partners) and the state in which they strike agreements on issues like price levels, wage increases, tax rates and pension entitlements. In these countries, collective bargaining is often done on a national level not between one corporation and one union, but national employers' organizations and national trade unions. At first controversial, the model became increasingly popular in West Germany and Austria, since in both states economic success (Wirtschaftswunder) was identified with it. From the 1960s, the social market economy was the main economic model in mainland Western Europe, pursued by administrations of both the centre right (usually led by Christian Democratic parties) and the centre left (usually led by Labour or Social Democratic parties).

Southern European states preferred large-scale public services, high salary growth rates and a low unemployment rate over low inflation, low national debt, low public expenditure and other economic health policies.

Following the fall of the Berlin Wall on 9 November 1989, most centre right parties gradually moved towards the highly capitalist economic policies of neoliberalism, and a significant portion of the centre left made a similar move, developing the "Third Way". Nevertheless, a commitment to some form of social market economy was present in the European Union Constitution (now in limbo following the referenda in France and the Netherlands).

TRADITIONAL ECONOMY

A traditional economy is an economic system in which resources are allocated by inheritance, and which has a strong social network and is based on primitive methods and tools. It is strongly connected to subsistence farming. In the majority of countries traditional economy has been replaced by command economy, market economy or mixed economy. However, it is found today mainly in underdeveloped, agricultural parts of South America, Asia, and Africa.

Advantages

Traditional economy fosters the sense of community, as it causes little friction among members and provides a sense of security and psychological comfort. Subsequently, there is no unemployment and low crime rate. A traditional economy allows for a greater degree of autonomy as no money or little is given to the government and there is no competition. It is also environmentally friendly, as the use of technology is limited.

Disadvantages

A traditional economy does not allow for much economic growth and development as changes are very slow and there is a lack of social mobility. A traditional economy does not take advantage of technology and there is relatively little promotion of intellectual and scientific development. With no incentives for entrepreneurs, the consumer choice is diminished, which leads to a lower standard of living.

12

Quality Control

In engineering and manufacturing, quality control and quality engineering are involved in developing systems to ensure products or services are designed and produced to meet or exceed customer requirements. These systems are often developed in conjunction with other business and engineering disciplines using a cross-functional approach.

HISTORICAL BACKDROP

Though terms like 'quality engineering' and 'quality assurance' are relatively new, the ideas have existed just as long as the very art of tool manufacture. Simple tools made of rock or bone were subject to familiar modes of failure.

They could be fragile, dull where they should be sharp, sharp where they should be dull, etc. When the first specialized craftsmen arose, manufacturing tools for others, the principle of quality control was simple: "let the buyer beware" (caveat emptor).

The first civil engineering projects, however, needed to be built to specifications. For instance, the four sides of the Great Pyramid of Giza are perpendicular to within 3.5 arcseconds.

CRAFT AND TRADESPERSONS

During the Middle Ages, guilds took the responsibility of quality control upon themselves. All practitioners of a particular trade living in a certain area were required to join the corresponding guild, and the guild instituted punishments for members who turned out shoddy products.

Royal governments purchasing material were interested in quality control as customers. For instançe, King John of England appointed a certain William Wrotham to supervise the construction and repair of ships. Some centuries later, but also in England, Samuel Pepys, Secretary to the Admiralty, appointed multiple such overseers.

Prior to the extensive division of labor and mechanization resulting from the Industrial Revolution, it was possible for a workman to control the quality of his own product. Working conditions then were more conducive to professional pride.

The Industrial Revolution led to a system in which large groups of men performing a similar type of work were grouped together under the supervision of a foreman who also took on the responsibility to control the quality of work manufactured.

Quality Assurance has developed a good deal during the last 80-90 years (in about 20 year intervals) from its inception to the current state of the art.

WARTIME PRODUCTION

During World War I, the manufacturing process became more complex, and the introduction of large numbers of workers being supervised by a foreman designated to ensure the quality of the work, which was being produced. This period also introduced mass production and piecework, which created quality problems as workmen could now earn more money by the production of extra products, which in turn led to bad workmanship being passed on to the assembly lines.

Due to the large amount of bad workmanship being produced, the first full time inspectors were introduced into the large-scale modern factory. These full time inspectors were the real beginning of inspection quality control, and this was the beginning the large inspection organizations of the 1920's and 1930's, which were separately organised from production and big enough to be headed by superintendents.

The systematic approach to quality started in industrial manufacture during the 1930's, mostly in the USA, when some attention was given to the cost of scrap and rework. With the impact of mass production, which was required during the Second World War, it became necessary to introduce a more stringent form of quality control which can be identified as Statistical Quality Control, or SQC. Some the initial work for SQC is credited to Walter A. Shewhart of Bell Labs.

This system came about with the realisation that quality cannot be inspected into an item. By extending the inspection phase and making inspection organizations more efficient, it provides inspectors with control tools such as sampling and control charts.

SQC had a significant contribution in that it provided a sampling inspection system rather that a 100 per cent inspection. This type of inspection however did lead to a lack of realisation to the importance of the engineering of product quality.

For example, if you have a basic sampling scheme with an acceptance level of 4%, what happens is you have a ratio of 96% products released onto the market with 4% defective items-this obviously is a fair risk for any company/customer-unless you happen to be one of the unfortunate buyers of a defective item.

POSTWAR PRODUCTION

After World War II, the United States continued to apply the concepts of inspection and sampling to remove defective product from production lines. However, there were many individuals trying to lead U.S. industries towards a more collabrative approach to quality. Excluding the U.S., many countries' manufacturing capabilities were destroyed during the war. This placed American business in a position where advances in the collabrative approaches to quality were essentially ignored.

After World War II, the U.S. sent General Douglas MacArthur to oversee the re-building of Japan. During this time, General MacArthur invited two key individuals in the development of modern quality concepts: W. Edwards Deming and Joseph Juran. Both individuals promoted the collabrative concepts of quality to Japanese business and technical groups, and these groups utilized these concepts in the redevelopment of the Japanese economy.

Quality Assurance

Quality Assurance covers all activities from design, development, production, installation, servicing and documentation, this introduced the rules: "fit for purpose" and "do it right the first time". It includes the regulation of the quality of raw materials, assemblies, products and components; services related to production; and management, production, and inspection processes. One of the most widely used paradigms for QA management is the PDCA (Plan-Do-Check-Act) approach, also known as the Shewhart cycle.

Failure Testing

A valuable process to perform on a whole consumer product is failure testing, the operation of a product until it fails, often under stresses such as increasing vibration, temperature and humidity. This exposes many unanticipated weaknesses in a product, and the data is used to drive engineering and manufacturing process improvements. Often quite simple changes can dramatically improve product service, such as changing to mould-resistant paint or adding lock-washer placement to the training for new assembly personnel.

Statistical Control

Many organizations use statistical process control to bring the organization to Six Sigma levels of quality, in other words, so that the likelihood of an unexpected failure is confined to six standard deviations on the normal distribution. This probability is less than four one-millionths. Items controlled often include clerical tasks such as order-entry as well as conventional manufacturing tasks.

Traditional statistical process controls in manufacturing operations usually proceed by randomly sampling and testing a fraction of the output. Variances of critical tolerances are continuously tracked, and manufacturing processes are corrected before bad parts can be produced.

Company Quality

During the 1980's, the concept of "company quality" with the focus on management and people came to the fore. It was realised that, if all departments approached quality with an open mind, success was possible if the management led the quality improvement process.

The company-wide quality approach places an emphasis on three aspects:-

1. Elements such as controls, job management, adequate processes, performance and integrity criteria and identification of records
2. Competence such as knowledge, skills, experience, qualifications
3. Soft elements, such as personnel integrity, confidence, organisational culture, motivation, team spirit and quality relationships.

The quality of the outputs is at risk if any of these three aspects are deficient in any way.

The approach to quality management given here is therefore not limited to the manufacturing theatre only but can be applied to any business activity:

- Design work
- Administrative services
- Consulting
- Banking
- Insurance
- Computer software
- Retailing
- Transportation...

It comprises a quality improvement process, which is generic in the sense it can be applied to any of these activities and it establishes a behaviour pattern, which supports the achievement of quality.

This in turn is supported by quality management practices which can include a number of business systems and which are usually specific to the activities of the business unit concerned.

In manufacturing and construction activities, these business practices can be equated to the models for quality assurance defined by the International Standards contained in the ISO 9000 series and the specified Specifications for quality systems.

Still, in the system of Company Quality, the work being carried out was shop floor inspection which did not control the major quality problems. This led to quality assurance or total quality control, which has come into being recently.

TOTAL QUALITY CONTROL

Total Quality Control is the most necessary inspection control of all in cases where, despite statistical quality control techniques or quality improvements implemented, sales decrease.

The major problem which leads to a decrease in sales was that the specifications did not include the most important factor, "What the customer required".

The major characteristics, ignored during the search to improve manufacture and overall business performance were:-

- Reliability
- Maintainability
- Safety

As the most important factor had been ignored, a few refinements had to be introduced:

1. Marketing had to carry out their work properly and define the customer's specifications.
2. Specifications had to be defined to conform to these requirements.
3. Conformance to specifications i.e. drawings, standards and other relevant documents, were introduced during manufacturing, planning and control.
4. Management had to confirm all operators are equal to the work imposed on them and holidays, celebrations and disputes did not affect any of the quality levels.

5. Inspections and tests were carried out, and all components and materials, bought in or otherwise, conformed to the specifications, and the measuring equipment was accurate, this is the responsibility of the QA/QC department.
6. Any complaints received from the customers were timorously and satisfactorily dealt with.
7. Feedback from the user/customer is used to review designs.

If the original specification does not reflect the correct quality requirements, quality cannot be inspected or manufactured into the product.

For instance, all parameters for a pressure vessel should include not only the material and dimensions but operating, environmental, safety, reliability and maintainability requirements.

To conclude, the above forms the basis from which the philosophy of Quality Assurance has evolved, and the achievement of quality or the "fitness-for-purpose" is "Quality Awareness" throughout the company.

13

Joint Stock Company

A joint stock company is a type of business partnership in which the capital is formed by the individual contributions of a group of shareholders. Certificates of ownership or stocks are issued by the company in return for each contribution, and the shareholders are free to transfer their ownership interest at any time by selling their stockholding to others.

NEED AND SIGNIFICANCE

Ownership of stock confers a number of privileges. The company is managed on behalf of the shareholders by an elected Board of Directors. Consequently, the share owner may attend an annual general meeting, and vote for directors and sometimes the principal officers. The shareholders receive an annual report, and vote upon the yearly audited set of accounts. Other resolutions upon important decisions can be put to them. There are other meetings, which may be called, either regularly or by special resolution of either the Board or the shareholders themselves.

Of course, individual shareholders can sometimes stand for directorships within the company, should a vacancy occur, but this is unusual. The shareholders are usually liable for any company debts that exceed the company's ability to pay. However, the limit of their liability only extends to the face value of their shareholding. This concept of limited liability largely accounts for the success of this form of business organisation.

Ordinary shares entitle the owner to a share in the company's net profit. This is calculated in the following way:

the net profit is divided by the total number of owned shares, producing a notional value per share, known as a dividend. The individual's share of the profit is thus the dividend multiplied by the number of shares that they own.

History

The Dutch started joint stock companies. In 1602, the Dutch East India Company issued the first shares on the Amsterdam Stock Exchange. It was the first company to issue stocks and bonds.

During the period of colonialism, the joint stock company was a financing model that allowed companies to raise large amounts of capital while lowering risk by diversifying contributed capital among multiple ventures. Europeans, initially the British, trading with the Near East for goods, pepper and calico for example, enjoyed spreading the risk of trade over multiple sea voyages. The joint stock company became a more viable financial structure than previous guilds or state regulated companies.

Transferable shares often earned positive returns on equity, which is evidenced by investment in companies like the British East India Company, which used the financing model to manage trade in India. Joint stock companies paid out divisions, dividends, to their shareholders by dividing up the profits of the voyage in the proportion of shares held.

Divisions were usually cash, but when working capital was low and it was detrimental to the survival of the company, divisions were either postponed or paid out in remaining cargo which could be sold by shareholders for profit in the market.

It also made it affordable to support early colonists in America. Jamestown, for instance, was financed by the Virginia Company. It is because of Joint stock companies that the colonization and settlement of America were made possible.

However, in general, incorporation was only possible by Royal charter or private act, and was limited owing to government's jealous protection of the privileges and advantages thereby granted. As a result, many businesses came to be operated as unincorporated associations with possibly thousands of members. Any consequent litigation had to be carried out in the joint names of all the members and was impossibly cumbersome.

In the UK, registration and incorporation of companies without specific legislation was introduced by the Joint Stock Companies Act 1844.

PRESENT STATUS

The joint stock company was a forerunner of contemporary corporate entities such as the American business corporation, the British public limited company, the French société anonyme, the German Aktiengesellschaft, the Japanese kabushiki kaisha, and the Korean jushik hoesa.

In some countries, "joint stock company" is used as an English translation for business forms that more closely resemble corporations.

While traditional joint stock companies still exist in some areas, they are generally considered an unattractive alternative to limited liability entities. Joint stock companies have recently been used in some fraudulent asset protection schemes in Texas.

INTERNATIONAL TRADE

International trade is the exchange of goods and services across national borders. In most countries, it represents a significant part of GDP. While international trade has been present throughout much of history, its economic, social, and political importance have increased in recent centuries, mainly because of Industrialisation, advanced transportation, globalisation, multinational corporations, and outsourcing. In fact, it is probably the increasing prevalence of international trade that is usually meant by the term "globalisation".

Empirical evidence for the success of trade can be seen in the contrast between countries such as South Korea, which adopted a policy of export-oriented industrialisation, and India, which historically had a more closed policy (although it has begun to open its economy, as of 2005). South Korea has done much better by economic criteria than India over the past fifty years, though its success also has to do with effective state institutions.

Trade sanctions against a specific country are sometimes imposed, in order to punish that country for some action. An embargo, a severe form of externally imposed isolation, is a blockade of all trade by one country on another. For example, the United States has had an embargo against Cuba for over 40 years.

Although there are usually few trade restrictions within countries, international trade is usually regulated by governmental quotas and restrictions, and often taxed by tariffs. Tariffs are usually on imports, but sometimes countries may impose export tariffs or subsidies. All of these are called trade barriers. If a government removes all trade barriers, a condition of free trade exists. A government that implements a protectionist policy establishes trade barriers.

The fair trade movement, also known as the trade justice movement, promotes the use of labour, environmental and social standards for the production of commodities, particularly those exported from the Third and Second Worlds to the First World.

Leading IMPORTERS in world trade in merchandise, data from WTO, 2004

Rank	Country	Valuebn US$	Share %	annual % change
1	United States	1525,5	16,1	17
2	Germany	716,9	7,6	19
3	China	561,2	5,9	36
4	France	465,5	4,9	17
5	United Kingdom	463,5	4,9	18
6	Japan	454,5	4,8	19
7	Italy	351,0	3,7	18
8	Netherlands	319,3	3,4	21
9	Belgium	285,5	3,0	22
10	Canada	279,8	2,9	14

Leading EXPORTERS in world trade in merchandise, data from WTO, 2004

Rank	Country	Valuebn US$	Share %	annual % change
1	Germany	912,3	10,0	21
2	United States	818,8	8,9	13
3	China	593,3	6,5	35
4	Japan	565,8	6,2	20
5	France	448,7	4,9	14
6	Netherlands	358,2	3,9	21
7	Italy	349,2	3,8	17
8	United Kingdom	346,9	3,8	13
9	Canada	316,5	3,5	16
10	Belgium	306,5	3,3	20

Standards may be voluntarily adhered to by importing firms, or enforced by governments through a combination of employment and commercial law. Proposed and practiced fair trade policies vary widely, ranging from the commonly adhered to prohibition of goods made using slave labour to minimum price support schemes such as those for coffee in the 1980s. Non-governmental organizations also play a role in promoting fair trade standards by serving as independent monitors of compliance with fairtrade labelling requirements.

ORGANISATION OF TRADE

Patterns of organising and administering trade include:

- State control-trade centrally controlled by government planning.
    - o Laws regulating Trade and establishing a framework such as trade law, tariffs, support for intellectual property, opposition to dumping.
- Guild control-trade controlled by private business associations holding either de facto or government-granted power to exclude new entrants.

- In contemporary times, the language has evolved to business and professional organisations, often controlled by academia. For example in many states, a person may not practice the professions of engineering, law, law enforcement, medicine, and teaching unless they have a college degree and, in some cases, a license.
- Free enterprise-trade without significant central controls; market participants engage in trade based on their own individual assessments of risk and reward, and may enter or exit a given market relatively unimpeded.
- Infrastructure in support of trade, such as banking, stock market,
- Technology in support of trade such as electronic commerce, vending machines.

International Organisations

- European Common Market
- GATT = General Agreement on Tariffs and Trade
- G8
- IMF = International Monetary Fund
- OPEC = Organization of the Petroleum Exporting Countries

Free Trade Areas

- Free trade organizations or free trade areas
  - European Free Trade Association
  - Free Trade Area of the Americas
  - NAFTA = North American Free Trade Agreement
  - South American Community of Nations

United Nations Umbrella

- UNCTAD = United Nations Conference on Trade and Development
- WTO = World Trade Organization

EXPORT-ORIENTED INDUSTRIALIZATION

Export-Oriented Industrialisation (EOI) is a trade and economic policy aiming to speed-up the industrialization process of a country through exporting goods for which the nation has a comparative advantage. Export-led growth implies opening domestic markets to foreign competition in exchange for market access in other countries. Reduced tariff barriers, floating exchange rate (devaluation of national currency is often employed to facilitate exports), and government support for exporting sectors are all an example of policies adopted to promote EOI, and ultimately economic development. Export-Oriented Industrialisation was particularly characteristic of the development of the national economies of Japan, South Korea, Taiwan and Singapore in the post World War II period. The purpose of international institutions such as the World Trade Organization, work in favour of such trade strategies and promote multilateral trade policy rules to put every nation on the same playing field. It has been mostly successful, although it can be sensitive to the market. The 1998 economic crisis hurt the economies of countries who used export-oriented industrialization. It is criticized for it's lack of product diversity, which makes the economies potentially unstable.

Export-oriented industrialization is often contrasted with import substitution industrialization. It grew as a reaction to import substition and has been more successful in increasing the per capita GDP relative to import substitution.

EXPORT PERFORMANCE

Export performance is the relative success or failure of the efforts of a firm or nation to sell domestically-produced goods and services in other nations. Export performance can be described in objective terms such as sales, profits, or marketing measures or by subjective measures such as distributor or customer satisfaction.

Performance Improvement

Performance improvement is the concept of measuring the output of a particular process or procedure, then modifying the process or procedure in order to increase the output, increase efficiency, or increase the effectiveness of the process or procedure. The concept of performance improvement can be applied to either individual performance such as an athlete or organizational performance such as a racing team or a commercial enterprise.

In Organizational development, performance improvement is the concept of organizational change in which the managers and governing body of an organization put into place and manage a program which measures the current level of performance of the organization and then generates ideas for modifying organizational behavior and infrastructure which are put into place in order to achieve a better level of output. The primary goals of organizational improvement are to improve organizational effectiveness and organizational efficiency in order to improve the ability of the organization to deliver its goods and/or services and prosper in the marketplaces in which the organization competes. A third area of improvement which is sometimes targeted for improvement is organizational efficacy which involves the process of setting organizational goals and objectives.

Performance improvement at the operational or individual employee level usually involves processes such as statistical quality control. At the organizational level, performance improvement usually involves softer forms of measurement such as customer satisfaction surveys which are used to obtain qualitative information about performance from the viewpoint of customers.

Performance Defined

Performance is a measure of results achieved. Performance efficiency is the ratio between effort expended and results achieved. The difference between current performance and the theoretical performance limit is the performance improvement zone.

Another way to think of performance improvement is to see it as improvement in four potential areas. First, is the resource INPUT requirments (e.g., reduced working capital, material, replacement/reorder time,and set-up requirements). Second, is the THROUGHPUT requirments, often viewed as process efficiency; this is measured in terms of time, waste, and resource utilization. Third, OUTPUT requirements, often viewed from a cost/price, quality, functionality perspective. Fourth, OUTCOME requirments, did it end up making a difference.

Performance is an abstract concept and it must be represented by concrete, measurable phenomena or events in order to be measured. Baseball athlete performance is abstract covering many different types of activities. Batting average is a concrete measure of a particular performance attribute for a particular game role, batting, for the game of baseball.

Performance assumes an actor of some kind but the actor could be an individual person or a group of people acting in concert. The performance platform is the infrastructure or devices used in the performance act.

There are two main ways to improve performance: improving the measured attribute by using the performance platform more effectively, or by improving the measured attribute by modifying the performance platform, which in turn allows a given level of use to be more effective in producing the desired output. For instance, in several sports such as tennis and golf, there have been technological improvements in the apparatuses used in these sports. The improved apparatus in turn allows players to achieve better performance with no improvement in skill by purchasing new equipment. The apparatus, the golf club and golf ball or the tennis racket, provide the player with a higher theoretical performance limit.

FINANCE

Finance studies and addresses the ways in which individuals, businesses, and organizations raise, allocate, and use monetary resources over time, taking into account the risks entailed in their projects. The term finance may thus incorporate any of the following:

- The study of money and other assets;
- The management and control of those assets;
- Profiling and managing project risks;
- As a verb, "to finance" is to provide funds for business.

The activity of finance is the application of a set of techniques that individuals and organizations (entities) use to manage their financial affairs, particularly the differences between income and expenditure and the risks of their investments.

An entity whose income exceeds its expenditure can lend or invest the excess income. On the other hand, an entity whose income is less than its expenditure can raise capital by borrowing or selling equity claims, decreasing its expenses, or increasing its income. The lender can find a borrower, a financial intermediary, such as a bank or buy notes or bonds in the bond market. The lender receives interest, the borrower pays a higher interest than the lender receives, and the financial intermediary pockets the difference.

A bank aggregates the activities of many borrowers and lenders. A bank accepts deposits from lenders, on which it pays the interest. The bank then lends these deposits to borrowers. Banks allow borrowers and lenders of different sizes to coordinate their activity. Banks are thus compensators of money flows in space since they allow different lenders and borrowers to meet, and in time, since every borrower, in theory, will eventually pay back.

A specific example of corporate finance is the sale of stock by a company to institutional investors like investment banks, who in turn generally sell it to the public. The stock gives whoever owns it part ownership in that company. If you buy one share of XYZ Inc, and they have 100 shares available, you are 1/100 owner of that company. You own 1/100 of the net difference between assets and liabilities on the balance sheet. Of course, in return for the stock, the company receives cash, which it uses to expand its business in a process called "equity financing". Equity financing mixed with the sale of bonds (or any other debt financing) is called the company's capital structure.

Finance is used by individuals (personal finance), by governments (public finance), by businesses (corporate finance), etc., as well as by a wide variety of organizations including schools and non-profit organizations. In general, the goals of each of the above activities are achieved through the use of appropriate financial instruments, with consideration to their institutional setting. Finance is one of the most important aspects of business management. Without proper financial planning, a new enterprise cannot even start, let alone being successful. As money is the single most powerful liquid asset, managing money is essential to ensure a secure future, both for an individual as well as an organisation

Personal Finance

Questions in personal finance revolve around:

- How much money will be needed by an individual (or by a family) at various points in the future?
- Where will this money come from (e.g. savings or borrowing)?
- How can people protect themselves against unforeseen events in their lives, and risk in financial markets?
- How can family assets be best transferred across generations (bequests and inheritance)?
- How do taxes (tax subsidies or penalties) affect personal financial decisions?

Personal financial decisions may involve paying for education, financing durable goods such as real estate and cars, buying insurance, e.g. health and property insurance, investing and saving for retirement.

Business Finance

In the case of a company, managerial finance or corporate finance is the task of providing the funds for the corporations' activities. It generally involves balancing risk and profitability. Long term funds would be provided by ownership equity and long-term credit, often in the form of bonds. These decisions lead to the company's capital structure. Short term funding or working capital is mostly provided by banks extending a line of credit.

On the bond market, borrowers package their debt in the form of bonds. The borrower receives the money it borrows by selling the bond, which includes a promise to repay the value of the bond with interest. The purchaser of a bond can resell the bond, so the actual recipient of interest payments can change over time. Bonds allow lenders to recoup the value of their loan by simply selling the bond.

Another business decision concerning finance is investment, or fund management. An investment is an acquisition of an asset in the hopes that it will maintain or increase its value. In investment management-in choosing a portfolio-one has to decide what, how much and when to invest. In doing so, one needs to:

- Identify relevant objectives and constraints: institution or individual-goals-time horizon-risk aversion-tax considerations
- Identify the appropriate strategy: active vs passive-hedging strategy
- Measure the portfolio performance

Financial management is duplicate with the financial function of the Accounting profession. However, Financial Accounting is more concerned with the reporting of historical financial information, while the financial decision is directed toward the future of the firm.

Shared Services

There is currently a move towards converging and consolidating Finance provisions into shared services within an organization. Rather than an organization having a number of separate Finance departments performing the same tasks from different locations a more centralized version can be created.

Finance of States

Country, state, county, city or municipality finance is called public finance. It is concerned with:

- Identification of required expenditure of a public sector entity
- Source(s) of that entity's revenue
- The budgeting process
- Debt issuance (municipal bonds) for public works projects.

Financial Economics

Financial economics is the branch of economics studying the interrelation of financial variables, s.a. prices, interest rates and shares as opposed to those concerning the real economy. Financial economics concentrates on influences of real economic variables on financial ones, in contrast to pure finance.

It studies:

- Valuation-Determination of the fair value of an asset
  - o How risky is the asset? (identification of the asset appropriate discount rate)
  - o What cash flows will it produce? (discounting of relevant cash flows)
  - o How does the market price compare to similar assets? (relative valuation)
  - o Are the cash flows dependent on some other asset or event? (derivatives, contingent claim valuation)
- Financial markets and instruments
  - o Commodities-topics
  - o Stocks-topics
  - o Bonds-topics
  - o Money market instruments-topics
  - o Derivatives-topics
- Financial institutions and regulation

Financial Mathematics

Financial mathematics is the main branch of applied mathematics concerned with the financial markets. Financial mathematics is the study of financial data with the tools of mathematics, mainly statistics. Such data can be movements of securities-stocks and bonds etc.-and their relations. Another large subfield is insurance mathematics.

Experimental Finance

The goals of experimental finance are to establish different market settings and environments to observe experimentally and analyze agents' behavior and the resulting characteristics of trading flows, information diffusion and aggregation, price setting mechanisms, and returns processes. Researchers in experimental finance can study to what extent existing financial economics theory makes valid predictions, and attempt to discover new principles on which such theory can be extended. Research may proceed by conducting trading simulations or by establishing and studying the behaviour of people in artificial competitive market-like settings.

Related Professional Qualifications

There are several related professional qualifications in finance, that can lead to the field:

- *Qualified Accountant Qualifications:* Chartered Certified Accountant (ACCA, UK certification), Chartered Accountant (CA, certification in Commonwealth countries), Certified Public Accountant (CPA, US certification)
- *Non-statutory Accountancy Qualifications:* Chartered Cost Accountant CCA Designation from AAFM
- *Business Qualifications:* Master of Business Administration (MBA), Doctor of Business Administration (DBA)
- *Finance Qualifications:* Chartered Financial Analyst (CFA), Association of Corporate Treasurers (ACT), Masters degree in Finance, Certified Market Analyst (CMA/FAD) Dual Designation, Master Financial Manager (MFM), Corporate Finance Qualification (CF)
- *Quantitative Finance Qualifications:* Master of Quantitative Finance (MQF), Master of Computational Finance (MCF), Master of Financial Mathematics (MFM).

14

Financial Plan

A financial plan is a written analysis of an individual's financial circumstances developed by a financial planner, in light of the individual's goals, resources, and current tax law, investment options, and insurance needs. Also, a financial plan can refer to a section of a business plan, which consists of three financial statements (the income statement, the cash flow projection, and the balance sheet) and a brief analysis of these three statements.

FINANCIAL PLANNING (BUSINESS)

Financial Planning is the task of determining how a business will afford to achieve its strategic goals and objectives. Usually, a company creates a Financial Plan immediately after the vision and objectives have been set. The Financial Plan describes each of the activities, resources, equipment and materials that are needed to achieve these objectives, as well as the timeframes involved. The Financial Planning activity involves the following tasks:

- Assess the business environment
- Confirm the business vision and objectives
- Identify the types of resources needed to achieve these objectives
- Quantify the amount of resource (labor, equipment, materials)
- Calculate the total cost of each type of resource
- Summarize the costs to create a budget
- Identify any risks and issues with the budget set.

Performing Financial Planning is critical to the success of any organization. It provides the Business Plan with rigor, by confirming that the objectives set are achievable from a financial point of view. It also helps the CEO to set financial targets for the organization, and reward staff for meeting objectives within the budget set.

FINANCIAL PLANNER

A Financial Planner or Personal Financial Planner is a practising professional who helps people to deal with various personal financial issues through proper planning, which include but not limited to these major areas: tertiary education planning, retirement planning, investment planning, risk management and insurance planning, tax planning, estate planning and business succession planning (for business owners). The work engaged in by this professional is commonly known as personal financial planning. In carrying out the planning function, he is guided by the financial planning process to create a detailed strategy tailored to a client's specific situation, for meeting a client's specific goals.

Aims and Objectives

People enlist the help of a financial planner because of the complexity of knowing how to perform the following:

- Providing direction and meaning to financial decisions;
- Allowing the person to understand how each financial decision affects the other areas of finance; and
- Allowing the person to adapt more easily to life changes in order to feel more secure.

Defining Personal Financial Planning

Personal financial planning is broadly defined as a process of determining an individual's financial goals, purposes in life and life's priorities, and after considering his resources, risk profile and current lifestyle, to detail a balanced and realistic plan to meet those goals. The individual's goals are used as guideposts to map a course of action on 'what need to be done' to reach those goals.

Along side the data gathering exercise, the purpose of each goal is determined to ensure that the goal is meaningful in the context of the individual's situation. Through a process of careful analysis, these goals are subjected to a reality check by considering the individual's current and future resources available to achieve them. In the process, the constraints and obstacles to these goals are noted. The information will be used later to determine if there are sufficient resources available to get to these goals, and what other things need to be considered in the process. If the resources are insufficient or absent to meet any of the goals, the particular goal will be adjusted to a more realistic level or will be replaced with a new goal.

Planning often requires consideration of self-constraints in postponing some enjoyment today for the sake of the future. To be effective, the plan should consider the individual's current lifestyle so that the 'pain' in postponing current pleasures is bearable over the term of the plan. In times where current sacrifices are involved, the plan should help ensure that the pursuit of the goal will continue. A plan should consider the importance of each goal and should prioritize each goal. Many financial plans fail because these practical points were not sufficiently considered.

Scope

Financial planning should cover all areas of the client's financial needs and should result in the achievement of each of the client's goals. The scope of planning would usually include the following:

- *Risk Management and Insurance Planning:* Managing cash flow risks through sound risk management and insurance techniques;
- *Investment and Planning Issues:* Planning, creating and managing capital accumulation to generate future capital and cash flows for reinvestment and spending;
- *Retirement Planning:* Planning to ensure financial independence at retirement;
- *Tax Planning:* Planning for the reduction of tax liabilities and the freeing-up of cash flows for other purposes;

- *Estate Planning:* Planning for the creation, accumulation, conservation and distribution of assets;
- *Cash Flow and Liability Management:* Maintaining and enhancing personal cash flows through debt and lifestyle management.

The Process

The personal financial planning process is generally accepted as a six-step process as follows:

Step 1: Setting goals with the client This step (that is usually performed in conjunction with Step 2) is meant to identify where the client wants to go in terms of his finances and life.

Step 2: Gathering relevant information on the client This would include the qualitative and quantitative aspects of the client's financial and relevant non-financial situation.

Step 3: Analysing the information The information gathered is analysed so that the client's situation is properly understood. This includes determining whether there are sufficient resources to reach the client's goals and what those resources are.

Step 4: Constructing a financial plan Based on the understanding of what the client wants in the future and his current financial status, a roadmap to the client goals is drawn to facilitate the achievements of those goals.

Step 5: Implementing the strategies in the plan Guided by the financial plan, the strategies outlined in the plan are implemented using the resources allocated for the purpose.

Step 6: Monitoring implementation and reviewing the plan The implementation process is closely monitored to ensure it stays in alignment to the client's goals. Periodic reviews are undertaken to check for misalignment and changes in the client's situation. If there is any deviation or significant change to the client's situation, the strategies and goals in the financial plan are revised accordingly.

What is a Financial Planner's Job Function?: A financial planner specializes in the planning aspects of finance, in particular personal finance, as contrasted with a stock broker who is only concerned with the actual investments, or with a life insurance intermediary who advises on risk products.

Financial planning is usually a six-step process, and involves considering the client's situation from all relevant angles to produce integrated solutions. The six-step financial planning process has been adopted by the International Organization for Standardization (ISO) and the details can be obtained from the organisation (Refer). Financial planners are also known by the title financial advisor in some countries, although these two terms are technically not synonymous, and their roles have some functional differences.

Although there are many types of 'financial planners', the term is used largely to describe those who consider the entire financial picture of a client and then provide a comprehensive solution. To differentiate from the other types of financial planners, some planners may be called 'comprehensive' financial planners.

Other financial planners may specialize in one or more areas, such as, insurance planning and retirement planning.

Licensing, Regulations and Self-regulation

The title of 'financial planner' is largely an unregulated term in many countries. Lack of regulation has allowed financial services personnel in these countries to use the title indiscriminately. Financial products intermediaries, such as life insurance and unit trusts agents, use the title to project a professional image to clients even when they are not trained in the professional aspects of financial planning. This has sometimes led to abuse. Clients may be deceived to receive financial planning services that are unprofessional, from unethical providers.

To protect the industry, financial planning professionals and practitioners from across the globe (starting from the United States) have begun to form trade organisations to provide self-regulations and to maintain some orderliness in the industry. Some, such as the FPA, have begun to organise high-level training programmes and certify members who successfully completed these programmes.

The title of 'financial planner' continues, however, to be used by individuals in the financial industry in most countries, as there are little or no legal barriers to prevent the use of the title. The governments in many countries where the financial planning profession is taking roots are beginning to play an increasingly active role in tasking themselves to ensure the market is orderly. More stringent laws and guidelines are being progressively introduced to keep the profession in check.

In Australia, the financial planning services are initially delinated by law by the granting of licence to deal in securities or advise on investments. Licences are issued under the stringent criteria by the Australian Securities and Investments Commission (ASIC), which has evolved these regulations vigourously over the years. Financial planning is now a highly regulated industry in Australia especially where financial advice to the public is involved. Practitioners who offer advice that could influence a client's decision to purchase a financial product must meet minimum training requirements and be licensed by the ASIC. The meaning of 'licenced' refers to Australian Financial Services Licence (AFSL) holders and representatives or authorised representatives of licence holders. Broadly, most people embarking in financial planning will start as an authorised representative of a licence holder.

Becoming a financial planner involves two main steps:

1. Meet the training requirements of Policy Statement 146;
2. Select a licence holder with whom to be affiliated.

The licence holder is the authorised representative, and will be ultimately responsible for the advice given by the planner. The licence holder therefore must make sure the representatives meet all compliance and training prerequisites. As of November 2005, there were approximately 4,300 licence holders registered with ASIC and over 42,500 authorised representatives in Australia.

In 2001, the Singapore government introduced the Financial Advisers Act (FAA) to regulate the conduct of financial advisory business in the country. The FAA does not, however, specifically require a high level qualification before an individual can use the title 'financial planner'. The Act also defines a financial adviser to mean a firm with a corporate structure which is properly licenced by the Monetary Authority of Singapore (MAS)to perform financial advisory business. In both the Australia and Singapore situation, there is no law specifically on 'holding out' oneself to be a financial planner.

Licensing of Financial Planners and Financial Advisers: The first country to introduce legislation that require a person to be licensed before he can hold himself out to be a 'financial planner' is Malaysia. This is quite unexpected as the financial planning concept is considered quite a new introduction in the Asian region as compared to those in the west, such as the United States and Australia where the profession is more established. The Securities Commission (SC) (refer) of Malaysia introduced legislation through amendments made to the Securities Industry Act in 2003 to regulate financial planning and the use of the title or related-title of 'financial planner' or to conduct activities related to financial planning.

In 2005, amendments to the Malaysian Insurance Act require those who carry out financial advisory business (including financial planning activities related to insurance) and/or use the title of financial adviser under their firm (which, like in Singapore, must be a corporate structure) to obtain a licence from Bank Negara (BNM). Some persons who offer financial advisory services, e.g. licenced life insurance agents, are exempted from licensing as a practising requirement.

One of the basic requirements to apply for a financial planner or financial adviser licence in Malaysia is that the key company officers, e.g. directors, must be a RFP designee (most, if not all Malaysian FChFP designees also carries the RFP designation). Subsequently, in September 2006, the CFP qualification is included as one of the alternatives that can be used by the financial adviser licence applicant. With this development, the demand for financial planning courses has begun to take root in more concrete forms in Malaysia. The licence applicant must also be a member of a self-regulatory organisation (SRO) in financial planning recognised by the authorities. For this purpose, the two SROs currently recognised by both the Security Commission and Bank Negara are the

Malaysia Financial Planning Council (MFPC) and the Financial Planning Association of Malaysia (FPAM). The purpose of this requirement is to ensure some form of self-supervision for persons practicing financial planning.

In some countries, e.g., the United States, financial planners must be registered as an investment advisor first. This requires an employee within a firm to pass the series 65 or 66 Registered Investment Advisor Exam. A private advisor or company can apply to the state and SEC for a RIA Registered Investment Advisor License or Status.

Being 'licenced' to practice financial planning is not the same as merely having a professional 'qualification' in financial planning. A person may be professionally qualified in financial planning, but without a licence required by the law, he cannot practice the trade in that country or call himself a financial planner there. As of now, there are quite a bit of qualifications related to financial planning that can be found in world. The most prestigious financial planning designations are those which are not just of advanced standing and well-known, but are also recognised by the relevant authorities for licensing purpose. The FChFP, RFP, CFP, ChFC, RFC, FFSI, CWM ™, MFP ™, or PFS, FPS designations are advanced financial planning or closely related qualifications that are independently offered and regulated by esteemed financial industry organizations but not all are recognised for licensing purpose.

In some places, individual employees within a licensed & Registered Investment Advisor firm such as a: brokerage, bank or insurance company may be exempt if providing complementary financial planning services in relation to their existing products and services. Moreover, financial planners should be extremely careful in providing estate planning or taxation advise for a fee, as these fields are highly regulated by government agencies that control the practice of lawyers and Certified Public Accountants (CPAs). The term "Investment Advisor" also includes any person who uses the title "financial planner" and who, for compensation, engages in the business, whether principally or as part of another business, of advising others, either directly or through publications or writings, as to the value of securities or as to the advisability of investing in, purchasing or selling securities, or who, for compensation and as part of a regular business, publishes analyses or reports concerning securities.

From the California Department of Corporations: A financial planner will be registered with the state if he or she has less than 25 million in AUM, and with the SEC if he or she has more than 30 million in AUM. The planner is required to present a client with the ADV Part II or equivalent before the client enters into a contract with the planner. No certification, tests or training ensure that any planner is suitable for the client or any investor, and it is important to read the ADV Part II, interview them, and fully understand any contract.

GLOBAL CERTIFICATIONS IN FINANCIAL PLANNING

In a newly emerging profession such as financial planning, there is a lack of regulation, especially in the early years of development. The need for some forms of self-regulation and the demand that a financial planner be competent and trustworthy have prompted several independent financial services organizations to introduce certifications and ethical benchmarks to meet these challenges in accordance to the need in each country. Those who meet the requirement of the certification process and ethical standards will be awarded a professional financial planning designation.

One of the oldest, most well-known financial planning certification service marks is the Certified Financial Planner (CFP), which has gained global recognition because of its active standard setting activities and worldwide presence. The CFP designation was first introduced in the United States in the early 1970's to meet the need of the consumers. The CFP mark now belongs to the CFP® Board of Standard's ("CFP Board"), USA, which has member associations worldwide.

The CFP Board was founded in July 1985 as the International Board of Standards and Practices for Certified Financial Planners, Inc., (IBCFP) by the College for Financial Planning (College) and the Institute of Certified Financial Planners (ICFP). The IBCFP became Certified Financial Planner Board of Standards Inc. (CFP Board) on February 1, 1994. As a professional regulatory organization acting in the public interest by fostering professional standards in personal financial planning, the CFP Board establishes and enforces education, examination, experience and ethics requirements for CFP® certificants. The CFP service mark is promoted worldwide through member associations, the FPAs.

Another well-known certification mark with a unique history is the Fellow Chartered Financial Practitioner (FChFP), which is conferred by the Asia-Pacific Financial Services Association (APFinSA). The FChFP designation is the first known professional designation in financial planning that is completely developed in Asia and the programs leading to the designation is tailored to each country's need by local professionals and practitioners who writes these courses. It is also among the earliest to be vigorously promoted in this region. The FChFP designation was pioneered by the National Association of Malaysian Life Insurance and Financial Advisors (NAMLIFA) and was first launched on 31st May 1996 to its members in Malaysia as an 8-module financial planning programme. The FChFP was adopted by APFinSA in 2001 (of which NAMLIFA is a member) as the highest professional financial services designation amongst its member associations in 11 countries. This development effectively made the FChFP designation a regionally recognised designation in financial planning.

Through the Insurance and Financial Practitioners Association of Singapore (IFPAS), Singapore was the second country to successfully introduce the FChFP designation to its practitioners in 2003. It was during this time that the original letters of the designation 'ChFP' was modified to 'FChFP' to prevent the public from confusing it with the CFP mark. The FChFP designation has since spread to all over the Asia-Pacific region and is quick gaining strength in places like Hong Kong, China and Taiwan.

The Registered Financial Planner (RFP) designation is conferred by the Malaysian Financial Planning Council (MFPC). The designation and the MFPC was created through the collaborative work of the Life Insurance Association of Malaysia (LIAM), National Association of Malaysian Life Insurance and Financial Advisors (NAMLIFA) and Malaysian Insurance Institute (MII) who also become the founding members of the

Association or Charter Promoter Organisations (ChPOs). Since then, other organisations such as the Malaysian Association of Chartered Financial Consultant (MAChFC) have joint the Association as a member.

The Personal Financial Specialist (PFS) credential was established for CPAs in the United States who specialize in personal financial planning. The credential is awarded exclusively to AICPA members who have demonstrated considerable experience and expertise in that area. As of today, the AICPA has granted approximately 3,300 CPA/PFS credentials.

In Australia, the financial planning specialisation, CPA (FPS), is available to those members of CPA Australia who can demonstrate their eligibility through experience and education within the financial services industry.

The objectives of the FPS designation are to:

- achieve public recognition for those who hold the specialisation enhance the quality of financial planning services that members provide;
- increase practice development and career opportunities for CPAs.

The FPS designation is available to CPAs, and is based on a points system, where a minimum of 100 points must be accrued. Although all CPA Australia members who provide financial product advice must be licensed by ASIC, a member does not have to be licensed to first obtained the CPA (FPS) designation. The Chartered Financial Consultant (ChFC) is another prestigious financial planning qualification, which is conferred by American College, USA). Since 1982, the ChFC has remained among the most extensive education available for professionals seeking a designation in financial planning. Todate, more than 41,000 individuals have attained this distinction. This designation has also spread to Asia, where designees are found in countries like Singapore, Malaysia, Indonesia, China and Hong Kong.

In Europe, the European Financial Planner (EFP) designation conferred by the European Financial Planning Association (EFPA) is gaining ground as a financial planning certification mark. The EFPA is the largest professional and educational organisation for financial planners and financial advisors in Europe and is the only Financial Planning Association created solely in the interest of European financial planning consumers and practitioners.

In one of the significant recent developments, several major financial services organisations with international/regional affiliations have grouped together to form the International Federation of Financial Standards Associations (IFFSA). The organisations that originally initiated the IFFSA concept are the European Financial Planner EFPA and the Asia-Pacific Financial Services Association (APFinSA). It is expected that more organisations will join as associates of this new entity.

The rest of the certification qualifications related to financial planning include: Fellow, Financial Services Institute (conferred by LOMA, USA); The highest known conditions set for conferment of a financial planning credential seems to be those of the CWM Chartered Wealth Manager (conferred by the AAFM) designation which requires an accredited MBA, PhD or CFA to apply (Note: This entry requirement is not uniform and only applies to some places where the AAFM operates).

Accredited Business School, Training Centers and Education Providers in Financial Planning: In America, more than 150,000 financial services professionals have earned advanced degrees and designations from The American College. Their leading financial planning programs include ChFC programme and courses leading to the CFP certification awarded by the CFP Board of Standards.

Another American organisation active in the promotion of financial planning courses is the International Association of Registered Financial Consultants (IARFC), which confers the Registered Financial Consultant (RFC) designation. The IARFC has introduced a financial planning self-study and examination process for Registered Financial Consultant applicants.

In Singapore, the Financial Planning Association of Singapore (FPAS) appoints educational providers to conduct tutorials for students interested in taking the CFP examinations. Two of its active education providers are Financial Perspectives and FTC. The Singapore College of Insurance (SCI) conducts localised courses leading to the ChFC designation which is awarded by The American College. Finally, the Insurance and Financial Practitioners Association of Singapore (IFPAS) uses the educational provider, Professional Education and Consultancy (PEC) to conduct tutorials for its FChFP students. These training companies, i.e. Financial Perspectives, FTC and PEC, also provide a host of other financial related trainings to the financial practitioners in Singapore.

As for Malaysia, the Financial Planning Association of Malaysia (FPAM) has active education providers such as IMS, IFPA, PNB, KDU and IBBM to conduct its CFP courses. The Malaysian Financial Planning Council (MFPC) also appoints education providers for its RFP courses. Some of them to date are MII, NAMLIFA, MIM-IMS, IBBM, OUM, Kolej Kasturi and Regent School of Economics. For the FChFP, the courses are conducted in-house by the National Association of Malaysian Life Insurance and Financial Advisors (NAMLIFA) and its branches throughout the country. Other Malaysian training providers active in supporting financial planning education in the non-designation domain include Brain Station Academy, AD Capital and Jon Wise.

Globally, cross-recognition agreements are being developed to facilitate the learning of financial planning. The 2 major accrediting agencies AACSB and ACBSP in the west, which accredit over 560 of the best business school programs, provides the Certification of MFP Master Financial Planner Professional from the American Academy of Financial Management, which is available to AACSB and ACBSP business school graduates with finance or financial services related concentrations.

15

Investment

FINANCE

Investment or investing is a term with several closely-related meanings in business management, finance and economics, related to saving or deferring consumption. An asset is usually purchased, or equivalently a deposit is made in a bank, in hopes of getting a future return or interest from it. Literally, the word means the "action of putting something in to somewhere else" (perhaps originally related to a person's garment or 'vestment').

TYPES OF INVESTMENT

The major difference in the use of the term investment between the economics field and the finance field is that economists refer to a real investment (such as a machine or a house), while financial economists refer to a financial asset, such as money that is put into a bank or the market, which may then be used to buy a real asset. An important thing to know about investing is that even when the times are tough that is the time when you most need to hold on to your investment.

Business Management

The investment decision (also known as capital budgeting) is one of the fundamental decisions of business management: managers determine the assets that the business enterprise obtains; these assets may be physical (e.g. buildings or machinery), intangible (e.g. patents, software, goodwill), or financial. Whatever the type of asset, the manager must assess whether the net present value of the investment to the enterprise is positive; the net present value is calculated using the enterprise's marginal cost of capital.

Economics

- In Economics, investment means the purchase (and thus the production) and/or stock of capital goods and/ or technology-goods which are not consumed but instead used in future production. Examples include building a railroad, or a factory, clearing land, or putting oneself through college. In measures of national income and output, investment is also a component of GDP given in the formula GDP = C + I + G + NX. The investment function in that aspect is divided into non-residential investment (such as factories, machinery etc) and residential investment (new houses).
- Investment is often modeled as a function of income and interest rates, given by the relation I = f(Y, r). An increase in income will encourage higher investment, whereas a higher interest rate may discourage investment as it becomes costlier to borrow money. Even if a firm chooses to use its own funds in an investment, the interest rate represents an opportunity cost of investing those funds rather than loaning them out for interest.

Finance

- In finance, investment means buying securities or other monetary or paper (financial) assets in the money markets or capital markets, or in fairly liquid real assets, such as gold as an investment, real estate, or collectibles. Valuation is the method for assessing whether a potential investment is worth its price.
- Types of financial investments include shares or other equity investment, and bonds (including bonds denominated in foreign currencies). These investments assets are then expected to provide income or positive future cash flows, but may increase or decrease in value giving the investor capital gains or losses.

- Trades in contingent claims or derivative securities do not necessarily have future positive expected cash flows-so are not considered to be assets, or strictly speaking, securities or investments. Nevertheless, since their cash flows are closely related to (or derived from) those of specific securities, they are often studied as or treated as investments.
- Investments are often made indirectly through intermediaries, such as banks, mutual funds, pension funds, insurance companies, collective investment schemes, or even investment clubs. Though their legal and procedural details differ, an intermediary generally makes an investment using money from many individuals, each of whom receives a claim on the intermediary.

Personal Finance

- Within personal finance, money used to purchase shares, put in a collective investment scheme or used to buy any asset where there is an element of capital risk is deemed an investment. Saving within personal finance refers to money put aside, normally on a regular basis. This distinction is important as investment risk can cause a capital loss when an investment is realized, unlike saving(s) where the more limited risk is cash devaluing due to inflation.
- In many instances the term saving and investment are used interchangeably which confuses this distinction. For example many deposit accounts are labeled as investment accounts by banks for marketing purposes. To help establish whether an asset is saving(s) or an investment you should consider where your money is invested. If the answer is cash then it is savings, if it is a type of asset which can fluctuate in value then it is investment.

Investment Management

Investing can be a complex activity and there have been countless books about investing that have been written over the years though certain books are considered classics because of their enduring principles that have stood the test of time. Many of the books on investing, including some of the seminal texts were written by investment managers and or famous investors like Peter Lynch, Phil Fisher or Benjamin Graham

Real Estate Investment

- Within real estate, money used to purchase property for the sole purpose of holding or leasing for income and where there is an element of capital risk is deemed a real estate investment. Real Estate investment is distinct from other forms of economic or financial investment in that a real estate is purchased.

FOREIGN DIRECT INVESTMENT

Foreign direct investment (FDI) is defined as a long-term investment by a foreign direct investor in an enterprise resident in an economy other than that in which the foreign direct investor is based. The FDI relationship, consists of a parent enterprise and a foreign affiliate which together form a transnational corporation (TNC). In order to qualify as FDI the investment must afford the parent enterprise control over its foreign affiliate. The UN defines control in this case as owning 10% or more of the ordinary shares or voting power of an incorporated firm or its equivalent for an unincorporated firm.

In the years after the Second World War global FDI was dominated by the United States, as much of the world recovered from the destruction wrought by the conflict. The U.S. accounted for around three-quarters of new FDI (including reinvested profits) between 1945 and 1960. Since that time FDI has spread to become a truly global phenomenon, no longer the exclusive preserve of OECD countries. FDI has grown in importance in the global economy with FDI stocks now constituting over 20% of global GDP. In the last few years, the emerging market countries such as China and India have become the most favoured destinations for FDI and investor confidence in these countries has soared. As per the FDI Confidence Index compiled by A.T. Kearney for 2005, China and India hold the first and second position respectively, whereas United States has slipped to the third position.

Types of FDI

- *Greenfield Investment*: direct investment in new facilities or the expansion of existing facilities. Greenfield investments are the primary target of a host nation's promotional efforts because they create new production capacity and jobs, transfer technology and know-how, and can lead to linkages to the global marketplace. However, it often does this by crowding out local industry; multinationals are able to produce goods more cheaply (because of advanced technology and efficient processes) and uses up resources (labor, intermediate goods, etc). Another downside of greenfield investment is that profits from production do not feed back into the local economy, but instead to the multinational's home economy. This is in contrast to local industries whose profits flow back into the domestic economy to promote growth.
- *Mergers and Acquisitions*: transfers of existing assets from local firms to foreign firms takes place; the primary type of FDI. Cross-border mergers occur when the assets and operation of firms from different countries are combined to establish a new legal entity. Cross-border acquisitions occur when the control of assets and operations is transferred from a local to a foreign company, with the local company becoming an affiliate of the foreign company. Unlike greenfield investment, acquisitions provide no long term benefits to the local economy--even in most deals the owners of the local firm are paid in stock from the acquiring firm, meaning that the money from the sale could never reach the local economy. Nevertheless, mergers and acquisitions are a significant form of FDI and until around 1997, accounted for nearly 90% of the FDI flow into the United States.
- *Horizontal Foreign Direct Investment*: Investment in the same industry abroad as a firm operates in at home.

- *Vertical Foreign Direct Investment*: Takes two forms:
  (1) backward vertical FDI: where an industry abroad provides inputs for a firm's domestic production process
  (2) forward vertical FDI: in which an industry abroad sells the outputs of a firm's domestic production

Types of FDI based on the Motives of the Investing Firm

FDI can also be categorized based on the motive behind the investment from the perspective of the investing firm:

- *Resource Seeking:* Investments which seek to acquire factors of production that are more efficient than those obtainable in the home economy of the firm. In some cases, these resources may not be available in the home economy at all (e.g. cheap labor and natural resources). This typifies FDI into developing countries, for example seeking natural resources in the Middle East and Africa, or cheap labor in Southeast Asia and Eastern Europe.
- *Market Seeking:* Investments which aim at either penetrating new markets or maintaining existing ones. FDI of this kind may also be employed as defensive strategy; it is argued that businesses are more likely to be pushed towards this type of investment out of fear of losing a market rather than discovering a new one. This type of FDI can be characterized by the foreign Mergers and Acquisitions in the 1980's by Accounting, Advertising and Law firms.
- *Efficiency Seeking:* Investments which firms hope will increase their efficiency by exploiting the benefits of economies of scale and scope, and also those of common ownership. It is suggested that this type of FDI comes after either resource or market seeking investments have been realized, with the expectation that it further increases the profitability of the firm. Typically, this type of FDI is mostly widely practiced between developed economies; especially those within closely integrated markets (e.g. the EU).

INTERNATIONAL SERVICES TRADE INFORMATION AGENCY

The International Services Trade Information Agency (ISTIA) is a non-profit international agency in Geneva, Switzerland. The ISTIA mandate is to provide capacity building to developing countries, least developed countries and economies in transition to collect, analyze and interpret trade in services information, including information relevant to foreign direct investment (FDI) and Foreign Affiliate Trade Statistics (FATS) in a manner which empowers them to participate more actively in trade in services negotiations, most notably in the context of the General Agreement on Trade in Services (GATS) of the World Trade Organization (WTO).

ISTIA was founded as a response to many official and informal requests on the part of developing country WTO Members for trade in services statistics-related technical assistance and capacity building in order that they might have better access to statistics for trade in services negotiations under GATS. Discussions on improvements of statistics for trade in services date back to the 1980s, during the time of the Uruguay Round under the General Agreement on Tariffs and Trade (GATT) talks of the Interim Commission for the International Trade Organization (ICITO), the functional predecessor to the WTO.

The two principal objectives of ISTIA capacity building for developing country and LDC governments are as follows. Firstly, ISTIA seeks to provide training to trade negotiators and policymakers on the fundamentals of globalization statistics, that could provide them with a deeper understanding of their work. These comprise trade in services statistics, which could provide insight into the services trade under the GATS Four Modes of Supply. As well, FDI statistics and Foreign Affiliate Trade Statistics, or "FATS" are important economic indicators in this realm. FATS are corporate financial statistics, aggregated at the national level, describing the operations of FDI-based enterprises, being multinational corporations or transnational corporations; some examples of FATS include statistics on levels of employment, value-added, capital expenditures, inter-and intra-firm trade, as they relate to the economies where FDI-enterprises are based. The second objective of ISTIA is to help national governments to improve the substance of trade in services statistics and FDI statistics by providing training on data collection methodologies which are conformant to International Monetary Fund (IMF) statistical standards, and recommendations of the United Nations Manual on Statistics on International Trade in Services (MSITS), created as a joint intergovernmental effort chaired by the OECD-Eurostat Inter-Agency Task Force on Statistics on International trade in Services.

ISTIA technical assistance will help the over 120 developing countries which require this form of assistance, to meet IMF and other criteria, while providing governments with information which is more useful for negotiations and policymaking, and which private sector enterprises in developing countries and LDCs can use to make evidence-based decisions.

ISTIA also works with private sector enterprises and industrial consortia as well as with academic institutions around the world to forward a wider knowledge of the new field of globalization statistics.

CASH FLOW

Cash flow is an accounting term that refers to the amounts of cash being received and spent by a business during a defined period of time, sometimes tied to a specific project. Measurement of cash flow can be used to evaluate the state or performance of a business or project.

Cash flow measurement can be used to determine problems with liquidity. Being profitable does not necessarily mean being liquid. A company can fail because of a shortage of cash, even while profitable. Cash measurement can be used to generate project rate of returns. The time of cash flows into and out of projects are used as inputs to financial models such as internal rate of return, and net present value.

Cash flow is used to examine income or growth of a business when it is believed that accrual accounting concepts do not represent economic realities. Alternately, cash flow can be used to 'validate' the net income generated by accrual accounting.

Classification

Cash flows can be classified into:

1. *Operational Cash Flows:* Cash received or expended as a result of the company's core business activities.
2. *Investment Cash Flows:* Cash received or expended through capital expenditure, investments or acquisitions.
3. *Financing cash Flows:* Cash received or expended as a result of financial activities, such as receiving or paying loans, issuing or repurchasing stock, and paying dividends.

All three together are necessary to reconcile the beginning cash balance to the ending cash balance.

Benefits from using Cash Flow

The cash flow statement is one of the three main financial statements of a company. The cash flow statement can be examined to determine the short-term sustainability of a company. If cash is increasing (and operational cash flow is positive), then a company will often be deemed to be healthy in the short-term. Increasing or stable cash balances suggest that a company is able to meet its cash needs, and remain solvent. This information cannot always be seen in the income statement or the balance sheet of a company. For instance, a company may be generating profit, but still have difficulty in remaining solvent.

Operating Cash flow as Proxy for Income

Many investors have lost faith in the value of published income statements. One way to by-pass them is to use cash flows instead. The feeling is that

- cash flows cannot be forged. This presumption is shown to be wrong by the following section.
- cash liquidity is necessary for survival. This is true, and even more true for businesses with limited access to financing.
- cash is tangible proof of income. The problem with this concept is that cash can be received as profit on a sale...

but also as proceeds from the sale of an asset with no profit. One asset is simply exchanged for another. This reality is expressed by non-cash expenses like depreciation, amortization and depletion. Capital assets wear out in the process of being used to generate sales. Part of the proceeds from the sale is a return of capital not income. The cash replaces the reduction in the asset's value.

Not withstanding the problems with GAAP, the growth of a business is better measured by Net Income than by Cash from Operations.

Dangers of Isolating Operating cash Flow

When analysts and the media refer to 'cash flow', they are most likely referring to "Operating Cash Flow". There are adherent problems in isolating only this type of flows, because business can easily manipulate the classification. Common methods of distorting the results include:

- Sales-Sell the receivables to a factor for instant cash. (leading)
- Inventory-Don't pay your suppliers for an additional few weeks at period end. (lagging)
- Sales Commissions-Management can form a separate (but unrelated) company act as its agent. The book of business can then be purchased quarterly as an investment.
- Wages-Renumerate with stock options.
- Maintenance-Contract with the predecessor company that you prepay five years worth for them to continue doing the work
- Equipment Leases-Buy it
- Rent-Buy the property (sale and lease back if you like).
- Oil Exploration costs-Replace reserves by buying another company's
- Research & Development-Wait for the product to be proven by a start-up lab. Then buy the lab

- Consulting Fees-Pay in shares from treasury since usually to related parties
- Interest-Issue convertible debt where the conversion rate changes with the unpaid interest
- Taxes-Buy shelf companies with Tax Loss Carry Forward's. Or gussy up the purchase by buying a lab or O&G explore co. with the same TLCF.

ECONOMY OF SOUTH INDIA

The Economy of South India is largely agrarian, dependent on monsoons, as are most people in India. Some of the main crops cultivated in South India include paddy, sorghum, millet, pulses, cotton, chilli, and ragi. South India was and still is the "promised land" as far as spice cultivation is concerned. Areca, coffee, pepper, tapioca, and cardamom are widely cultivated on the Nilgiri Hills and Kodagu. But frequent droughts in Northern Karnataka, Rayalaseema and Telangana regions are leaving farmers debt-ridden, forcing them to sell their livestock and sometimes even to suicides. Scarcity of water has been a major problem for past few years in these regions along with cities like Chennai and Hyderabad.

Education is highly valued in the south Indian community, and is seen as a gateway to a better livelihood. Many of the nation's most prominent physicists and mathematicians have been South Indians. Kerala, while possessing a literacy rate above 98% also has the highest unemployment rates in India. The population growth rate of these states is also beginning to decline rapidly relative to North India.

Information Technology is a growing field in South India. Bangalore is India's Information Technology hub, and is home to over 200 software companies. It is often referred to as the "Silicon Valley of India".

Chennai, Tamil Nadu ranks next only to Bangalore in the software exports in India and grossed over Rs 100,000,000,000 in 2005.

Chennai houses the automobile manufacturing giants in the country. More than 35% of heavy vehicles produced in the country, such as cars, buses, lorries, trains and bicycles, are produced in Chennai, and it is referred to as the Detroit of South Asia. The manufacturing units of BMW, Flextronics, Motorola, Dell, TVS, Mitsubishi, Ford, Hyundai, Nokia and Saint Gobain are some of the international players in Chennai.

Hyderabad is a currently the most happening place in India. Hyderabad is the first destination for Microsoft Development Center in India. Hyderabad is known as Pearl City.

Hyderabad is also known as GeNome Valley of India (Number of Biotech and Pharma Industries) like Avra Laboratories, Bharat Biotech International, Bijam Biosciences, Biological E. Ltd, Bioserve Biotechnologies, Dr Reddy's Laboratories, Genotex International, GVK Bio, Indian Immunologicals Ltd, Indigene Pharmaceuticals, Jupiter Biosciences, Krebs Biochemicals, Microbiomed Products, Nuziveedu Seeds, Prabhat Agri Biotech, Satyam Computer Services, Shantha Biotechnics, Tata Consultancy Services and Vimta Labs are the Top Players.

Hyderabad convention center is the south Asia's largest convention center. Guntur is the Cotton source for nearly 50% production in India. Andhra Pradesh Government is planning to establish Cotton Mills around Guntur to Make the city Cotton city surpassing the Current Cotton City Coimbatore. Currently Guntur district Port/Nizam Patnam is built up to make the plan implemented. Czek Repablic is Investing 10,000 crores for this Project.

Kerala lags behind many of the Indian states in terms of production and per capita income, but in terms of Human Development Index and life standard of the people, Kerala is ahead of most other states in India. This peculiar paradox is often termed as the "Kerala Phenomenon" or Kerala model of development by experts.

There is also a large amount of disparity within Southern India. As IT companies have entered the economic arena, their high level of pay has raised the economic standing of young and educated professionals, while the poor has become less and less able to afford basic necessities. It is not uncommon to see the shacks of homeless people propped up against the buildings of large multinationals. The poor, unable to afford sending their children to school, remain in a cycle of life completed separated from that of this more affluent upper class.

Andhra Pradesh

Agriculture has been the chief source of income for the state's economy. Two important rivers of India, the Godavari and Krishna, flow through the state. Rice, tobacco, cotton, mirchi, and sugarcane are the local crops. The state has also started to focus on the fields of information technology and biotechnology.

Hyderabad, the capital of Andhra Pradesh, is the fifth largest cosmopolitan city in India, rich in culture, enduring history and industrial growth.

Hyderabad beat IT heavyweight Bangalore to bag the Fab City project, which will host India's first major silicon chip manufacturing facility. Its Due to the Governments Unique FDI Policies and the City Infrastructure.

The advent of Information Technology growth in India, the so called "Blue Chip Revolution", has fostered the growth of Hyderabad's economy. The city is sometimes referred to as "Cyberabad" because of the large number of IT firms in the city. Andhra Pradesh has witnessed a major jump in software exports. Hyderabad's IT export revenue was Rs. 81,450,000,000, an increase of 62% from fiscal 2004. For Andhra, fiscal 2004 is particularly significant as the 62% growth in exports in fiscal 2005, was almost double the 37% it grew in 2003-2004. Other cities such as Vizag and Vijayawada have shown growths in IT exports on an annual basis. Vizag's contribution was Rs 700,000,000, while it was Rs 240,000,000 from Vijayawada.

State Owned APSRTC Bus Service-entered Guinness World Record for owning the largest fleet of buses IN 1999.

AP is the largest producer of rice in India

Rajiv-(Internet Village) Initiative by AP Government. Government's plan is to establish Broadband Network across the State by connecting Districts with 10 GB/s and Up to Mandals with 1 GB/s and up to Villages with 100 MB/s

Bandwidth with in Jun 2007. Infosys signs MoU Andhra for expansion in Hyderabad Plans to ramp up headcount to 25,000 with an added investment of Rs. 1250 crore

Karnataka

Karnataka's net state domestic product of $47 billion is the fifth largest in India. Between 1992-2002, Karnataka attracted the fourth highest total Foreign Direct Investment approvals in India, to the tune of Rs. 21,566 million. Karnataka accounts for one third of India's Information technology exports. For the year 2006, the state is expected to bring in 37% of all IT revenues amounting to 37,000 crores ($8.2 billion). Nearly 50% of IT companies and 40% of Bio-Tecnology companies are based here. Agriculture in Karnataka, like most of India, employs 80% of the population. Agriculture and its allied activities account for 49% of the state's income. The coastal plains of Karnataka, which include Uttara Kanara and Dakshina Kanara are cultivated with rice and sugarcane. Coffee and Tea are also grown on the slopes of the Western Ghats in the district of Kodagu Chikmagalur and Hassan. Karnataka produces 70% of India's coffee, of which about 50% is exported.. The black soil in the northwest of the state, is hospitable for the growth of cotton, onion, course cereal, sunflower and peanuts.

The forests of the Malnad region produce timber, bamboo and sandalwood. Karnataka is the only exporter of sandalwood in the country. Most of the world's sandalwood oil is produced in Karnataka. All of India's gold comes from the Kolar district of Karnataka. Karnataka is also rich in minerals which form the bulk of the raw materials for iron and steel industries in the state such as the one at Bhadravati. All of India's Iron ore comes from the Malnad region.

The first power station in Asia was set up in Karnataka at Shivanasamudra in 1902 to produce hydroelectric power. Karnataka has 18 power stations which generate annually 16,513 million units. The state, however generates insufficient power and is forced to buy electricity from neighboring states.

Bangalore, the capital of Karnataka, is home to several public sector undertaking aircraft companies, such as Hindustan Aeronautics Limited (HAL), HMT Hindustan Machine Tools,

Bharat Heavy Electronics Limited (BHEL), National Aeronautics Limited and also Indian Space Research Organization (ISRO). Bangalore, often referred to as the Silicon Valley of India has the largest number of international and local Information Technology and business process outsourcing (BPO) companies in the country.

A number of "IT Parks" have been set up by the Karnataka State Electronics Development Corporation Limited (KEONICS) including Bangalore's "Electronics City" and IT parks in Mysore, Mangalore and Hubli. Bangalore is also home to prestigious higher institutes of learning such as the Indian Institute of Science (IISc) and the Indian Institute of Management (IIM Bangalore).

Kerala

The interior of a building in the Technopark, at Thiruvananthapuram (Trivandrum). 70% of the state's IT exports are from Technopark

Kerala's economy is predominantly agrarian. In terms of industrialisation, Kerala lags behind many of the Indian states, but in terms of Human Development Index and life standard of the people, Kerala is ahead of most other states in India. In fact, in certain development indices it is on a par with some of the developed countries. This peculiar paradox is often termed as the "Kerala Phenomenon" or Kerala model of development by experts.

Kerala follows a socialist welfare economy. Kerala's emphasis on social welfare also resulted in slow economic progress. There are few major industries in Kerala, and the per capita GDP is lower than the national average. Remittances from Keralites working abroad, mainly in the Middle East, make up over 60% of the state's gross domestic product.

However, today, the state is emerging as a future IT center of India, owing to its high internet connectivity (undersea cable landing points), along with skilled labour. The government has established two IT Parks in the state at Trivandrum and Kochi. The Technopark at Trivandrum is the second largest IT park in Asia. Kochi is a safe natural harbour, and hence on the most important ports of India. A container transhipment terminal has been proposed in Kochi. The construction of the proposed mega Deep Water Container Transshipment Port at Vizhinjam near Trivandrum is expected to boost up the economy of the state. Vizhinjam is having a natural depth of 24m, which requires no annual dredging, thus making it the deepest port in Asia. Situated close to Trivandrum city, Vizhinjam is very close to international shipping route and East-West shipping axis.

Agriculture is still the most predominant economic activity in the state. Coconut, tea and coffee are grown extensively, along with rubber, cashew and spices. Spices commonly cultivated in Kerala include pepper, cardamom, vanilla, cinnamon and nutmeg. Much of Kerala's agriculture is in the form of home gardens.

Unemployment is typically high in Kerala. Traditional low-wage cottage industries such as the processing of coconut fiber and cashew or weaving employ most workers. More than a fourth of Kerala's workers provide services.

Kerala boasts an Indian Institute of Management at Kozhikode. One of the two ship building yards of India is in Kerala at Kochi. The Southern Naval Command of India has its headquarters in Kochi, and the Southern Air Command Head Quarters is in Thiruvananthapuram (Trivandrum). There are three international airports in Kerala, Trivandrum, Cochin and Calicut. Cochin International Airport is the first International Airport in India that has been built without the Federal Government's stake.

Kerala is also one of the tourist hot-spots of India. It was proclaimed as one of the ten paradises on earth by the National Geographic traveller. The state has also won a large number of awards for its tourism initiatives. Its tourism logo and slogan have global superbrand status.

Tamil Nadu

Tamil Nadu's net state domestic product is the largest in South India and third largest in India. It is one of the most industrialised states in India. It ranks third in the country in total foreign direct investment (FDI) (Rs. 220,582,640,000).

The State's investment constitutes 9.12% of the total FDI in the country. According to the 2001 Census, Tamil Nadu has the highest level of urbanization (43.86%) in India, which accounts for 6% of India's total population and 9.6% of the urban population. Chennai is referred as the Gate way of South India. Chennai is the Second leading Software exporter in India. Companies such as Cognizant, Covansys, Xansa, Verizon, iSoft and many others are Chennai based companies in India.

Infosys has set up India's largest software development centre to house 25,000 software professionals at an estimated investment of Rs 1,250 crore (Rs 12.5 billion) in Chennai. India's largest IT park is housed at Chennai. Unlike other States in India the state has many software tier II cities such as Coimbatore, Trichy, Madurai and Hosur. Chennai has become the most preferred BPO hub in India and South Asia. Chennai is sometimes referred to as the "Health Capital of India" or the "Banking Capital of India", having attracted investments from International corporations and the World Bank.

Tamil Nadu has a network of about 110 industrial parks/ estates that offer developed plots with supporting infrastructure. Also, the Government is promoting other industrial parks like Rubber Park, Apparel Parks, Floriculture Park, TICEL Park for Biotechnology, Siruseri IT Park, Agro Export Zones among others. 56% of India's total knitwear exports come from Tirupur, Tamil Nadu.

The heavy engineering manufacturing companies are centered around the suburbs of Chennai. Chennai boasts presence of global car manufacturing giants like Ford, Hyundai, BMW and Mitsubishi as well as home grown companies like MRF, TI Cycles of India, Ashok Leyland and TVS. Chennai is also home to one of the Indian Institutes of Technology, IIT Madras.

Kalpakkam nuclear power plant, Neyveli Lignite Corporation, and the Narimanam natural gas plants provide sources of fuel and energy for the nation. 55% of electricity from wind power produced in India from wind mills comes from Tamil Nadu. The town of Sivakasi is the leader for Printing, Fireworks, Safety matches Production in India. It contributes to 80% of India's total Safety Matches Production, 90% of India's Total Fireworks Production and 60% of India's Total Offset Printing Solutions and ranks as one of the highest Tax payer towns in India. Sivakasi and Tirupur in Tamil Nadu are 100% employed towns, among a few towns in India.

Tamil Nadu is leading producer of kambu, cholam, ground nut, oil seeds and sugarcane in India. At present Tamil Nadu is Third biggest producer of Rice in India, next to Andhra Pradesh and Punjab where there is perennial source of irrigation.

Biovalleys in Tamil Nadu include Biotechnology Incubator Park Near Chennai,, Women's Biotechnology Park Kelambakkam, Medicinal Plants Biotechnology Park, Madurai, Marine Biotechnology Park, Madapam and Bioinformatics and Genomics Centre (BGC), Chennai.

□□□

Bibliography

Albright, K. B.: *Enhancing Kansas Communities*, Manhattan, Kansas State University, 1991.

Anne, Farrar: *An American Vision: Far Western Landscape and National Culture, 1820-1920*, New York, New York University Press, 1990.

Arlin, F.: *Private and Commercial Recreation*, New York, Wiley, 1977.

Ashworth, G.J.: *Marketing Tourism Places*, London, Routledge, 1990.

Baker, Priscilla: *Touring Historic Places: A Manual for Group Tour Operators and Managers of Historic and Cultural Attractions*, Washington, DC: National Trust for Historic Preservation, 1995.

Baum, T.: *Managing the Development and Implementation of National Human Resource Policies for Tourism*, England, Wiley, 1994.

Berry, S.: *Conservation, Capacity and Cashflows—Tourism and Historic Building Management*, England, Wiley, 1994.

Brown, Tommy L.: *Economic and Social Significance of Recreational Access for the Rural Community*, Morgantown, West Virginia University, 1993.

Cater, Erlet: *Ecotourism: A Sustainable Option?*, New York, John Wiley & Sons, 1994.

Clayne, R.: *Leisure and Recreation: Introduction and Overview*, Philadelphia, Lea and Febiger, 1977.

Clough, Richard: *Construction Project Management*, New York, John Wiley & Son, 2000.

Copps, D. H.: *Views from the Road: A Community Guide for Assessing Rural Historic Landscapes*, Washington, DC, Island Press, 1995.

Daniel J. Decker: *Economic and Social Significance of Recreational Access for the Rural Community*, Morgantown, West Virginia University, 1993.

David W. Marcouiller: *Ethnic Variation in Leisure and Recreational Interests*, Chicago, Council of Planning Librarians, 1994.

David, H.: *Views from the Road: A Community Guide for Assessing Rural Historic Landscapes*, Washington, DC, Island Press, 1995.

Davies, I.: *Competency Based Learning: Technology, Management, and Design*, New York, McGraw-Hill, 1973.

Dennis, L.: *Public Policy Management and Public Policy*, New York, Longman, 1999.

Donald E. : *Public Personnel Management: Contexts and Strategies*, Upper Saddle River, NJ: Prentice Hall, 1998.

Donald R. Field: *National Parks and Rural Development: Practice and Policy in the United States*, Washington, DC, Island Press, 2000.

Edward, J.: *Ethnic Variation in Leisure and Recreational Interests*, Chicago, Council of Planning Librarians, 1994.

Elkinton, L. C.: *Back Road Adventures: A Private Enterprise Model for Nature Study on Private and Public Land*, Morgantown, West Virginia, 1990.

Epperson, A. F.: *Private and Commercial Recreation*, New York, Wiley, 1977.

Frame, J. Davidson: *Managing Projects in Organizations: How to Make the Best Use of Time, Techniques, and People*, San Francisco, Jossey-Bass, 1995.

Frew, E.: *International Charter Travel—a New Opportunity for Australian Tourism*, England, Wiley, 1994.

Gawthrop, L.C. : *Public Sector Management Systems and Ethics*, Bloomington, Indiana University Press, 1984.

Gerald, K.: *The Less Developed Countries in the International Economy*, Cambridge, Cambridge University Press, 1975.

Gibson, L. J.: *Economic Adaptation*, Boulder, Westview Press, 1993.

Glatthorn, Allan: *The Teacher's Portfolio: Fostering and Documenting Professional Development*, Rockport, Active Publications, 1996.

Goldman, George: *Impact of Visitor Expenditures on Local Revenues*, Corvallis, Oregon, 1994.

Gregory, J.: *Marketing Tourism Places*, London, Routledge, 1990.

Gwen, Lowman: *Ecotourism: A Sustainable Option?*, New York, John Wiley & Sons, 1994.

Helleiner, G. K.: *The Less Developed Countries in the International Economy*, Cambridge, Cambridge University Press, 1975.

Hervik, Peter: *Social Categories and Lived Identity in Yucatan*, New York, Harwood, 1999.

Hilchey, Duncan: *Agritourism in New York State: Opportunities and Challenges in Farm-Based Recreation and Hospitality*, New York, Cornell University, 1993.

Hyde, A. F.: *An American Vision: Far Western Landscape and National Culture, 1820-1920*, New York, New York University Press, 1990.

Ireland, Lewis: *Quality Management for Projects and Programs*, Upper Darby, PMI, 1991.

Iso-Ahola, S. E.: *Social Psychological Perspectives on Leisure and Recreation*, Springfield, Illinois, Thomas, 1980.

Jensen, C. R.: *Leisure and Recreation: Introduction and Overview*, Philadelphia, Lea and Febiger, 1977.

Jepson, E. J.: *Ethnic Variation in Leisure and Recreational Interests*, Chicago, Council of Planning Librarians, 1994.

Johannis, Theodore B.: *Sociology of Leisure*, California, Sage, 1971.

Jon, A.: *Guidebook for Creating Wetland Interpretation Sites, Including Wetlands and Ecotourism*, New York, Association of State Wetland Managers, 1992.

Kando, T. M.: *Leisure and Popular Culture in Transition*, St. Louis, Mosby, 1980.

Kaplan, Max: *Leisure in American: A Social Inquiry*, New York, Wiley, 1960.

Kiel, L. D. : *Managing Chaos and Complexity in Government*, San Francisco, Jossey-Bass, 1994.

Kotler, Philip: *Marketing for Hospitality and Tourism*: New Jersey, Prentice-Hall, 1998.

————: *Marketing Places: Attracting Investment, Industry, and Tourism to Cities, States, and Nations*, New York, Free, 1993.

Krippendorf, Jost: *The Holiday Makers: Understanding the Impact of Leisure and Travel*, London, Heinemann, 1987.

Kuehn, Diane: *Considerations for Agritourism Development*, New York, Sea Grant, 1998.

Kusler, J. A.: *Guidebook for Creating Wetland Interpretation Sites, Including Wetlands and Ecotourism*, New York, Association of State Wetland Managers, 1992.

Laufer, Alexander & Hoffman, Edward: *Project Management Success Stories: Lessons of Project Leaders*, New York, John Wiley & Son, 2000.

Lay, J.: *Economic Adaptation*, Boulder, Westview Press, 1993.

Linda, C.: *Back Road Adventures: A Private Enterprise Model for Nature Study on Private and Public Land*, Morgantown, West Virginia, 1990.

Lock, Dennis: *Project Management*, New York, Wiley, 1996.

Machlis, Gary E.: *National Parks and Rural Development: Practice and Policy in the United States*, Washington, DC, Island Press, 2000.

Martin, Martin; Teagarden, C. Claude; and Lambreth, Charles: *Contract Administration for the Project Manager*, Upper Darby, PA, 1983.

Mastran, Shelley: *Getting Started in Heritage Area Development*, Washington, DC, National Trust for Historic Preservation, 1997.

Nakazawa, A.: *Impact of Visitor Expenditures on Local Revenues*, Corvallis, Oregon, 1994.

Neil, B.: *Sociology of Leisure*, California, Sage, 1971.

Nelson, Bob and Economy, Peter: *Managing for Dummies*, Foster City, IDG Books, 1996.

Pinto, Jeffrey K. and Kharbanda, O.P.: *Successful Project Managers: Leading Your Team to Success*, New York, Van Nostrand Reinhold, 1995.

Robert, K.: *Building Effective Project Teams*, New York, Wiley, 2001.

Robert, T.: *Practical Public Management*, New York, Marcel Dekker, 1995.

Rosenburg, Marc J.: *E-Learning: Strategies for Delivering Knowledge in the Digital Age*, New York, McGraw-Hill, 2001.

Seppo, E.: *Social Psychological Perspectives on Leisure and Recreation*, Springfield, Illinois, Thomas, 1980.

Thomas, M.: *Leisure and Popular Culture in Transition*, St. Louis, Mosby, 1980.

Wysocki, R. K.: *Building Effective Project Teams*, New York, Wiley, 2001.

Index

J

K

L

M

N

O

P

Q

R

S

□□□